LIVING FULLY FREE

Step into the Incredible *Life* that Awaits You

BY
MICHAEL & CYNDI HINSON

SILVERSMITH
PRESS

Published by Silversmith Press–Houston, Texas
www.silversmithpress.com

Copyright © 2025 Michael and Cyndi Hinson
Edited by Nicole Norris

All rights reserved.

This book, or parts thereof, may not be reproduced in any form or by any means without written permission from the publisher, except for brief passages for purposes of reviews. For more information, contact the publisher at office@publishandgo.com.

The views and opinions expressed herein belong to the author and do not necessarily represent those of the publisher.

Unless otherwise indicated, Scripture quotations are taken from the Holy Bible, New International Version, (NIV).

ISBN 978-1-961093-33-1 (Softcover Book)
ISBN 978-1-967386-00-0 (eBook)

CONTENTS

Acknowledgement	*1*
Author's Note: What to Expect	*3*
1 ~ The Truth	*7*
2 ~ A New Beginning	*21*
3 ~ Preparing the Heart	*33*
4 ~ The Truth About Repentance	*49*
5 ~ The Truth About Forgiveness	*67*
6 ~ Who Has Your Heart?	*89*
7 ~ Truths of the Kingdom	*107*
8 ~ Trials of Life	*139*
9 ~ The Power of Words	*161*
10 ~ The Power of Thoughts	*185*
11 ~ Truth About Covenants	*203*
12 ~ Truth About Deliverance and Strongholds	*231*
13 ~ Sins of the Father	*257*
14 ~ Truth About Salvation	*275*
15 ~ Addictions & Other Issues of the Heart	*283*
Appendix: List of Healing Prayers	*305*

ACKNOWLEDGEMENT

We would like to thank all our friends and family for your unwavering support and encouragement during this season of writing and ministering. Without you, this book would not have become a reality.

To our 4 amazing daughters, Nicole, Michelle, TC and Khala: your lives, love and support mean more to us than you know, and we are extremely grateful to be called your Mom and Dad. We love you! To our oldest daughter Nicole Norris, thank you for your time, skills and input to so brilliantly edit the book for us. You've been overwhelming us with your creativity and talent all your life, not sure why we still get surprised by it, but we do.

AUTHOR'S NOTE: WHAT TO EXPECT

In our travels, we have met people everywhere trying to replace the loneliness, depression, broken hearts, grief, anxieties, fears, abuses, and addictions in their lives with anything they believe would help. Assisting people through this process required significant effort and did not always result in lasting change. We knew there had to be a better, more effective way.

It was while we were pursuing the "better way" that something miraculous happened. In an experience, one could not properly explain with mere words, everything we had learned through our life's study of the Word of God and through years of ministry came together like the pieces of a puzzle. What was once an incomplete picture is now a seamless and complete image. **It was so amazingly simple that we could not believe we had not seen it before.**

Before this experience, we concentrated our efforts on the broken areas that needed attention. This seemed like the proper way. However, it could take time, and it did not work for everyone or consistently produce lasting change.

When we saw the full picture, we understood our focus should be on what was right, not what was wrong. Upon presenting what was right (the Truth), what was wrong (the broken and hurting areas of their lives) were displaced. From that moment on, everyone's life was empowered in ways we had never imagined. **To our surprise, it was all so easy!**

Not only were their lives significantly altered, but those who had this experience also reported positive impacts on the people around them. Loneliness, depression, broken hearts, grief, anxieties, fears, abuses, and addictions as well as many other issues of the heart were healed with such ease that it was startling.

A surprising number of physical illnesses that were not directly addressed were healed as well. People went from hurting and lack to helping others in the very areas they had overcome. **Their lives took on a fullness they had not previously experienced.**

Those who were healed had something in common: they yielded their hearts to God and allowed Him to change them. You cannot successfully restore your life on your own. However, God will do it for you in unimaginable ways when you follow His simple Truths within this book. When we say unimaginable, we mean that if you are lacking or hurting in any way, you cannot imagine how easy it is to be healed and to Live the rest of your life Fully Free. **Join us on this journey!**

Scan the QR code to watch a special message from Michael and Cyndi—a personal note just for you!

CHAPTER 1

THE TRUTH

Mary had been struggling with a mild form of depression for years. She also had physical ailments that hindered her ability to work effectively. Her doctor diagnosed her with chronic fatigue syndrome and told her she could be developing Fibromyalgia. Adding to these problems, she had lost the intimacy with her husband that once was the cornerstone of their relationship. She could not remember how or when it left, she just knew it was gone. She still loved her husband and longed for the intimacy they had once shared.

Mary was busy taking care of her family and serving the best that she could. However, she felt an emptiness inside that was never satisfied. To protect herself from the pain inflicted by others, she had built a wall around her heart that now resembled a prison. She felt trapped within it, and it felt like the walls were closing in on her.

She searched for answers to her problems and felt better for periods of time after receiving ministry, but the changes never seemed to last. Hope for permanent change faded away as she realized that many of her friends were experiencing similar problems. She was merely going through the motions of life looking for something different. She began to believe this was just life and she had to resign herself to it.

Mary was at a service when she asked for prayer for her physical symptoms. After asking a few questions, she told her story. We explained that the solution to her problems was easy. With basic instruction, followed by prayers, she could be healed. Mary's story is very typical of people in need and her response to the statement, "This is easy" was just as typical. Surprise, confusion and unbelief plainly showed on her face.

She explained, "You are not the first person that I have come to for prayer. Afterwards, I often feel better for a while, but nothing seems to last." We explained that we would instruct her from the Word of God in a way she had not heard before and also lead her in some unique prayers. When we were through, she would be forever changed. She cautiously agreed.

After the instruction and prayers, Mary's heart could hardly hold the joy that filled her soul. She declared a love for her husband she had not felt in years. She had a renewed strength and life burning deep inside her heart. She felt closer to God, her friends, and her spouse, than she could ever remember. To her surprise, she looked years younger and the pains that once racked her memories and body were now completely gone. The pressure that squeezed around her heart and the flood of negative thoughts that ran through her mind were gone as well.

Mary later reported that after ministry, she had slept effortlessly through the night and experienced a peace that she had not known before. Her mind was quiet and still for the first time in her life. She began to understand who she truly was and what she had been called to do in life. She was truly content and full of joy.

The Truth

Over a year later, Mary was not only still healed and free; she was ministering to her friends and loved ones and reporting about the changes in their lives as well. She said two things that we hear in testimonies everywhere we go. "I had no idea it could be this easy." And "I never knew this kind of contentment and joy was possible."

What caused this dramatic change? Mary had an encounter with God and His Truth. His kingdom's truths are quite simple and easy to understand. However, they are immensely powerful and life changing. Once they are acknowledged and become part of your being, the promises of God manifest in your life in miraculous ways, and you will never be the same after this encounter.

Along this journey, we will explain some truths you may have heard before from a different perspective. We will also travel through some areas where you might have a partial understanding but not a complete life-changing revelation.

If you are reading his book because you find yourself feeling like you have a grasp on the truths in God's word regarding healing but are unable to figure out how to apply them to your life, you are in good company. You may have learned some concepts without the life changing truths that empower them, and you are suffering needlessly because of this misunderstanding.

God wants you to be free, content, healed and made whole!

God loves you so much and cares so deeply about your every need. He has already made a provision for your healing and freedom, and our desire is to help guide you into the fullness of what He has for you today. He wants you to be free, content, healed and made whole! You have heard us say this a few times already, but once again: it is easy!

The following chapters contain revelations which bring life and permanent change. The same joy and peace that Mary now holds dear, so many others also received when they embraced these truths. You can receive them as well, with the same outcome, and see God's kingdom advance in and through your life.

If you were drawn to this book because of its cover or title, you may identify with one of these scenarios:

1. You are called to minister to others, and your heart's desire is to see them healed, set free and living their lives to the fullest. You may find this book especially useful. We have seen people made whole again in such a simple straightforward way, that it is hard to imagine until you experience it for yourself. Often the ones healed cannot believe it was so easy, yet there they stand... restored, healed, with the ability to minister to others.
2. You may be searching for fulfillment in your life that is missing. Like Mary, you may experience occasional comfort, but it does not last, leaving you even more frustrated. You may have lost the intimacy in your relationship with your spouse, your family, friends, or with God, and nothing you do is enough to get it back. You also may have never experienced true intimacy and are questioning the possibility of ever having it. You may have gone around the mountain of trials and tribulations one too many times,

The Truth

leaving you without the strength for another trip. This can result in feeling isolated, lost and alone, having lost hope with no clear direction out of your circumstances.

In addition, you may have encountered trusted friends that have wounded you by their words or by their actions. Those hurts can accumulate, and suddenly the "mountain" of hurt appears insurmountable. In this condition, it is easy to believe that you are doomed to spend the rest of your life in a wounded state, longing for a way out.

Like Mary, maybe you have built a wall around your heart to protect yourself from the pain and now you are trapped behind it. You can identify this by asking yourself: "Do I feel bitter, weary, hopeless, depressed, or even dead inside. You may be stuck in this "survival mode," tired and frustrated, just living your life to get through another day in hopes that somehow something will miraculously change tomorrow.

Although family or friends may surround you, you feel separated and alone. There may be constant activity going on in your head that you cannot seem to shut off even when you try to sleep. The pressures of today and the worry about tomorrow create a fear and anxiety that just never ends.

We have to acknowledge these fears and pain are very real. But you are definitely not alone. There are multiple ways one can become wounded, broken, grieved, or even completely shut down. Life can be hard and is often difficult, and things do not always seem to work out the way you thought they would. Sometimes, horrible things occur that should never have happened, and you are left wondering "Why?"

If you are at any stage of what we described, we have something important to tell you: We know where you are and understand what your condition may be at this moment. We understand the struggle you are having. When you continue through this book and apply the truths in it, you can be free of your pain and feelings of separation. There is something that happens, in ways unimaginable, when the kingdom of our God overtakes the kingdom of this world within your life.

We have yet to find anyone who was not changed when they applied these truths in their life.

Your life can be full of joy and contentment like you may have never known. It does not have to involve years of counseling to be free and forever changed. You should not need continuous sessions of ministry to guide you through a variety of emotions and incidents. We once believed these methods were the way to find the answers, as well. But we have experienced a better way. Jesus did not counsel people to be comforted with their problems. He brought healing and deliverance. That is the model He gave us. Following His example, you can find freedom in a short amount of time, and it is easy. We are not saying that you should not seek the counsel of others, or that you should not go to the elders for prayer for life's issues. The Bible instructs us to do this. We are simply saying that healing is simple and that continuous ministry for the same or similar issues may be a sign that you need something else. You may need a new perspective.

You might be thinking this all sounds too good to be true. We say emphatically, "Not at all!" We have yet to find anyone who was not changed when they applied these truths in their life. When you are hurting, especially if you have been feeling that way for a long time, it is easy to get stuck thinking that no amount of prayer or ministry will work. That is a natural reaction based on your circumstances, but it is not the truth.

Jesus declared in John 10:10, *The thief comes only to steal and kill and destroy; I have come that they may have life and have it to the full.* He would not have said it if it were not possible. It is not a "pipe dream" or some sweet sentiment. It may be difficult to believe now, but you can have a healed heart and live a content, fulfilled life. A life full of joy and peace, as promised in the Word, is available to you. It is real and accessible to you today. We have seen these truths work for people who were once in pain and had lost vision for their lives.

You will have the knowledge you need in order to be free and to stay free. You will also have the tools to help others.

You may be asking, "Why hasn't it happened before now?" The answer could be one of many reasons, such as God's timing (Ecclesiastes 3:3) or a lack of knowledge (Hosea 4:6). The good news is since you are reading or listening to this, God's timing for your healing is now. When you follow the simple instructions taught in God's Word, you will not only have the knowledge you need to get free and to stay free, but you will also have the tools to help others as well.

God does not make promises to us in His Word, telling us of the wonderful life we could have, only to keep how to have it a secret. He did not intend our lives to be so difficult that we would never be able to find fulfillment in it. Man's reasoning has made it difficult. In actuality, God did the most amazing thing: He designed a purpose for our lives that is greater than we can imagine. To access this, He simply requires us to trust Him and live within His purpose for our lives.

While doing that sounds easy enough, if you have been wounded and hurt, it can be difficult and frightening. It is hard to trust when you have been wounded and betrayed by people you once trusted. It is hard to hope that things can be different when you have endured disappointment after disappointment and lost your hope. It is hard to open your heart to love as you once did after being wounded by people you once loved. Finally, it may be hard to understand a God who says He loves you but created the world where all of this happened to you.

At this point, you will need to decide in your heart how you will proceed. You can either accept things as they are and try to live your life resistant to your difficult circumstances, or you can choose to be willing to examine your life from an unfamiliar perspective. We all have a choice when it comes to applying God's truth to our lives. If you honestly want God's plan of contentment and fulfillment for your life, we will guide you through this process and teach you what has healed so many

The Truth

hearts and changed so many lives in ways they could not have imagined.

If you want to restore anything to its original condition, you need to know what the original was supposed to look like. Otherwise, how would you know if restoration had truly taken place?

Let us start at the beginning. We came from God. He made us in His image. *Then God said, "Let us make man in our image, in our likeness." So, God created man in his own image, in the image of God he created him; male and female he created them,* (Genesis 1:26-27).

Every living thing on earth can only reproduce after its own kind. You will not find a duck giving birth to a chicken. A duck will reproduce a duck that looks like its parents, acts like its parents, and will eventually live like its parents. All living things will have certain natural characteristics "woven" into their being that are inherited from their parents.

One of the first steps is to recognize that **God is our Father**. Scripture states we were made in His image. We were all "cut from the same bolt of cloth." God wove fibers of His "DNA" through us so we would resemble Him. You are His "offspring" and when you were created, you inherited certain characteristics that make you like your Father. When we live contrary to who He is, we live in opposition to who we were made to be, and our life loses its fulfillment. Under these conditions, we are working against His creation, and the fruit of our lives reflects this fact. We feel a loss of joy and contentment and become weary. If you do not know the true character and nature of God, you will by default, give Him your own.

**If you do not know the nature and character
of God, you will give Him your own.**

Wholeness comes when we overcome those things that oppose our likeness to Him. When you accomplish this, you begin to emulate who He is, and your life takes on the meaning He intended for you. You then reflect His very being, taking on His character and nature, and work in unity with what He created. There is no greater fulfillment.

This is God's plan for your life. When you have this understanding in your heart, you will not be in pursuit of anything else. Completeness in this life will come to you, you will not have to search for it. You can live life to the fullest and you can have contentment and peace in everything, and it is surprisingly easy to attain.

Though most of us know this, many have gone down paths that have made this life hard, and after years of striving for it, this completeness appears unobtainable. However, nothing could be further from the truth. This amazing life is achieved as a byproduct of understanding the simple truths about who you are now and who God originally intended you to be. The problem lies in the fact that most of us do not have this settled in our hearts where it becomes a life-changing revelation. If you do not have the conviction of this truth yet, do not worry. God will make the changes in you as you follow His purpose.

It is sometimes difficult for us to understand that we may have been wrong in our beliefs, especially when our hearts

The Truth

are set on doing what is right. It may be scary to consider changing the beliefs you have been living with, but we will ask you a question: How has your current belief system been working for you? The Bible declares that we can judge our lives by its fruit (Matthew 7:17-18). What is the fruit of your life now?

You cannot continue to do the same thing over and over and expect different results. That is a form of insanity. For example, you cannot plant corn year after year and expect wheat to grow. If you want something different to take place in your life, something must change. This is easier than you can imagine. If you are feeling fear, doubt, or unbelief currently, do not worry, it is only natural. If you are fighting with hopelessness, then the thought of having to do one more thing may seem overwhelming and more than you think you can manage. We must tell you again that applying these truths from God's word is amazingly simple. You will not be alone through this process. The Holy Spirit will show you His Truths and bring life-changing revelation in ways you cannot imagine!

You can have a freedom and peace that you have never known before, and it is only pages away from your present reality.

You can have a freedom and peace that you may have never known before, and it is only pages away from your present reality. When you follow this journey through to the end, you will experience new understanding. Like others, you will look back and declare, "That was so easy!" Not only that, but you will be more equipped to help others through similar circumstances and point them to the answers for their life situations as well.

So, as we begin to embark on this powerful life-changing journey, you can say the simple prayer below, trust God and be open to the possibilities of seeing your life from a new perspective. This promises to be an exciting new understanding that can bring healing and freedom for the rest of your life.

> *"Father, if there is anything in this book that You want me to have, then I ask You to open my eyes to see Your truth, my ears to hear Your voice, and my heart to hear and receive what You are saying to me. Give me the ability to look at my life honestly and the strength to make the changes that are needed so that I become who You created me to be and reflect who You are to others. Father, I thank you for the healing that is coming to my heart and for fulfillment in my own life. Amen."*

Scripture References

There is a time for everything, and a season for every activity under heaven: a time to be born and a time to die, a time to plant and a time to uproot, a time to kill and a time to heal, a time to tear down and a time to build.

(Ecclesiastes 3:1-3)

The Truth

My people are destroyed from lack of knowledge. Because you have rejected knowledge, I also reject you as My priests; because you have ignored the law of your God, I also will ignore your children.

(Hosea 4:6)

Likewise, every good tree bears good fruit, but a bad tree bears bad fruit.
A good tree cannot bear bad fruit, and a bad tree cannot bear good fruit.

(Matthew 7:17 -18)

CHAPTER 2

A NEW BEGINNING

We need to lay a solid foundation for the truths presented in this book on which to build from and will spend a little time doing so. Before that happens, we should correct any misconceptions you have about ministry to the heart. Through this instruction, you may gain valuable knowledge that will lead you to life changing revelation. This foundational information will be of immense value when you minister to the hearts of others in the future.

For clarification, the heart, as we will refer to it in this book, is not the physical heart that pumps our blood. It is the heart as described in the New Testament of the Bible and is closely interchangeable with the word "soul," as used in the Old Testament. The heart/soul does have a marriage with the spirit and the two are inseparable in a regenerated man but are recognized separately by their characteristics and nature.

The heart is the center, motivating part of our being. It is made up of your mind (your thinking, not your brain), your will, and your emotions. You are a spirit being, who has a heart/soul and lives in a body. The Bible confirms this: *May God himself, the God of peace, sanctify you through and through. May your whole spirit, soul and body be kept blameless at the coming of our Lord Jesus Christ,* (1 Thessalonians 5:23).

We do not consider ourselves as human beings having spiritual experiences, but rather, we are spirit beings living a human experience on this earth. By restoring the spirit and the soul to its intended state, the human experience is always changed for the good. When the heart/soul is complete (restored), you prosper in every area of your life (3 John 1:2).

When we talk about healing the heart, we are talking about the restoration of the heart to its original state, pure, free, and unencumbered before God and men, the way God intended it to be. King David, a man after God's own heart, declared the need for it in Psalms 51:10, *Create in me a pure heart, O God, and renew a steadfast spirit within me.*

It is important to point out that the healing of your heart is <u>not</u> the healing of the old man or fixing the broken areas of your past. The old man is your old nature, the one you had before you asked Jesus into your heart. That nature died when Jesus came into your heart, and you were given a new nature. Simply put, you can have either the new nature or the old one, but you cannot have them both <u>without conflict</u>.

Maybe you do not understand the truth of this and are living from the past trying to fix old problems. From this position, you are prone to repeat the same mistakes as you attempt to fix one thing at a time. This approach will not achieve the fulfillment of life that God offers. You can often become stuck in this position, believing it is the right thing to do. However, it is an endless spiral that ends with fleeting hope. When you are

A New Beginning

hurting and lost, it is difficult to interact with others through any other lens.

If you are born again, <u>the old man is dead</u> and not capable of being healed. It is useless to attempt to do so. *Knowing this, that our old man was crucified with Him that the body of sin might be done away with, that we should no longer be slaves of sin,* (Romans 6:6). However, the thinking of your old nature that does not line up with God's will for your life may still be alive. You will be able to identify this pattern of belief because it will be in opposition to His purpose for your life. This "stinkin' thinkin'" needs to line up with the truth. If this unregenerated thinking is alive in you, it can be a powerful force that can wreak havoc with your life until it is renewed.

Without salvation, complete healing will never truly come. There will always be something missing. If you are not positively sure that Jesus lives in your heart and that He is Lord of your life, this is easily remedied. We would like to present a relationship with God from a unique perspective than you may have ever known. Please turn to the Salvation chapter of this book and then return here when you know that Jesus is Lord of your life.

Avoiding Hell seems like a viable reason to give your life to the Lordship of Jesus Christ. However, those who attempt to walk with Jesus for this reason often do so from a fear-based reasoning. A relationship based out of this type of fear is difficult to maintain at best and does not offer the contentment Jesus promised. Proverbs 9:10 tells us that *the fear of the Lord is the beginning of wisdom,* not the fear of Hell. Avoiding Hell was not why the disciples followed Christ, and it should not be our reason either. If that is why you offered your heart to the Lord, we understand why your life is missing fullness. That can change right now! Once again, we invite you to stop reading here and turn to the Salvation chapter of this book before continuing.

At this moment, your heart may not be able to comprehend a relationship with the God who allowed you to experience the pain and hurt that led you to this point. Like the laws of gravity, the Truths addressed in this book will work for everyone when they are appropriately applied in your life. At any time during your journey through these chapters you can turn to the Salvation chapter and know by experience a new life with Jesus.

The heart consists of your mind (what you think), your will, and your emotions. God addresses each of these areas in His Word.

Mind: As stated in Romans 12:2, "*Do not conform any longer to the pattern of this world but be transformed by <u>the renewing of your mind</u>. Then you will be able to test and approve what <u>God's will</u> is, his good, pleasing, and perfect will.*"

Will: The will of your heart needs to be conformed to that of the Lord's as stated in Romans 8:29, "*For those God foreknew he also predestined to be conformed to the likeness of his Son, that he might be the firstborn among many brothers.*"

Emotions: We were created in the image of a God who also has emotions. But He instructs us to find a way to express those emotions in a healthy way, not allowing ourselves to fall into sin. *Do not let the sun go down while you are still angry* (Ephesians 4:26).

Now that you understand what restoring the heart is about, let us explore why God created those feelings and emotions that make us who we are. If you are walking down the street and you step off a curb, you may twist your ankle severely. God designed you so that a pain would shoot up your leg, telling your brain there is a problem that needs immediate attention. Having a pain in your ankle does not mean that you are broken. You would be broken if you injured your ankle severely and no signal went to your brain to tell you there was a problem. If you continued to use your wounded ankle, you would make the problem worse and cause other complications. The presence of pain or discomfort is part of God's design to tell you when part of your body needs attention.

The presence of pain or discomfort is part of God's design to tell you when part of your body needs attention.

These natural signals are not just at work in your physical body, they are also at work in your heart. God made you so that your heart would feel pressure, aching and even severe pain. These feelings tell you when your heart needs attention. Emptiness and separation are also signs of a heart-related problem. If someone says something unkind, we feel pain. If someone we love betrays our trust, we might describe ourselves as being "heartbroken."

God created you with the ability to feel deep emotions in your heart. Since the heart we are talking about is your heart/soul and not your physical heart, the pain and pressure is not only felt in your chest but is often felt in your stomach, or as we say in the South, in your belly. It is also possible to feel this heart pain from your head to your toes. Everyone has experienced these symptoms at one time or another.

Unfortunately, you may have been taught to continue through life ignoring the signals from your heart. You could have been told to "get over it." It is only an emotional response which will fade away over time. You may be able to acknowledge that you were hurt by the experience, but then still find yourself trapped or struggling, unable to move past it.

When painful things happen, we continue with life the best we can. We plod through our days collecting additional wounds, becoming more sensitive and fearful with each step, and often causing us to look to external things for relief or comfort. We have seen many people caught in different types of addiction because of painful emotional wounds that have not been properly addressed.

Every person suffering with a wounded, broken or empty heart feels a sense of separation. Hopelessness can set in, and a slow death begins. Sadly, some people even wish for death thinking it will be an end to their mental and emotional torment. This is more common than some people want to believe, and now more medical professionals are finding that many of the physical illnesses they are treating have roots in heart/soul problems.

Every person suffering with a wounded, broken or empty heart feels separation.

A New Beginning

It has been said that "time heals all wounds." This statement is not true. "Time" has no power. Time only puts distance between the source of the wound and the person who was injured. Left unattended, your wound will not go away unless it is healed. Can you imagine someone not getting treatment for a serious physical wound without lasting negative results?

Consider the following scenario that can follow two different paths but have similar outcomes.

Years ago, we heard John and Paula Sanford give this powerful example. A hunter shoots a deer. However, the bullet only cuts through the back hip and does not kill the animal. Now, one of two things can happen at this point. The open wound can become infected and begin to fester. The wounded area on the animal's hip will be painful and sensitive. Even the slightest use of the hip or leg causes pain. Trying to minimize the pain, the deer will restrict its movement to avoid further injury. Normal sounds and noises now produce fear and anxiety, causing the animal to run away unnecessarily. If the injury is not treated, the infection spreads and begins to poison other parts of the body, causing complications not associated with the original wound. The open wound becomes an invitation for insects to feed, and a place to lay their eggs. Eventually, gangrene can set in and will spread through the deer's body, resulting in a slow and painful death.

This scenario could follow another path. When the bullet hits the deer, the wound could simply close over, callous and harden. The tissue will be less flexible and may still cause pain with any movement or be numb having no feeling at all. The wounded area will not look the same and will now function differently. The deer may not be able to run as fast or jump as high as before. As the deer loses some of its mobility, it becomes more vulnerable to predators. Thus, this callused condition causes a disability that makes the deer more likely to be wounded again or even killed.

So, it is with our hearts. If a wounded heart does not receive proper attention, it can become sensitive to even the slightest touch and fearful of another injury. Poison from the infection within the heart slowly progresses into other parts of the body. Sleeplessness, anxiety, aches, and pain develop. Illnesses without related causes become the new focus as the heart condition fades behind other ever increasing health issues. Quality of life can be diminished.

Instead of flies laying eggs within the wound like the analogy that we shared earlier, seeds are planted in the heart. Seeds of bitterness, resentment, anger, strife, hatred, and other such things find their way into our hearts, causing separation and pain. As these seeds take root in your heart, they grow and intertwine. The resulting condition leaves the heart unrecognizable from its previous state. At this point it can then be difficult, if not impossible, to identify the original cause. Death of the heart can be inevitable and could lead to the actual death of the person if not dealt with. In other words: if your heart stops functioning, you stop functioning.

The second path mentioned in our hunting analogy leads to callousness and hardening of the wounded heart. In its hardened and often unrecognizable state, the heart can lose its range of motion (emotions). We can become less sensitive to others. Intimacy in our relationships can be lost, although a constant quest. In this callous state, our hearts become more vulnerable to being wounded again or become numb as a means of protection and escape. Those who experience this often feel empty or dead inside.

**If your heart stops functioning,
you stop functioning.**

It is important that you know you cannot restore your own wounded heart. We cannot even think of a reason for you to keep trying. However, there is One who will do it for you when you open your heart to His purposes. He is Jesus Christ, Jehovah-Rapha, the Healer of hearts. He will make the changes within you and bring healing to your heart in ways that are miraculous.

There is one prerequisite for accessing this healing. You must be as honest with yourself as possible as you read through this book. When you are open and transparent before the Lord, it allows the Healer to move in ways you may have never seen happen before in your life. Once again, this process is quite simple. This is not a methodology or a science, but a series of biblical truths that leads to the abundant life to the fullest. These truths always work!

If you still have doubts or unbelief that God will heal you, or you are feeling hopeless, be assured that there is no damage or injury that God cannot restore. God can and will heal your heart. You do have a bright future ahead of you, and you will live your life to the fullest. We have seen Him do it over and over again, even for those who felt like healing was impossible for them. And best of all, it was easy.

As the father of a house full of girls, when they were young, occasionally, one would come into our bedroom in the middle of the night and say, "Dad, I am afraid." When I asked "why?" she would say, "I don't know why, I am just afraid." I would take her back to her room, tuck her in bed and do one of three things. I would tell her stories followed by a prayer. If they fell asleep, I would go back to my room. If they did not fall asleep right away, I would sit beside them on their bed until they fell asleep. Since their beds were small, sometimes I would take a pillow and lay on the floor beside their bed. Occasionally, I would nod off before they would, only to wake up feeling warm air blowing across my face. Upon opening my eyes, I would discover a face only inches from my own, checking to see if I was still awake. Of course, this "checkup" would startle me and ensure that I would stay awake until they were sound asleep.

Something particularly important happened when one of my daughters came into our room and told me that she was afraid. No longer was her fear her responsibility, at that point it became mine. I was her father and wanted the best for her. However, before I could do anything to help her, she had to come to me for help.

If you are experiencing fear, worry or anxiety, be assured that the Father will never leave you. Just as I watched over my daughters, comforting them, and protecting them, God will never leave you (Hebrews 13:5). Come to Him with an open heart, lay your burdens in His arms and watch Him make the changes in your heart. You will find the peace, security, and

A New Beginning

strength for which you are longing. Start by repeating this prayer from your heart:

Father, I am afraid the things in my heart will not change and the conditions in my life will continue as they are or even get worse. I have tried everything I know to do and have not found lasting answers. I am willing to give You all my fears and concerns and I lay them down at Your Altar.

Father, I ask You to help open my heart to hear any truths You have for me or to correct any false beliefs. I am willing to change my direction where You show me a truer path from Your Word. I ask You to give me Your peace and show me Your love. Father, thank You for what You are going to do in me and in others through me, in Jesus' Name. Amen."

Scripture References

Dear friend, I pray that you may enjoy good health and that all may go well with you, even as your soul is getting along well.

(3 John 1:2)

The fear of the Lord is the beginning of wisdom, and knowledge of the Holy One is understanding.

(Proverbs 9:10)

God has said, "Never will I leave you; never will I forsake you."

(Hebrews 13:5)

CHAPTER 3

PREPARING THE HEART

We are just one chapter away from presenting the truth with the power to change your life and heal your heart. As we prepare for that part of our journey, here are a few things that will help bring clarity.

When I (Michael) was 15 years old, I received my civilian pilot's license. After flying for three years, I planned to join the Army to become a helicopter pilot. Compared to other applicants who had no flying experience, I figured I was a "shoe-in." To my dismay, the Army did not agree. Even though I had three years' experience, I had learned a completely different method of flying. The Army would have to un-train me and then retrain me to fly by military methods and rules. Because this was often difficult and time-consuming, they found it was easier to start with new raw recruits who had not learned the "wrong" method of flying. I had been flying successfully for years and could not comprehend that there was another way to fly. However, there was another way, it was just not my way.

You may have heard it said, "the shortest distance between two points is a straight line." If you are going to a particular destination, you usually have multiple choices as to how to get there. Even though the shortest path may be the most direct way with the quickest results, you have the freedom to choose a longer, more "scenic" route. Sometimes our choice of direction is based only on roads or paths we are familiar with. However, our knowledge of the area may be limited to only a familiar path, unaware that there may be a better or easier way to reach our destination.

Although some things we discuss in the following chapters may be new concepts, many of these "places and destinations" may also be familiar to you. We might just be taking you there via a different route. Our current perspective has a lot to do with our ability to see. There are many examples of hikers getting lost in the woods, and when they are eventually found, they are only ten or fifteen feet from the trail. The foliage was just too thick for them to find their way through without help. It is entirely possible to be only a short distance from your destination and still be unable to find a path to it. Small corrections in direction can have big results in the end. Please keep an open heart and an open mind while we present an easier, better way to live the life you desire.

Those who are hurt, broken, empty or lost will search anywhere and everywhere for help. They are often willing to try anything for relief, but most have found only temporary solutions. There are several teachings that have entered the church as a way of restoring the heart. Although these methods appear to be truth at first glance and have offered temporary relief to some, they have also shipwrecked others and caused much pain. These methods do not represent the full Truth of God. We offer a brief explanation of why.

The first method to discuss is psychology. Psychology is the study of the human mind and its mental states as well as the study of human and animal behavior. Its focus is on how to relate to and work through problems, issues, and conditions, but it offers few real cures. Psychology may teach you how to live with your current "condition" or offer chemicals to change the various brain, hormonal and chemical functions of your body. However, psychology does not recognize spiritual causes of these conditions because it does not know of them. We are surprised to see churches so eagerly absorb psychology into their counseling programs when so many of its beliefs and teachings contradict the Word of God.

We are not against psychologists. We are thankful for the research they have done and for what they have mastered in identifying specific problems. However, we are emphasizing that the Truth of God is not psychology's foundation for healing. Their leaders can present you "facts" about your condition in the light of their own understanding and education, but that does not make it truth. Their findings and beliefs cannot be our standard, and their methods, which often contradict the Word of God, rarely produce lasting fruit.

Only the Truth of God can produce lasting fruit in your life. This Truth is superior to all other "truths" or facts, no matter what the person presenting them to you believes. We know by experience that the truths found in the Word of God bring healing. This Truth is written by God and is about God. We were created in His image and only His Truths have the power to change our lives. When we act contrary to who He is, we act contrary to our own true nature and live unfulfilled lives.

Psychology has no concept of this truth. We have seen people get healed through counseling and are not opposed to some of it. However, there is a better way as outlined in the Word of God.

The second method we will discuss here is teachings that includes the "healing of memories." This has also been called "inner healing" or "healing of the emotions." Those that practice this type of healing (we did for decades until we found a better way) probe the mind for hidden and buried memories so the negative memories can be revealed, identified, and healed. This sounds like the right idea at first, but it is not, even when caring people present it. Most people who do this type of ministry have loving hearts and want to help them by fixing the broken areas of their past.

The philosophy of these teachings claims that healing comes through the uprooting of negative memories and hurts caused by others earlier in life, some as far back as the womb. These memories and hurts may be hidden in our subconscious mind and may have to be dug up for healing to occur. Those who practice this believe that if the memory is in your subconscious, it is an authentic experience. Unfortunately, this belief discounts the powerful influence of the stories we absorb from books, television, movies, and other sources of the world media.

The person receiving this type of ministry is often at the mercy of whatever or whoever is influencing their memories. It is common for the person who is receiving this type of ministry to feel better temporarily but they can end up with an altered sense of reality of the situation. By this time, some may experience an altered perception of who God is as well. God created us with a powerful and creative imagination, and it sometimes takes only a small suggestion to create a vivid picture and lasting memory in our minds.

Some prayer ministers desire to see the person healed so badly that they want the memory, whether real or perceived, to include Jesus being present while the hurt is taking place. Some inner healers use a "technique of visualization." The fact that these teachings cannot be found in the Bible, does not seem to affect those who practice it. These techniques require you to turn inward for the answers every time you experience a negative emotion. Those who practice this say you cannot deny their results, but they also admit that it could take a lifetime to root out all the negative memories. Moreover, even after a lifetime of trying, you may continue to feel incomplete until you die and go to heaven.

**The old man is dead, however,
your thinking needs to be renewed**

This is <u>not</u> the message of the Kingdom that Jesus brought to us and offers only temporary fulfillment until the next negative emotion emerges. In truth, this is just another attempt to heal the "old man" who is dead and does not need to be healed. The "old man" needs to be buried for the last time. However, your 'thinking' needs to be renewed and many in this type of ministry disagree on how to do it.

Most people who are teaching this type of inner healing have sincere hearts for God and a real desire to see His people set free.

LIVING FULLY FREE

If you are someone who has been doing the type of ministry described above, we would like to speak directly to you for a moment. Before you throw this book down and conclude that there is not a better way, we ask you to please continue reading. See for yourself if the truths that are presented here offer a more complete result with less effort. At this point, we ask you to do what we did when confronted with the same choice. Search out the Truth for yourself and ask the Lord if this might be a better way. It will require some time and effort on your part but will prove to be valuable to you and those you are called to help in the future.

Significant lasting results come when you deal with the root cause of the problem according to the Word of God, not by some other method. The "healing of memories" produces some immediate fruit that feels good, but it rarely deals with the root cause in a way that brings complete healing. Its focus is inward. If you do not receive total healing, you will need to return for a deeper dive. This could continue indefinitely.

True fruit always contains the seed that makes it capable of being reproduced.

The Bible says, *by their fruit you will recognize them*, (Matthew 7:20). However, <u>true fruit always contains the seed that makes it capable of being reproduced</u>. In that way, it becomes lasting fruit. Otherwise, fruit would soon die and decay leaving you with nothing. Jesus did not talk about a temporary

Preparing the Heart

healing. He did not mention short-term deliverance with a need for repeated ministry for the rest of your life for the same issues. Nowhere in the Bible can you find Jesus say He was shedding His blood for a partial healing or temporary fix. NO! His declaration was one of eternal life, freedom, and healing for the rest of your life. The Bible tells us, *He whom the Son has set free, is free indeed,* (John 8:36). Ministry that produces short-term results only deals with the branches of the tree, or the symptoms, but has not pulled the tree up by its roots. Without the removal of the root cause according to the principles in the Bible, you will find your problems to be chronic in nature, never completely resolved.

A danger in psychology and inner healing teaching is that it forces you to turn inward in a continual spiral, constantly looking for more wounds. Its negative focus can be endless, looking for perfection. Anything that turns you inward toward self will turn you <u>away</u> from the Cross of Jesus Christ, where all healing is found. The fruit of that inward turn is 'I' centeredness which leads to death. Inner healing uses "the mind" as its operating table where anything can and often does happen. We disagree strongly with this because we have ministered to many hurting people who were casualties of this mindset. There is a way to avoid this process altogether by focusing on the powerful, life-changing Truth in God's Word.

The Bible says, *Therefore, if anyone is in Christ, he is a new creation; old things have passed away; behold, all things have become new,* (2 Corinthians 5:17-18 NKJV). Dead things should not and do not need to be healed, and you can wear yourself out trying to do so. However, the thinking of your old man may be alive and active. As we are told in Scripture, your old way of thinking needs to be changed.

Man is the most unusual creature on earth. While other animals are born with inherent abilities from birth, we are born with only a few basic instincts. We need constant care and ongoing teaching to survive on our own. As babies, we must be shown how to walk, or we will never walk. We must be talked to in order to learn how to talk, and we must be shown love to learn how to love. We learn from what others teach us. Thus, we are the product of other people's influence. We live within a belief system taught to us by others.

This is easily understood by comparing the many cultural differences that exist around the world. Whether we examine a nuclear family, or comparatively a large nation, each group of people has their own collection of beliefs. Children brought up within a particular culture continue in those beliefs because it is what they have been taught. Our perceptions from the teachings and influences of others become the foundation of our internal belief systems and will dictate how we interact with the world around us. Your interpretations of these teachings and the influences others have on your life make up your thinking (your beliefs). However, what happens if you have believed things that are not true, and are living your life as if they were the truth?

**Dead things should not and
do not need to be healed.**

Preparing the Heart

When I (Michael) was a young boy, my mother dressed me in a light blue suit to go to a family reunion. I must admit I did not like that suit and did not want to go anywhere wearing it. My mother insisted that I looked good in that blue suit. As I was getting out of the car, my aunt spotted me and stopped dead in her tracks. With a loud voice, she blurted out, "Boy, you sure do look good in blue!" Her words poured into my being like molten lead into a cold mold and they forever formed an indelible impression in my mind. To this day, I believe that I look good in blue, in comparison to other colors.

Imagine a scenario where the words spoken to me were not edifying, but instead were harsh, ugly, and damaging and I had absorbed them as the truth? The words, whether positive or negative, had the same possibility to be poured into the mold of my heart and to become what I now believe. If my aunt had told me I looked like a tulip, which was my perception, I doubt I would own a blue shirt today. What I have learned through my experiences makes up the foundational beliefs I stand on today. How I perceived those experiences makes up the "thinking" part of my heart.

We are affected not only by reality but also by our perception of reality. This is illustrated in a story told about two brothers who shared the same room while they were growing up. The younger brother had been blind from birth. When the older brother turned ten, he was given the responsibility to make sure his younger brother was properly dressed each day. One day, thinking he was being funny, he told his younger brother there was a right and left sock. Further amusing himself, he often told his brother he had his socks on the wrong foot. Years later, it took two roommates in college a month to convince the younger brother that he had been taught something that was not true. He had believed a lie.

While that may seem funny, far-fetched, and even a bit sad, it does bring us to the point. You are a product of what you have learned through your experience and have become what you have believed. This will happen whether what you were taught was the truth or a lie. You act out of and live according to what you believe. If you believe lies, you will continue to believe them <u>as</u> truth until you are enlightened to <u>the</u> Truth. A lie believed as truth will affect your life as if it were true. You may be wondering, "How do I know if what I believe is a lie or the truth?"

If you believe lies, you will continue to believe them until you are enlightened to the Truth.

The answer is quite simple. Look at the lasting fruit produced by what you currently believe. The fruit of your life is the evidence of the condition of your heart. Ask yourself, "Would you want everything in your heart reproduced in those you love"? Your heart's condition was formed through what you believe. Because of what you believe and how you act because of those beliefs, your fruit will be self-evident.

The Bible tells us, *as a man thinks in his heart, so he is*, (Proverbs 23:7 NKJ). Fortunately for us, God was gracious and did not leave it up to our imaginations or reasoning to define what good fruit should be. He spelled it out clearly for us in Scripture. In people, good fruit is recognized as love, joy, peace, patience, kindness, goodness, faithfulness, gentleness, and self-control with humility (Galatians 5:22-23). Bad fruit is recognized as pride, selfishness, bitterness, rage, anger, brawling and slander, along with every form of malice (Galatians 5:19-21).

Even though hurt people often have a combination of good and bad fruit, most do not believe they produce any bad fruit. Almost everyone believes in their heart that their motives are pure and that they just occasionally act badly or stray from their own good nature. Some believe these actions are not born out of their own heart but from the influences and inappropriate actions of others. They believe they are only reacting badly because of someone else's bad behavior. So, what is the truth?

How can you tell if your heart is pure and produces good fruit or if you are deceived? Again, the answer is quite simple: listen to the words that come out of your mouth. These words alone can paint a picture of what lives within your heart. The Bible says, *either make the tree good and its fruit good, or else make the tree bad and its fruit bad; for a tree is known by its fruit. Brood of vipers! How can you, being evil, speak good things? For out of the abundance of the heart the mouth speaks. A good man out of the good treasure of his heart brings forth good things, and an evil man out of the evil treasure brings forth evil things,* (Matthew 12:33-36).

Examine the condition of your heart for a moment. Are your words destructive or are they life giving? Are you talking about the faults and shortcomings you see in those around you, or are you edifying and building them up despite their faults? What comes out of our mouths reveals what is in our hearts. Words paint a vivid picture of our heart that others can see even when we cannot.

LIVING FULLY FREE

It is common for people who are hurting and under pressure to act and speak differently than when there is no pain or pressure from a trial or hardship. Consider this: if you squeeze grapes, you will get grape juice. Putting oranges under pressure produces orange juice. Squeeze a lemon and you will not get sweet apple juice or anything other than lemon juice. You can only get out of something that which is already in it.

**You can only get out of something
that which is already in it.**

You do not know what is truly on the inside of you until a situation comes along that begins to apply pressure. What is deep down inside of you, during normal daily life, may never have reason to rise to the surface, so it lays hidden and dormant. But, when life gets challenging and difficult, you will see what you are really made of, instead of what you want to believe about yourself. These situations and the resulting "unveiling" of your true self, are not pleasant and can even be painful and embarrassing. We have all gone through it.

It has been said that adversity will always introduce a man to himself. If we believe lies, the ungodliness of those lies will show up in our lives as bad fruit and will come out of our mouths accordingly. When these lies are rooted into your heart, they leave you hurting and incomplete.

Another way to tell whether you are walking in truth or not is if there is a battle going on within you. This might be exhibited by a constant "war" of arguments in your mind, knots in your stomach, or fear, doubt and unbelief which keep you from sleeping at night. It could also come in the form of negative thoughts that keep replaying in your mind. These situations can be disturbing and hard to process. Peace might feel like a distant friend. There is a resolution available in those moments and we are going to discuss them further as we progress through this book. Those who walk in the Truth do not have this battle.

We have often found that if the truth is presented to someone who is deceived, that person may process the truth through his or her false beliefs and end up poisoning that truth. It is now only partially true. For example, many in the church chant, "The truth will set you free." That is only half of the Scripture, thus it is an inaccurate statement or just a partial truth.

Indeed, the Scripture tells us, *then you will know the truth, and the truth will set you free*, (John 8:32). This passage contains the hope of freedom, but it cannot stand alone without the context of the verse before it, and thus the two verses are inseparable. Verse 31 is what makes this all work. *To the Jews who had believed him, Jesus said, "If you hold to my teaching, you are really my disciples. Then you will know the truth, and the truth will set you free"* (John 8:31-32). The word "hold" in this text means to continue in or obey, to remain faithful to.

Only after holding to His teachings, can we process His Truth as the Truth. After holding and knowing Him, the Truth will set you free! Jesus said, "I am the way, and the truth, and the life," John 14:6. Jesus is the Truth. If you hold to His teachings, it says, "...you will know the truth," and the Truth (Jesus) will then set you free! You may have heard concepts like this before, but we now want to offer "His teachings" in a way so that you can truly experience Truth. We will present commonly misunderstood truths in the light of His teachings. The results can be life changing.

Knowing the Truth will not end all life's hardships, but it will help you get through every one of them. Truth will not keep your heart from being wounded and hurt, but you will never be alone as you experience them. Truth will keep your heart soft and pure and will quickly produce healing when and where it is needed. Your life will reflect the nature and character of God through every circumstance, and you will shine.

It is possible that not everything you have been taught in the past is the life-giving Truth of God. If the fruit of your life and the words of your mouth are not consistent with a pure heart, then allow the Lord to do a work in you as you repeat the parts of this prayer that apply to you:

Father, I confess the fruit of my life is not what it could be and that my thinking needs to change. I also recognize by the words of my mouth that my heart needs to change. I do not have consistent peace and that needs to change. Jesus, I am willing to open my heart to You and trust You to make the necessary changes within my heart. In Jesus' name, I pray. Father, I thank You, for the change that is coming to my life, amen!

Now we are ready to focus on the instructions that can heal your heart. These Truths are simple, and we will go through them together. All these teachings are based on His Word, and that is where we will go next to find the answers. Keep your heart open

Preparing the Heart

as we present some old ideas from an entirely new perspective in hopes that you may see the revelatory Truth that always brings healing and freedom. The Word of God produces good fruit that lasts.

Scripture References

Watch out for false prophets. They come to you in sheep's clothing, but inwardly they are ferocious wolves. By their fruit you will recognize them. Do people pick grapes from thorn bushes, or figs from thistles? Likewise, every good tree bears good fruit, but a bad tree bears bad fruit. A good tree cannot bear bad fruit, and a bad tree cannot bear good fruit. Every tree that does not bear good fruit is cut down and thrown into the fire. Thus, by their fruit you will recognize them.

(Matthew 7:15-20)

But the fruit of the Spirit is love, joy, peace, patience, kindness, goodness, faithfulness, gentleness, and self-control. Against such things there is no law.

(Galatians 5:22-24)

The acts of the sinful nature are obvious: sexual immorality, impurity, and debauchery; idolatry and witchcraft; hatred, discord, jealousy, fits of rage, selfish ambition, dissensions, factions, and envy; drunkenness, orgies, and the like. I warn you as I did before, that those who live like this will not inherit the kingdom of God.

(Galatians 5:19-21)

CHAPTER 4

THE TRUTH ABOUT REPENTANCE

Let us start at the beginning with the story of Adam and Eve. You think that you know this story. However, do you really know the messages within the story and how they relate to you today? Take the time to read Genesis chapter 1-3.

Picking up the story in Chapter 2: *The LORD God took the man and put him in the Garden of Eden to work it and take care of it. And the LORD God commanded the man, "You are free to eat from any tree in the garden; but you must not eat from the tree of the knowledge of good and evil, for when you eat of it you will surely die"* (Genesis 2:15-17).

Moving forward to Chapter 3: *Now the serpent was craftier than any of the wild animals the LORD God had made. He said to the woman, "Did God really say, 'You must not eat from any tree in the garden'?" The woman said to the serpent, "We may eat fruit from the trees in the garden, but God did say, "You must not eat fruit from the tree that is in the middle of the garden, and you must not touch it, or you will die". "You will not surely die," the serpent said to the woman. "For God knows that when you eat of it your eyes will be opened, and you will be like God, knowing good and evil." When the* *woman saw that the fruit of the tree was good for food and pleasing to the eye, and desirable for gaining wisdom, she took some and ate it. She also gave some to her husband, who was with her, and he ate it. Then the eyes of both of them were opened, and they realized they were naked; so, they sewed fig leaves together and made coverings for themselves. Then the man and his wife heard the sound of the LORD God as he was walking in the garden in the cool of the day, and they hid from the LORD God among the trees of the garden. But the LORD God called to the man, "**Where are you**?" He answered, "I heard you in the garden, and I was afraid because I was naked; so, I hid." And he said, "**Who told you that you were naked? Have you eaten from the tree that I commanded you not to eat from?**" The man said, "The woman you put here with me, she gave me some fruit from the tree, and I ate it." Then the LORD God said to the woman, "**What is this you have done?**" The woman said, "The serpent deceived me, and I ate"* (Genesis 3:1-13).

Why did God ask Adam if he had eaten fruit from the tree of knowledge of good and evil? Certainly, God already knew the answer. God was aware of what Adam had done. The Creator of the universe does not ask man questions seeking knowledge, but rather to reveal to man what lies within his heart. So why did God ask Adam this question?

The Creator of the universe does not ask man questions seeking knowledge, but rather to reveal to man what lies within his heart.

The Truth About Repentance

Consider another question. At this point in the story, after eating from the tree of the knowledge of good and evil, had man fallen? Adam had disobeyed God. However, had he fallen? The answer lies in the fact that God even asked Adam the question above. If man had already fallen, there would have been a swift pronouncement of judgment instead of an inquiry.

If you know the true nature of God, you can better understand the reason He questioned Adam. Two truths about God are at work here that cannot change. The Bible says in 1 John 1:9, *if we confess our sins, he is faithful and just and will forgive us our sins and purify us from all unrighteousness.* In addition, Hebrews 13:8 tells us: *Jesus Christ is the same yesterday and today and forever.*

By approaching Adam with His question, God was giving Adam the opportunity to take ownership of his disobedience and repent. He gave Adam a choice. He later gave it to Adam's son, Cain, after he had killed his brother Abel. (Genesis 4:10-12) Additionally, He gave that same chance to King David after he had taken Bathsheba and killed her husband, Uriah. (2 Samuel 12:1-13) Today, He also gives that opportunity to anyone who wants to continue to walk in agreement or in unity with Him. In doing so, you will eventually take on His character and nature, His plan from the beginning.

Look at what Adam did with his opportunity to take responsibility for his actions. He not only told God that it was not his fault, but he continued to point out that it was *the <u>woman</u> that <u>You</u> gave me.* He was saying, "Not me! Not me! IT WAS NOT ME!" Instead of taking the responsibility and repenting for what he had done, Adam not only pointed a finger at Eve, but, ultimately, he blamed God. He accused God as the responsible party, since after all He had put the woman in the Garden to start with! This is a perfect picture of the Adamic nature at work. It was, "Not me! It is not my fault."

The same nature was at work in Eve who quickly blamed the serpent when God gave her the opportunity to confess. After Cain murdered his brother, Abel, in Genesis 4:9 God asked Cain where his brother was? Sadly, Cain followed in the footsteps of both his mother and father. When the door was open for him to become accountable for his actions, he answered, "I don't know."

"Not me" and "I don't know" are the trademarks of the Adamic nature. "It was not my fault." 'It was that person who cut me off in traffic." Or "It was that boss of mine at the job You gave me Lord." Maybe you have even caught yourself thinking, "It was that mother, father, or that spouse You gave me, Lord. But it was "NOT ME!" The Adamic nature blames someone else but does not take ownership/responsibility for its own actions. If you want to continue to walk in unity with God and His creation, it is necessary to identify the Adamic "not me" nature in your life and get rid of it. How different would things have been if, when God approached Adam, he had instead accepted responsibility for his actions and asked for forgiveness?

We are all born with the Adamic nature of "not me" within us. A perfect example comes to mind from the days when our girls were young. I (Michael) can still see the milk jug that one of the girls had left out of the refrigerator on the kitchen table all night long. The jug had lost its original shape and had swollen so large that it looked as if it were about to explode.

When I discovered the problem, I questioned the girls, "Who

left the milk out all night?" I turned to each one asking, "Did you do it?" Respectfully, each child claimed it was, "Not me!" When questioned further as to who might possibly be responsible, they each responded with a resounding, "I don't know!" The old one-two punch of the Adamic nature at work!

Based on what you read in the Bible, do you understand that God foreknew Adam was going to fall and man would need a Savior? We believe the answer is found in 1 Peter 1:20 *He (Jesus) was chosen before the creation of the world but was revealed in these last times for your sake.* It was God's plan from the very beginning to restore the hearts of men. His plan has not changed. God made a provision for restoration before the creation of the world.

God always gives us the opportunity to take ownership and repent so that we can be restored, no matter what we have done. Cain needed to repent for jealousy and the murder of his brother. King David had to repent for lust, premeditated murder, and adultery. In the midst of an angry, bloodthirsty crowd in John 8, Jesus, full of love, compassion, and forgiveness, reaches out to the woman caught in adultery. He offers another chance at life by pardoning her for her actions. Whenever you are willing to confess your sins and take responsibility (ownership) for your heart's attitudes, Jesus readily offers the same opportunity to you as well.

Another misconception has been taught from the Adam and Eve story. Some believe that God no longer walked with man after Adam and Eve were banished from the Garden of Eden. This belief claims God's heart changed towards man and His feelings towards him changed because man was not perfect. This is simply not true. (Genesis Chapter 4) The Bible is the story of

God desiring to commune with man after Adam was expelled from the Garden. Malachi 3:6 *"I the Lord do not change."*

God's original plan is for us to walk with Him in a deep intimate relationship.

God designed us for fellowship with Him. His plan is for us to walk with Him in a deep, intimate relationship. God's desire was not to force us to come to Him, but to allow us to choose to love Him. He desires that we would choose Him as our Father and come to Him for help, healing, forgiveness, fellowship, and love. Remember, when we walk with Him, we will in time take on His nature and character (2 Corinthians 3:18).

Sin separates us from Him, and repentance restores our relationship with Him. God designed man with the ability to choose to sin when He created him. He also knew that few if any could maintain the laws, rules, and regulations of the Old Covenant, so He planned a perfect way to reconcile us to Himself. <u>He sent His Son</u>, Jesus Christ.

Jesus came so God could live within us, and we could once again live a life in unity with Him and His creation. His provision was not just for this life, but also for eternity (John 3:16). God is offering forgiveness and healing to you today as well because He truly is *Jesus Christ, the same yesterday and today and forever,* (Hebrews 13:8).

Look at another aspect of the story. *The man and his wife heard the sound of the Lord God as he was walking in the Garden, and they hid from the Lord God,* (Genesis 3:10). When we know we have done something wrong, we often attempt to hide from the Lord as well as from others around us. We may do this by avoidance or by trying to bury ourselves in our work, hobbies, or other activities. We all know someone that uses sarcastic comments or hurtful words to keep people at a distance. There are some who try to avoid sin's guilt by losing themselves in the world's media in hopes of forgetting a particular situation or problem, only to find the issue remains when the entertainment is over. Some camouflage their actions by creating and presenting an acceptable "personality" to others because they fear their true selves would not be loved or accepted. Others may turn to alcohol or drugs as a haven until these false hiding places eventually become problems as well. Man's Adamic nature tries to cover up sinful actions with deception, avoidance and lies.

Most are willing to confess the sins to God that they would not mind everyone knowing. However, the sins we do not want anyone to know about we mistakenly believe we can hide from God as well. This thinking is based on the false belief that He does not already know the intimate parts of our lives. Also, do not make the mistake of believing that God's silence about your sin is somehow an endorsement or acceptance of your actions. It is not.

God's silence about your sin is not an endorsement or acceptance of your actions.

The Word is truly clear on this subject. *Nothing in all creation is hidden from God's sight. Everything is uncovered and laid bare before the eyes of him to whom we must give account,* (Hebrews 4:13). What you mistake as acceptance, due to His silence, is merely the separation that your sin has caused between you and your Creator. He is not sitting in silent agreement with your ungodly actions or character. In reality, He is waiting for you to choose to come to Him with a repentant heart so you may be reconciled to Him and have the life promised to you. He will never reject you when you humbly approach Him seeking a restored relationship.

There are many reasons why people try to hide their sin or the sin of others, but the result of hiding is always the same: separation from God. Job stated it best: *I have concealed my sin as men do, by hiding my guilt in my heart because I so feared the crowd and so dreaded the contempt of the clans that I kept silent and would not go outside* (Job 31:33-34).

Some sins hidden within your heart may not have originated from you.

Some sins hidden in your heart might not even be <u>your</u> sin. People who were verbally, physically, or sexually abused as children, may have hidden the sin in their heart as if they were the author, conspirators of it, or even deserved it. Was it their sin? No! However, they have hidden it in their hearts, believing that somehow the sin committed against them was a result of their own actions. These people carry the false belief that they were at some point responsible for the abuse they received as children. Unfortunately, those who believe this lie will carry it into every part of their life until they hear and embrace the truth and accept God's healing.

The Bible states in Hebrews 11:4 that *Abel was a righteous man.* He was a righteous man, yet he died because of sin, his brother's sin. The Bible confirms in Romans 6:23a that *the wage of sin is death.* It does not always have to be your sin that causes the death. Fortunately, there is freedom for you, even if you are suffering from the effects of someone else's sin that was committed against you. This freedom is provided through Jesus Christ.

He (Jesus) was chosen before the creation of the world but was revealed in these last times for your sake, (1 Peter 1:20). God always had a plan for restoration. Within that plan, He had to have a path for those who would choose to follow Him. Preparation was necessary for man to be ready to receive Jesus and the message He would bring. When the time was right, and in fulfillment of prophecy, God sent a man, a voice, to compel people to come. That man was John the Baptist.

John loudly voiced man's need for repentance of sin. Mark 1:5 states: *The whole Judean countryside and all the people of Jerusalem went out to him.* Do you suppose all these people would have listened to this man if something life changing had not happened to them? Others would not have come to John either unless they had seen the changes in their friends and family members who had already heeded John's words.

John prepared the way for the people of Judea by leading them in repentance of their sins. He prepared the hearts of people to hear Jesus, and eventually be healed by Him. Those who would not repent, like the Pharisees who believed they had no sin to repent of, were unable to hear Jesus' words or comprehend who He was. It was through repentance and blood sacrifice that God would restore all things unto Himself. Through our repentance and the blood of Jesus, He restores all things today.

**Repentance means you change
your ways or habits.**

After people went to John the Baptist and repented (changed), their hearts were prepared to hear the life-giving words of Jesus. According to some definitions, the word "repent" means that you recognize the wrong in something you have done. Subsequently, you feel so much regret about a sin, past action, or inaction, that you change your ways or habits. <u>Change</u> is the keyword here. True repentance is characterized when we cease to love and practice sin. Remember, it is a form of insanity to continue to do the same thing (no change) and expect different results.

When your heart is hurting and bound by pain, the idea that you must do one more thing can sometimes be overwhelming, even if doing that one thing means you will be free. You may not believe this now, but doing what we propose is quite easy. This change will not make your life more difficult, but instead, will make it more fruitful. There is hope, although it may not seem that way if you view things only from the unrepentant side of your heart where you are carrying the weight, guilt, shame, and fear from sin.

The Truth About Repentance

Before we go any further with repentance, we need to clarify something men call the "age of accountability." Sin is simply a willful act of disobedience against God. A young child may be too immature to understand their sinful actions are an act of disobedience towards God, even if they are aware that their actions are in disobedience to their parents. Understanding <u>why</u> something is wrong is just as important as knowing that it is wrong. It is the parent's responsibility to make the child aware of the effects of their actions and of their eventual accountability to God (Proverbs 22:6). Until they become aware of this responsibility to God, the child is sanctified through the believing parent (1 Corinthians 7:14). This covering by the parent is continued until the child reaches the age of accountability or maturity.

The "age of accountability" is a time in our young lives when we cross over from our parent's spiritual "protection" to becoming accountable to God for our own actions. Based on the ancient Jewish belief, a child goes from childhood to adulthood at the age of thirteen.

However, the "age of accountability" is best identified as when the child reaches puberty and is capable of reproduction. The age for this varies between children, as does their awareness of God. After this age, the child becomes responsible to God for his actions as well as to his parents and other governing authorities. Children may not receive proper training in this area and carry guilt and condemnation into their adult life for their past actions.

By now, you should fully understand that you are personally responsible to God for anything (sin) that would separate you from the life He promised you <u>after</u> the age of accountability. If you still carry any sin in your heart, you are separated from God to some degree. You might be asking, "When I gave my life to the Lord, didn't He wash away all my sin?" Of course He did! You have been brought into His wonderful light (1 Peter 2:9). However, if you have not renewed your mind (Romans 12:2) with the Truth of God's Word (Ephesians 5:26), you could still believe lies that keep you separated from the life that God offers you. This is more common than people are willing to admit but is easy to correct. How would you know if this is you? The fruit of your life will reflect this condition.

You became a saint—a holy believer transformed out of the kingdom of darkness into the Kingdom of light—the day you asked Jesus into your heart, and you are no longer a sinner. The old desires and nature that once ruled you were replaced with the nature of your Lord and Savior, Jesus Christ. However, if you believe you are a sinner, then by faith you will sin. You will need to renew your mind, the way you think, to take on the new identity that Jesus offers you.

If you believe you are a sinner, then by faith, you will sin!

Not to complicate the matter even more, but sin can be more than just doing something wrong. It is also possible to commit the sin of omission, which is not doing what you should do in a certain situation. You can be hurt when you or someone else fails to do the right thing. The Bible states in James 4:17, *Anyone, then, who knows the good he ought to do and does not do it, sins.*

Therefore, it is possible to sin by not doing what you ought to do. We have all been victims of this type of sin and a lot of us are perpetrators of it.

Finally, the Bible goes on to teach us that anything not done in faith, is sin. Romans 14:23 explains *everything that does not come from faith is sin.* If you act or react out of fear, doubt, unbelief, or anything else that is not faith, you have opened the door to sin. Understand that sin is not really the problem but is simply a symptom of the root problem. Sin is the result of walking out of unity (out of agreement, not in accord) with God, His purpose, and His creation. There are some who just read the statement above and determined that sin is no big deal, since it is just walking out of accord with God. There is no "bigger" deal. Sin leads to death for both you and others!

The reason we are pointing out that there are many ways for sin to exist within your life is to bring about an awareness of it hiding within your heart. If it is there, you need to repent for it (take ownership). We are not identifying sin to bring judgment or condemnation, but to begin the process for freedom, healing, and restoration. We believe, there is more grace in Jesus than sin in you! If you are aware of sin in your life, know that God is faithful and just to forgive you when you confess your sins to Him (1 John 1:9). It is His nature to do so.

There is a common misconception that can capture the heart of those who miss the mark (sin). They can take on their sin as a part of their identity. This is especially true for people who have repeated the same sin. For example: perhaps you committed adultery, so you are now and forever an adulterer. The same can be true for any sin. Have you lied, been greedy, cheated, been a drunkard, addict, or a gossiper? God's Word tells us to take ownership of the sin and then repent (change). You are not to take ownership, repent, and then let it become part of your identity, secret or otherwise.

When I (Michael) was a teenager growing up in rural South Carolina, I worked on a family farm during the summers. I would often jump out of the second story window of the barn to get down as opposed to using the ladder. One day when I did, I landed on a board that had a large nail sticking up out of it. The nail went all the way through the bottom of my shoe and up out the top of my foot. Clearly the nail had entered my body, and was now a part of me, but I never once had the thought "I AM a nail!"

We do not become our sins. It does not matter how frequently you have sinned or repeated the same sin. In addition, there is not a statute of limitations on asking forgiveness for your sins. No matter when or where sin entered your life, ask for forgiveness today. If you know of any type of sin in your heart, it is time to get rid of it and be reconciled to the One who made you. If this describes you, then repeat this prayer from your heart.

> *Father, I confess that I have hidden sin in my heart. You said in Your Word that You would forgive me if I confessed my sin and that You will cleanse me from all unrighteousness. Father, I take responsibility for this sin (name of the sin or sins), I repent and will not repeat these sins again. Father, I ask You to forgive me. and to place these sins on the cross of Jesus. I thank you for washing me clean and making me whole, in Jesus' name. Father, I thank You for Your forgiveness and Your love. Amen.*

The Truth About Repentance

If you are still feeling guilt or shame because of sin or sins, consider this: guilt comes from the belief that you have caused harm to someone else. Shame comes because others (may) know what you have done wrong. These feelings should not exist in those that have repented and have embraced God's forgiveness. If you are still feeling guilt and shame, it means you are still identifying with the sin and are believing a lie. If you have repented, you only need to accept the forgiveness purchased for you because of the love of Jesus. He no longer associates that sin with you, and you need to know the truth of it in your heart. You are not the nail.

Most people know God forgives those who repent, but some believe that their sin is unforgivable or that God will not forgive them because they are different. This is a lie. It is not the truth and those who buy into this lie suffer needlessly.

Keep in mind that it does not have to be your sin that causes a problem. You may be hurt because of someone else's sin. However, what happens if they did not, cannot, or will not repent? What can you do then? Although this is an extremely hard place to be in, it is easily remedied, as you will see in the next chapter.

Scripture References

But the Lord said, "What have you done? Listen! Your brother's blood cries out to me from the ground! Now you are cursed and banished from the ground, which has swallowed your brother's blood. No longer will the ground yield good crops for you, no

LIVING FULLY FREE

matter how hard you work! From now on you will be a homeless wanderer on the earth."

(Genesis 4:10-12)

Then the Lord sent Nathan to David. And he came to him and said to him: "There were two men in one city, one rich and the other poor. 2 The rich man had exceedingly many flocks and herds. 3 But the poor man had nothing, except one little ewe lamb which he had bought and nourished; and it grew up together with him and with his children. It ate of his own food and drank from his own cup and lay in his bosom; and it was like a daughter to him. 4 And a traveler came to the rich man, who refused to take from his own flock and from his own herd to prepare one for the wayfaring man who had come to him; but he took the poor man's lamb and prepared it for the man who had come to him." 5 So David's anger was greatly aroused against the man, and he said to Nathan, "As the Lord lives, the man who has done this [a]shall surely die! 6 And he shall restore fourfold for the lamb, because he did this thing and because he had no pity." 7 Then Nathan said to David, "You are the man! Thus says the Lord God of Israel: 'I anointed you king over Israel, and I delivered you from the hand of Saul. 8 I gave you your master's house and your master's wives into your keeping and gave you the house of Israel and Judah. And if that had been too little, I also would have given you much more! 9 Why have you despised the commandment of the Lord, to do evil in His sight? You have killed Uriah the Hittite with the sword; you have taken his wife to be your wife and have killed him with the sword of the people of Ammon. 10 Now therefore, the sword shall never depart from your house, because you have despised Me, and have taken the wife of Uriah the Hittite to be your wife.' 11 Thus says the Lord: 'Behold, I will raise up adversity against you from your own house; and I will take your wives before your eyes and give them to your neighbor, and he shall lie with your wives in the sight of this sun. 12 For you did it secretly, but I will do this thing before all Israel, before the sun.'" 13 So David said to Nathan, "I have sinned against the Lord." And Nathan said to David, "The Lord also has put away your sin; you shall not die.

(2 Samuel 12:1-13)

Then the Lord said to Cain, "Where is your brother Abel? "I don't know," he replied. "Am I my brother's keeper?"

(Genesis 4:9)

But whenever anyone turns to the Lord, the veil is taken away. 17 Now the Lord is the Spirit,
and where the Spirit of the Lord is, there is freedom.

(2 Corinthians 3:18)

For God so loved the world that he gave his one and only Son, that whoever believes in him shall not perish but have eternal life.

(John 3:16)

Train a child in the way he should go, and when he is old, he will not turn from it.

(Proverbs 22:6)

For the unbelieving husband has been sanctified through his wife, and the unbelieving wife has been sanctified through her believing husband. Otherwise, your children would be unclean, but as it is, they are holy.

(1 Corinthians 7:14)

But you are a chosen people, a royal priesthood, a holy nation, a people belonging to God, that you may declare the praises of him who called you out of darkness into his wonderful light.

(1 Peter 2:9)

Do not conform any longer to the pattern of this world but be transformed by the renewing of your mind. Then you will be able to test and approve what God's will is his good, pleasing, and perfect will.

(Romans 12:2)

To make her holy, cleansing her by the washing with water through the Word.

(Ephesians 5:26)

If we confess our sins, he is faithful and just and will forgive us our sins and purify us from all unrighteousness.

(1 John 1:9)

CHAPTER 5

THE TRUTH ABOUT FORGIVENESS

As we continue the quest for Truth, let us examine a foundational truth. The truth of the cross of Jesus. All healing takes place at the cross of Jesus Christ. Any avenue in healing that takes you anywhere other than the cross is not going to produce lasting fruit. Unfortunately, people may have an inaccurate or distorted view regarding the cross. Because of this, they have misunderstood what Jesus did, why He did it, and the responsibility believers have because of His sacrifice.

We receive many questions about the cross, from "why did Jesus have to die" to "why did God require a sacrifice?" Once again, let us start with Adam and Eve. After their fall, they were removed from the Garden of Eden and sent out into the world. Initially, they were wearing a covering of fig leaves that they made to hide themselves (Genesis 3:6). However, read what happened in Genesis 3:21, *The LORD God made garments of skin for Adam and his wife and clothed them.* God made the very first sacrifice by taking the skins from animals to cover Adam and Eve's nakedness.

From that time on, the people of God and the priests sacrificed animals and used the blood to cover or atone for the sins of man. *For the life of a creature is in the blood, and I have given it to you to make atonement for yourselves on the altar; it is the blood that makes atonement for one's life* (Leviticus 17:11). This fact is again confirmed in Hebrews 9:22, *In fact, the law (of the Old Covenant) requires that nearly everything be cleansed with blood, and without the shedding of blood there is no forgiveness.*

The Bible tells us in Hebrews 9:27-28, *Just as man is destined to die once, and after that to face judgment, so Christ was sacrificed once to take away the sins of many people.* This is confirmed in Jesus' own words in Matthew 26:28, *This is my blood of the covenant, which is poured out for many for the forgiveness of (our) sins.* Again, it is confirmed in 2 Corinthians 5:21, *God made him (Jesus) who had no sin to be sin for us, so that in him we might become the righteousness of God.* Just as God clothed Adam and Eve, the Bible tells us in Galatians 3:27, *for all of you who were baptized into Christ have clothed yourselves with Christ.*

So, what happened on the cross? Jesus willingly chose to be a sin offering for us so we could become the righteousness of God (2 Corinthians 5:21). He was completely and truly innocent and could have rightly claimed it was "Not me!" Instead, as though He was guilty, He took responsibility and accepted the penalty of death for our sins. He died for us. He unselfishly made a way for us to return to our Father. He paved the way by paying our debts for us.

There was something else He did that was revolutionary. What did He do that was so different? He chose to forgive. He was unjustly judged and crucified. He could have easily condemned the entire world, but He did not. Until that time, it was expected that an eye was taken for an eye lost by another, a tooth was taken for a tooth lost by another, a life lost for every life taken by another (Exodus 21:24). Jesus forgave those who killed him (Luke 23:34). It was His forgiveness that shook the world, and it was His forgiveness that allowed the curtain in the Holy of Holies to spontaneously tear from top to bottom (Mark 15:38). Not so that man could get in, but so that the Lord God would remove the old heart of stone from man and replace it with a new heart of flesh. (Ezekiel 36:26, 27) Through the sacrifice of Jesus' blood. God's dwelling place is now in the hearts of men who receive Him. *Don't you know that you yourselves are God's temple and that God's Spirit lives in you?* (l Corinthians 3:16).

Jesus reconciled us to God through the work of the cross (Ephesians 2:16), by tearing down the wall that separated us from Him. God's Spirit now lives within His people. Only through the cross and sacrifice of Jesus Christ do we have forgiveness of our sins.

Our next question is, "does God forgive sin?" Think about it. If God could simply forgive sin without cost, why did Jesus have to die on the cross? Why didn't God just wave His arm and proclaim all sins were forgiven, or blow His breath across the earth and declare our sins forgiven? The shedding of blood from animal sacrifices to make atonement for people's sins would never have been necessary if God could simply forgive sin without cost. Much of the Old Testament could have been left out of the Bible because God would not have had to spell out the details of what animals to sacrifice for what sins and so forth. The truth is that God <u>forgives the sinner</u>!

The Truth is that God forgives the sinner!

God's Word states, *"For the wages of sin is death, but the gift of God is eternal life in Christ Jesus our Lord,"* (Romans 6:23). God forgives the <u>person</u> of their sins. You may need to read that sentence again, because there is a very life changing truth in it. Jesus died <u>because</u> of sin but He did not die <u>for</u> sin. There is an enormous difference. Jesus died to redeem people from sin, not to redeem sin. <u>Sin cannot be redeemed</u>. Do you understand the difference? God made a way to separate the sin from His people. In Psalms 103:12, the Bible says, *as far as the east is from the west, so far has He removed our transgressions <u>from us</u>*. He separates sin from His people, and He <u>chooses</u> to remember the sin no more. He makes this fact clear in Isaiah. *I, even I, am he who blots out your transgressions, for my own sake, and remembers your sins no more* (Isaiah 43:25). God is not an old man that lost his memory. Instead, He has separated you from the sin so that it is no longer associated with you. A completely different picture.

Jesus died to redeem people from sin, not to redeem sin.

God forgives people who sin and not sin itself. When Jesus taught His disciples to pray the Lord's Prayer He said:

This, then, is how you should pray:
"'Our Father in heaven, hallowed be your name, your kingdom come, your will be done.
on earth as it is in heaven. Give us today our daily bread.

The Truth About Forgiveness

Forgive <u>us</u> our debts,
As we also have forgiven <u>our</u> debtors (people)
And lead us not into temptation,
but deliver us from the evil one."

(Matthew 6:9-13)

In this well-known and often quoted passage of Scripture, Jesus is not talking about forgiveness of "sin" but rather about forgiving His people who had committed sin. The correct translation would be that God forgives (us of our) sins. Jesus taught His disciples to ask God to forgive <u>us</u> our debts/sins in verse twelve, not to simply forgive our debts/sins. Can you see the difference?

Why is the wording of this so important? Is this just a matter of semantics or is it something much bigger? For years, some people have been taught that God simply forgives sin. This teaching lends itself to making sin permissible because it is forgivable and has few or no other consequences. This belief, however, is a lie and good people who have believed it are hurting needlessly.

Those who have been taught that God simply forgives sin, in turn, try to forgive other peoples' sin and ungodly acts done towards them. It is hard, if not impossible, to do. This misconception is common in people with hurting hearts. It is especially true in people who have tried to forgive certain actions repeatedly without success. When we try to forgive the <u>sin</u> (the ungodly action) others committed against us instead of the person, we are acting contrary to God's own nature. We will not succeed. He does forgive the person when their sin is placed under the blood (on the cross) where it is separated from the person. We are called to forgive just as He forgave us: *Bear with each other and forgive whatever grievances you may have against one another. Forgive as the Lord forgave you* (Colossians 3:13).

God forgives YOU of your sins when you repent for them.

God does not simply forgive your sin; He forgives <u>you</u> of your sins when you repent for them. We must do the same: forgive the <u>person</u>, not what they did against us.

Only Jesus has the authority to forgive sin. *God made him who had no sin to be sin for us, so that in him we might become the righteousness of God,* (2 Corinthian 5:21). Jesus said *"I want you to know that the Son of Man has authority on earth to forgive sins,* Matthew 9:6a. *This will take place on the day when God judges people's secrets through Jesus Christ, as my gospel declares,* (Romans 2:16).

We met Sue when she came to get prayer for a bad back. She had been in serious pain for years, and at that moment you could see the pain on her face. Multiple surgeries and endless trips to the chiropractor had not solved her problem. Even the medicine she was taking for the pain hardly made a difference any longer. She also could not remember the last time she got a full night's sleep. She was growing weary and believed that she would have to spend the rest of her life in pain. Her pain was so severe that while waiting for prayer, she had to sit down. We asked her how long she had been in this condition, and she answered, "For about four years."

Our next question was, " What happened to you four years ago?" At first, she responded, "Nothing happened." However, she suddenly stopped and began to tell us how her now ex-husband had run off with a coworker taking everything they owned with him. He had committed other "indiscretions" before, but this time he left with the other woman. He took the family business and all their money, leaving her with nothing. Even her kids were no longer close to her because of the bitter battle that had taken place and all the things she had said to them about their father.

Sue was devastated. The thoughts of what he had done to her consumed every waking moment. The pain in her back, the pressure around her heart and the knot in her stomach had become part of everyday life. It was obvious she was still upset. She did not have one kind thing to say about the man. We asked if she had forgiven him. She replied, "Yes, I forgive him all the time. It seems like I must forgive him every day because the hurt and the anger rise up inside of me. But I do not want this anymore." This unfortunate situation had consumed her life, and she felt trapped.

{A note for those called to minister to others. We did not ask for specific details. If you start asking for details about sins when you are ministering or praying for someone, you are headed for a train wreck. Details generally do not matter when it comes to forgiveness. They can distract you. Sin is sin and it does not need to be qualified or measured as big or small or justified as worthy of forgiveness. When praying for people who have been promiscuous, never allow one detail. You would be allowing them to paint whatever images they want in your mind. You never need any details of sinful action. <u>Quite simply, sin is sin</u>.}

Now, back to the story about Sue. We explained to Sue that what her husband had done to her was simply sin. Call it what it was. Be honest. His actions and his conduct were indeed sin. She was devastated because of them.

First, we taught her about the separation of sin by forgiving the person, not the sin. We took a simple box of tissues and did what we now commonly refer to as "tissues for issues." We explained the box of tissues would represent her ex-husband and the tissues inside the box would be his sins. My hand would represent the cross of Jesus Christ. After this basic explanation, we led her in a simple prayer of forgiveness while she took a tissue (her husband's sin) out of the box and placed it in my hand (the cross). This prayer changed Sue's life:

> *"Father, what my ex-husband (his name) did to me was sin. Take this sin from him, put it on the cross of Jesus Christ, and separate it from him. I forgive my ex-husband and on the Day of Judgment when I am before Your throne, I will hold no accusation against him. Father, forgive my ex-husband (his name) and have mercy on him. Even now I release him of this sin. Father, bless him in Jesus' name, Amen."*

At that moment, tears were streaming down our faces because we knew she had prayed this from her heart. As we watched

The Truth About Forgiveness

Sue's face through our tears, Sue looked ten years younger. I (Michael) wiped my eyes to make sure I could focus clearly. To my amazement, she did look younger. Suddenly, the expression on her face changed and she jumped out of her chair. The pain was gone! She jumped up and down. Joy washed over her face. She was absolutely glowing. God had touched her and totally healed her back as well as her heart. A warm smile came across her face and the peace of God filled her heart.

She continued to forgive him for betraying the children as well as several other things, each time removing another tissue (his sin) from the box and placing it in my hand (the cross). When it was all over, she prayed sincerely from her heart; "Father, I bless my ex-husband (she stated his name)." This happened years ago, and we have seen Sue since then. She now lives in a beautiful home on the St. Johns River and is very content. God has richly blessed her abundantly in every area of her life and now she has a fantastic relationship with her children.

Over the years, she has seen her ex-husband on special occasions such as the children's graduations and marriages. She explained her heart hurt for him because the fruit of his choices in life was evident. However, she was quite comfortable anytime she was around him. She was no longer "eaten up" with bitterness and unforgiveness. She had forgiven him from her heart and God had restored her.

When we reflect the nature of God through forgiveness, miraculous things happen. Since that time, we have seen so many people restored and healed through this simple but effective process.

The tissue box simply stands for the person who was forgiven, and the tissues represent their sins. On their own, these props have no meaning. They are used only to show the concept of the separation of people from their sins. That old saying that "a picture can paint a thousand words" is the goal. Seeing this simple demonstration with the natural eye brings a powerful spiritual revelation that changes lives forever. Also placing the tissue in my hand only stands for the cross and has nothing to do with the death of Jesus on the cross. My hand is not Jesus' hand. However, He does live in my heart and in the heart of every believer. He can work through my hands as well as yours when you allow Him.

Through the cross of Jesus, we have forgiveness from our sins. But there is a condition to this truth that is not always taught. The Bible tells us, *for if you forgive men when they sin against you, your heavenly Father will also forgive you. But if you do not forgive men their sins, your Father will not forgive your sins,* (Matthew 6:14-15). This is a condition of the New Covenant. It is absolute. Jesus made it noticeably clear, but many of God's people do not understand the full scope of this condition and may act causally when it comes to forgiveness.

Jesus explains it in Matthew 18:23-35; *Therefore, the kingdom of heaven is like a king who wanted to settle accounts with his servants. As he began the settlement, a man who owed him ten thousand talents was brought to him. Since he was not able to pay, the master ordered that he and his wife and his children and all that he had be sold to repay the debt. The servant fell on his knees before him. "Be patient with me," he begged, "and I will pay back everything." The servant's master took pity on him, canceled the debt, and let him go.*

But when that servant went out, he found one of his fellow servants who owed him a hundred denarii. He grabbed him and began to choke him. "Pay back what you owe me!" he demanded. "His fellow servant fell to his knees and begged him, "Be patient with me, and I will pay you back." But he refused. Instead, he went off and had the man thrown into prison until he could pay the debt.

When the other servants saw what had happened, they were greatly distressed and went and told their master everything that had happened. Then the master called the servant in. "You wicked servant,' he said, "I canceled all that debt of yours because you begged me to. Shouldn't you have had mercy on your fellow servant just as I had on you?' In anger his master turned him over to the jailers to be tortured, until he should pay back all he owed. This is how my heavenly Father will treat each of you unless you <u>forgive your brother from your heart</u>."

Forgiveness smells like Heaven.

Jesus made payment for our sins by His death on the cross (Hebrews 9:28), and as followers of Christ, we, in turn, <u>must forgive</u> others of their sins. As Jesus pointed out in the story above, *for with the measure you use, it will be measured to you* (Luke 6:38). <u>You</u> set the standard of your own forgiveness. People who forgive others reflect God's nature and gain the fruit of that nature. People who do not forgive mimic the "accuser" and will eventually reap the reward of that unforgiveness (Revelation 12:10).

There is another aspect of forgiveness we need to address. Sometimes, we carry unforgiveness in a hidden way by picking up the banner of what was done to others. In this instance, we mistakenly think we are exchanging our personal unforgiveness for something more noble. We hear statements like, "I can forgive them for what they said to me, but not what they said to my children." We are willing to lay down our cause and pick up someone else's banner related to the sin done to them. We do this with the belief that we are justified in our unforgiveness on their behalf. This is a deception, and it is easy to fall into this trap.

Many are hurting, lost, and dying because of unforgiveness. Let us make something perfectly clear. Unforgiveness is the poison you drink, hoping the other person will get sick! You may not have thought about it in quite this way before, but it is a true picture of what you are doing when you refuse to forgive. What the other person did was sin, and this action or sin does not deserve forgiveness but deserves death.

It is a lie to believe that unforgiveness can keep someone from hurting you again. When you hold unforgiveness against anyone, you live outside of God's purposes. Instead of heaping pain and hurt on the one who hurt you and sinned against you, you end up heaping more pain and hurt on your own heart. People often refuse to forgive because they believe they can get back at the person who hurt them by withholding forgiveness, or they believe forgiveness gives that person a license to continue their sinful actions. This form of unforgiveness has no resemblance to God's nature and is certainly not His plan for your life.

We heard a saying recently that describes it perfectly. *Forgiveness smells like Heaven.* There is something miraculous that takes place when you emulate the nature and character of God by forgiving others. Not only do you receive freedom from that which once bound you, but God then moves in your life and your circumstances start changing for the better.

Unforgiveness is the poison you drink hoping the other person will get sick.

We have another question to ask. Is there anyone from your present or past who would change your "mood" or comfort level if they sat down beside you right now? Another way of asking this is: if you went out to a restaurant for dinner, is there anyone from your life that would upset your meal if they sat at the table next to you? If so, why? Take the time to answer this question honestly from your heart.

If they have committed a sin against you, it is understood that they do not deserve forgiveness. You did not deserve forgiveness either, yet because of love, Jesus offered it to you. You were given forgiveness without deserving it and told that you, in turn, should freely give forgiveness to a world that does not deserve it either. Forgiveness is a gift that blesses the giver more than the recipient.

When ministering to a person who has been hurt repeatedly by the same individual, we often hear that the offender has neither repented of their sin nor asked for forgiveness. To forgive them would seem like giving them permission to repeat the offense. Forgiveness is not based on a person deserving it.

Using their actions or potential future offenses as an excuse not to forgive only further separates you from God's own nature and will eventually cause your heart to both darken and harden. Remember you will not be forgiving the sin. The sin is placed on the cross. You will, however, be forgiving the person. That person will still be accountable to God for their own sin. Read that again. They will still be accountable to God for their sin even after you have forgiven them.

Jesus told people who did good things only to those who would return the favor, that they were no different from the tax collectors (Matthew 5:46). This was not a compliment. The tax collectors would sit at the entrances (gates) around the wall of Jerusalem to collect the taxes due to Caesar. In that day, you would not be allowed into the city unless your debt (taxes) was paid. You could not trade your goods or worship at the temple until all your debt was paid. Hurting people build a wall around their hearts and refuse to let certain people go beyond that wall until they pay the debt they believe is owed to them. That perceived debt could be an unresolved issue, an admittance they were wrong, or some other act of injustice. It could even be ongoing. You might even believe the wall around your heart is keeping you safe from harm but, instead, it has become a prison. Whether you sense it or not, you have lost intimacy in your relationships. It has cut you off not only from those around you, but from God as well. If this example describes you, then you are no different from the tax collectors. You are not living within God's nature and your heart is hurting. The good news is you do not have to stay in this condition.

After Jesus taught the disciples about forgiveness, Peter asked for clarification on this subject. *Then Peter came to Him and said, "Lord, how often shall my brother sin against me, and I forgive him? Up to seven times?" Jesus said to him, "I do not say to you, up to seven times, but up to seventy times seven,"* (Matthew 18:21-23, NKJV).

If my brother sins against me 490 times, one of us may need serious counsel. However, in this passage, Jesus is saying it is God's nature to forgive repeatedly. It should be our nature as well. Paul explains it best in Colossians 3:12-14, *Therefore, as God's chosen people, holy and dearly loved, clothe yourselves with compassion, kindness, humility, gentleness, and patience. Bear with each other and forgive whatever grievances you may have against one another. Forgive as the lord forgave you.*

At this point you may be thinking, "The people who sinned against me did not ask for forgiveness, so I do not have to forgive them." Jesus did not say we should only forgive those who ask for forgiveness. He simply said, "Forgive those who trespass against you." Again, it is important to point out that your forgiveness does not release them from their accountability to God for their actions. They will stand before the judgement seat of God. However, it does release them from their responsibility to you for their debt. It releases you from carrying the weight of unforgiveness and allows you to display the grace of God in your own life. Stephen, a man of grace and power, understood this powerful principle of God. As he was being stoned to death, Stephen asked God to forgive the people who were killing him (Acts 7:60).

Before we go any further, it is important to address those reading this who are currently being physically or sexually abused. It is not our intention for you to forgive the perpetrators of any crime and return to your abuser. <u>You need to get to a **safe place** at once!</u> Separate yourself now from the one that is hurting you! There are hotline numbers at the end of this chapter that you can call to receive help. After you are safe, you can begin the forgiveness and healing process.

In conclusion, there are no excuses not to forgive another. Remember you will not be forgiving the sin; you will be forgiving the <u>person</u>. They will still be accountable to God for their sins but will now be free from your judgement no matter how accurate the judgement. To begin this process in your own life, follow these instructions. Use a box of tissues as a demonstration of the separation of sin from the person who sinned against you. Pull one tissue out for each sin as you say this prayer from your heart:

> *"Father, I choose to forgive (name of the person) for what they did. What they did to me is sin. Father, take this sin from them and put it on the cross of Jesus Christ and separate it from <u>(name of the person)</u> and on the Day of Judgment when I stand before Your throne, I will hold no accusation against them. Even now, they are free, in Jesus' name. Father, I ask you to bless them. Amen."*

Continue to repeat this prayer until it is no longer needed. Take your time and search your heart. Ask the Father to show you anyone else you may need to forgive. Do not confine this process to a time limit. Forgiveness is not a one-time stopping place <u>but a place you will live for the rest of your life</u>. It is God's nature to forgive. To walk in agreement in our covenant with Him, it <u>must</u> be your nature as well.

The Truth About Forgiveness

This is the perfect time to apply the second half of Matthew 6:14 to your own life. *For if you forgive men when they sin against you, your heavenly Father will also forgive you.* Ask the Father if you have any other sins within your heart. It is easier for you to understand your forgiveness when you have forgiven others. With the measure you use, it will be measured to you (Luke 6:37-38). Search your heart again and if you have any unconfessed sins, repent of them, and continue in them no longer. Repeat this prayer from your heart:

"Father, I repent for (name of the sin). Father, forgive me this sin, separate it from me and put it on the cross of Jesus Christ. Father, You said you would forgive me just as I forgave (name of the person you just forgave). Father, I thank You for forgiving me of this sin, in the name of Jesus. Amen."

Repeat this process, as necessary. Take time to open your heart to the Spirit of God about any hidden thing that may need attention.

There is an obstacle that can make it difficult if not impossible to forgive others from the heart. When we have been treated unjustly by others, we may tell as many people as possible what happened (from our perspective) in an effort to get them to agree with our position. Our words of accusation, no matter how accurate, create a stronghold against the person or persons we are accusing. We, in essence, join forces with the accuser of the brethren and create a stronghold against those who harmed us. Until we are willing to renounce our words and agree not to repeat them again, we may find it hard if not impossible to forgive. (More on these subjects in the Words and Stronghold chapters.) To be free to forgive, all we must do is repent for the words we spoke about them. Until we do, our own words stand as a testimony against them. If you find it difficult to forgive, then repeat this prayer.

> *Father, I have spoken many words against (<u>name of person or persons</u>) that should not have been said no matter how accurate they were. This is sin. I renounce the words I spoke against them and will not repeat them in the future. Father, forgive me for this sin.*

> *Father, I choose to forgive (name of the person) for what they did. What they did to me is sin. Father, take this sin from them and put it on the cross of Jesus Christ and separate it from (<u>name of the person</u>) and on the Day of Judgment when I stand before Your throne, I will hold no accusation against them. Even now, they are free, in Jesus' name. Father, I ask you to bless them. Amen.*

Finally, we are aware of a teaching that says you need to forgive yourself. Forgiveness is referenced over 120 times in the Bible, and not once is forgiving yourself ever mentioned. This is an "I" centered thinking, exalting "self" over the finished work of Christ on the cross, that is an <u>affront,</u> an insult, to the cross of Jesus Christ. It turns people inward to forgive themselves instead of humbly accepting God's forgiveness through the cross. Anything that turns you inward will also turn you away from the cross. Jesus bought your forgiveness with His blood on the cross. To be free, you simply must receive and accept His forgiveness.

Otherwise, you are saying your faith in <u>your</u> forgiveness of self is greater than your faith in <u>His</u> forgiveness.

Forgiving yourself is an "I" centered thinking that exalts yourself over the cross of Christ.

Once repentance has completed its work in you and you have changed your direction back towards the Kingdom of God, you are free of sin and do not need to forgive yourself, as if that were possible in the first place. In other words, what part of you would forgive the other part of you and with what or whose authority could you do it?

Though it is true that you can be upset, angry or even hate your own actions, resulting in feelings of guilt, self-condemnation, or shame, forgiving yourself is not the answer. If, after you have repented, you are still operating from a place of guilt and shame, it will lead you into a false sense of spirituality and in turn create a false sense of humility. However, this is not the type of humility God seeks from us. It mimics it but does not give you access to what true humility offers. True humility places God on the throne of your life and allows Him to move on your behalf.

If you are led by guilt, shame, or condemnation after you have repented, you have joined forces with the accuser who is deceiving you with the intent of keeping you from walking in the truth. Forgiving yourself may feel right in the moment, but it does not restore you back into right relationship with the

Father. The whole purpose of repentance is reconciliation with God (2 Corinthians 7:10). True repentance is not only turning from sin but also turning towards a life that mirrors God's grace. If you have found yourself in this situation, repent now so that restoration will begin.

> *"Father, I have not fully accepted your forgiveness and carry guilt, shame and/or condemnation. I did not fully understand the finished work on the cross and allow it to change me. Father, I repent, forgive me of this sin, separate it from me and put it on the cross of Jesus Christ. Father, I thank You for forgiving me of this sin, in the name of Jesus. Amen."*

Scripture References

When the woman saw that the fruit of the tree was good for food and pleasing to the eye, and also desirable for gaining wisdom, she took some and ate it. She also gave some to her husband, who was with her, and he ate it.

(Genesis 3:6)

God made him who had no sin to be sin for us, so that in Him we might become the righteousness of God.

(2 Corinthians 5:21)

Eye for eye, tooth for tooth, hand for hand, foot for foot.

(Exodus 21:24)

The Truth About Forgiveness

Jesus said, "Father, forgive them, for they do not know what they are doing."

(Luke 23:34)

The curtain of the temple was torn in two from top to bottom.

(Mark 15:38)

I will give you a new heart and put a new spirit in you; I will remove from you your heart of stone and give you a heart of flesh. And I will put my Spirit in you and move you to follow My decrees and be careful to keep My laws.

(Ezekiel 36:26-27)

And in this one body to reconcile both of them to God through the cross, by which He put to death their hostility.

(Ephesians 2:16)

So, Christ was sacrificed once to take away the sins of many people; and He will appear a second time, not to bear sin, but to bring salvation,
to those who are waiting for Him.

(Hebrews 9:28)

Then I heard a loud voice in heaven say: "Now have come the salvation and the power and the kingdom of our God, and the authority of his Messiah. For the accuser of our brothers and sisters, who accuses them before our God, day, and night, has been hurled down.

(Revelation 12:10)

LIVING FULLY FREE

If you love those who love you, what reward will you get? *Are not even the tax collectors doing that?*

(Matthew 5:46)

Then he fell on his knees and cried out, "Lord, do not hold this sin against them." When he said this, he fell asleep.

(Acts 7:60)

Godly sorrow brings repentance that leads to salvation and leaves no regret, but worldly sorrow brings death.

(2 Corinthians 7:10)

HOTLINE NUMBERS WITH 24 HOUR HELP SERVICE

National Child Abuse Hotline	1-800-422-4453
Missing or Exploited Children	1-800-843-5678
Domestic Violence National Hotline	1-800-799-7233
National Sexual Assault Hotline	1-800-656-4673

CHAPTER 6

WHO HAS YOUR HEART?

When we met Angela, she told us how much she was hurting inside and that she felt lonely from a lack of intimacy in her marriage. She had been married for over 15 years and the closeness she once shared with her husband was gone. She could not think of a date or a specific incident that had caused the intimacy to leave. It just declined slowly, but surely, over the years. She believed she still loved her husband, but the intimacy that once was the hallmark of their love was gone, and she missed it. She desperately wanted it back in their relationship but had no idea how to make that happen.

Angela had purchased just about every book on relationships she could find at the Christian bookstore. She grasped at anything and everything that might hold the key to her situation. The information in the books and on the internet helped with different issues concerning the relationship but did not improve their intimacy. Nothing helped that. As a last resort, she convinced her husband to go to their pastor for counseling. This resulted in improved communication about their marital situation, and some additional issues in their relationship were resolved and healing took place. However, the intimacy she desired was still missing.

She was beginning to think that there was no hope for total restoration. The harder she tried to work on things, the more frustration she felt. Instead of growing closer to her husband again, all the "good things" Angela tried left her feeling frustrated. She finally confided in her mother, hoping for the voice of experience to offer some words of wisdom. Instead, her mother told her a loss of intimacy happened in every marriage. That it was just part of growing old together, and Angela needed to adjust and get over it. We wholeheartedly disagree!

As we prayed with Angela, she revealed her husband had done some things in the past that had hurt her deeply. Angela had forgiven him and believed those things were no longer an issue for her. However, over the years her husband continued to do minor things that hurt her. He had not always met her expectations, so she often felt neglected and disappointed. These disappointments caused her to withdraw her heart from her husband. She had taken back a part of her heart and began searching for a logical reason to give it back to her husband again.

When people have a problem with intimacy, we often ask this question, "What could your spouse do to win your heart back?" Think about that for a minute. We get answers that range from "a few things" to a list so long it would use up a ream of paper.

Our next question to them is the same: "If your spouse did everything on your list, would you instantly give your heart back? Or would you want to give the relationship time to see if their actions were temporary or lasting?"

Who Has Your Heart?

The answer is always, "I would give it some time." Next, we ask, "How long would you need to wait after they completed these things on your list until you could give them your heart again?" The answers vary from "a few weeks" to "possibly years."

Repeating this back to them, "So you are saying that if your spouse does 'all these things' and maintains a specific behavior for a certain length of time, you will give your heart back to them?"

Most answered with a resounding "YES!" Others are still not sure they would give their heart back, and this could be for any number of reasons.

We then ask, "When you first began the relationship, did your spouse have to complete a list of things to do before you gave your heart to them? Did you wait a certain amount of time for things to be established between the two of you before this happened?" The answer is always "No."

The truth is that no spouse could ever do enough to earn the right to your heart. They did not do enough to earn your love in the first place. You chose freely to give it to them. Contrary to many beliefs, no one can make you give your heart to them. No matter what they do or how hard they try to earn your heart, and no matter who they are or what chemistry exists between the two of you, giving your heart to someone is always your choice.

When you take back (withdraw) part of your heart from your spouse, you are acting contrary to the One who made you. You are no longer acting within His nature. God's love for you is unchangeable and unconditional, a precious gift which you did not earn. You were designed to love your spouse with all your heart. To do otherwise will always result in separation. The one most affected by this separation is the one withdrawing a part of their heart from the other. This withdrawing of the heart, as we call it, is a hardening of the heart.

You were designed to love your spouse with all your heart.

As each hurt or offense would come or whenever her expectations were not met, Angela would unconsciously harden part of her heart towards her husband as protection from further pain. Although she stated she always forgave him when he would hurt her, she became guarded and slowly lost the ability to trust him with her heart. She built a protective barrier around her now calloused heart, so what he did, or did not do, could no longer cause pain. Angela had once freely given her heart to him, loving without conditions. She did not realize her heart had become indifferent and numb, robbing her of intimacy with the man she loved most. Somewhere along the way, she had taken part of her heart back and the link to intimacy was gone.

Some people believe once you give your heart to someone you can never take it back. However, one look around will tell you this is not true. The evidence of strained relationships and family unit breakdowns is all around us. You make a choice every day, in every relationship, to give or take back your heart. People have said, "I fell out of love." No, they chose to withdraw their heart, and their love. Love is a choice. Can a baby do anything to earn your love? No. You choose to give your love to them. You always have a choice to love, even with God.

Who Has Your Heart?

We told Angela if she wanted intimacy in her marriage, she had to be willing to lay down her "list" and unconditionally give her heart back to her husband even though he did not deserve it. If you are in this condition, you also have that choice.

At this point, fear may have reared its ugly head. You may be afraid to give 100% of your heart back to the person who is responsible for some of the pain you feel. Fear claims you will be safer isolated behind the protective walls of your hardened and calloused heart. This fear slowly suffocates your heart behind those walls, until death ensues. At this point, you go through the motions of life without fully experiencing it.

This type of fear offers a future with less pain, but it is a loss of life and a never-ending search for the intimacy you surrendered. To those experiencing this fear, we ask an amazingly simple question: "How is this relationship without intimacy working for you now?"

We explained to Angela that giving her heart back to her husband would not necessarily change him, but it <u>would</u> change her. By choosing to love her spouse with all her heart, she would also be choosing to reflect God's nature. If she decided to hold onto her heart and withdraw from her husband, she would be acting against His nature and bear the fruit of that conflict in her heart.

We led Angela into a prayer of repentance for hardening her heart. As she made a conscious choice to give her heart back to her spouse, joy flooded her heart and her face. Without hesitation, she experienced a connection with her husband that she had not felt in years.

Following these types of reconciliations, we are always amazed at the reports received. For instance, Angela reported later that her husband appeared to have "changed" after she gave her heart back to him. People can appear to look and act differently when we look at them with eyes (and a heart) of intimacy. However, something much greater was at work in this situation. It is a principle of the Kingdom. When we walk in opposition to God's nature, we have conflict in our life. When we walk in agreement (unity) with His nature, the promises of God become alive in us. When Angela repented and gave love with all her heart, she emanated God's nature. Every area of her life began to reflect that love.

If you have come to the realization that you have taken back part of your heart from your spouse and want fullness back in your marriage, repeat this prayer from your heart:

Father, I confess that I have taken back part of my heart from my spouse. It is contrary to Your nature, and I ask You to forgive me for hardening my heart. I am willing to lay down my list of expectations at your altar. I will not make them requirements to meet before I give them my love and my heart. I (your full Christian name) choose to give (full Christian name of your spouse) 100% of my heart from this day forth, in Jesus' name. Father, I thank you for restoring my marriage and the intimacy in my relationship with my spouse. Amen.

We fully understand there are those who have "taken back" a part of their heart because of major offenses like betrayal, abuse, adultery, deception, addiction, control and tyranny. We are not suggesting you trust your heart again to people in any of these circumstances until you are in a safe place, they repent, and the issues are resolved. Only then can you begin the healing process. In the meantime, please seek help through a church or Christian support group.

The testimony of Angela's marriage is an excellent example of what can happen in your relationship with God as well. There are people who once had a close intimate relationship with God and are now doing everything they can to regain it. They have the belief that if they just read the Word more, prayed more, attended church more, gave more or attended one more worship or teaching conference they could regain the intimacy that is missing in their lives. Although every one of these things is important and will enhance your relationship with the Father, they are not the path to regaining intimacy.

The intimacy you once experienced in your relationship with God began when you freely gave the Father your heart. That act alone will once again bring you back to intimacy with Him. It is hard to believe anyone can lose intimacy with the Father when He is perfect, unlike a spouse. The Father's love never changes, but ours can. He never ignores or leaves us, but we can ignore or leave Him. Unfortunately, things happen that can draw us away from our first love. It does not mean that we do not "love" the Lord or that we are not serving Him. However, it can mean the cornerstone of that love, intimacy, is now gone and the relationship is different from what it once was.

Repent and do the things you did at first.

Jesus addressed this subject with the church in Ephesus. *You have forsaken your first love. Remember the height from which you have fallen! Repent and do the things you did at first* (Revelation 2:4-5).

Just like Angela, who still loved her husband, had lost intimacy with him, you can love God but lose intimacy with Him as well. Not because God did things that hurt you or wounded you, but usually because you have expectations that God has not met. You may feel disappointed and let down, sometimes even abandoned by God when life does not turn out how you hoped it would. It is tempting to blame God for the actions of others and choose to hold back a part of your heart from the very One who can heal it.

Just as we often do with our earthly relationships, we make a mental list of the things we want God to do for us. If God will meet our requests, then we will trust Him again. Doesn't it sound silly when you read it in plain, simple English? Life's circumstances or heartaches can cause us to believe that we cannot trust God with our hearts. He did not do anything to hurt us. He did not abandon us. He is not responsible for the actions of those who hurt us. Unfortunately, our "perception" of Him is altered because of a false belief. It is a lie.

Previously, we discussed reality versus our perception of reality. Which reality is truth, and which one is not? It is possible for you to take back your heart from God, piece by piece (hardening) over time because of your misperceptions of God through your life experiences. <u>God does not change, but our perception of Him can.</u>

For example, you might have prayed for something specific to happen in your life, such as the healing of a loved one, but God did not intervene the way you were hoping He would. It could be that you went through an extended, difficult trial, and you called on God to help, but He did not come through in the way you planned or in your timing. You could have prayed and believed for your spouse, your child, or a friend for a long time without any obvious change in them. The list of these examples could be endless. You prayed, believed, and stood in faith, but the outcome was not as you anticipated. You may believe there is something about you that makes you unworthy or different, believing God no longer desires intimacy with you as He does with others. This is a lie.

Even though it can be tough to admit, we can feel hurt by events in our lives that God allowed to happen. We can become disappointed when we go to God in prayer and do not see the results we expected. Has this happened to you? Remember the importance of being open and honest with yourself to bring about changes in your life? Be honest now.

You may have experienced a painful incident, and as a result, you closed your heart off behind the wall we talked about in the last chapter. You may have even reacted with a vow such as, "I will never love like that again!" or "I'll never serve anyone like that again!" If it was a pastor or church leader who hurt you, the vow might have been, "I will never go to church again until…" These examples of promises to yourself could go on and on in an infinite combination of things you will never do again or <u>never</u> allow someone else to do to you. At their core, they are declarations of a hardened heart. You may have done what Angela did with her husband and unknowingly withdrawn part of your heart from God. You may have been striving for intimacy with Him, not understanding why it was gone in the first place.

LIVING FULLY FREE

It is also possible you never gave 100% of your heart to God when you first called on His name. By holding back any part of your heart, you have not experienced true intimacy with your Father. Without surrendering all your heart, your Christian Walk has been hard because you are trying to live your life by your own strength, not His. This is identified by a never-ending struggle within your heart between the purposes of God and your own desires.

The Bible tells us in Luke 9:24: *For whoever wants to save his life will lose it, but whoever loses his life for me will save it.* If you are hanging on by your own strength, you are tired and weary. You may avoid the church and Christian scene entirely, just showing up for special meetings occasionally. You may have taken your heart back because someone who professed Christ hurt you. Whether it was a pastor, church leader, teacher or just another Christian, this hurt was real.

You may be able to forgive what happened to you personally, only to pick up a similar offense that happened to someone else. This injustice to someone else could become your new battle cry. You then carry their offense in your hardened heart. You blame God for allowing an offense to happen and then are upset with God when He does not bring justice to the one who hurt you or your friend. Most believe they can get God's attention by taking back part of their heart from Him. This is simply a form of "blackmail." Those who practice this believe it will motivate God to correct the injustice.

When you are in a storm of pain and suffering, you do not always think about what you are doing in clear terms. When we explain to individuals the bird's eye view of their circumstances in clear, simple black-and-white terminology, they are often repelled by the truth they see in it. Usually, they are remorseful and repent immediately.

There is something that these people have in common. Just like the "to do" list that Angela had for her husband, these people have an unwritten list of things that God needs "to do" to gain their heart back. Some may not have a "list" but are instead eagerly waiting for God to pursue them with signs that would confirm His pursuit.

God never changes, even when our perception of Him does.

Let us make something truly clear. God <u>never</u> changes, even if our perception of Him does. If you have asked Him into your heart, He is living there no matter how you feel. He is waiting for you to resume the intimacy you once had. He desires that you give Him all your heart with no stipulations on giving Him your love again. He waits for you to return to your First Love and to live in alignment with His character and nature. If you recognize that intimacy is missing in your relationship with God, repeat this prayer from your heart:

> *Father, I confess that there is a lack of intimacy in our relationship, and I want that close intimacy with You again. I am willing to lay all the conditions that I was expecting You to meet at Your altar. I ask You to forgive me for allowing*

my heart to be hardened towards You. I (your full Christian name) choose to give 100% of my heart to You, Father, from this day forth, in Jesus' name. Father, I thank You for Your love that endures forever. Amen.

We are not claiming this, or any prayer will protect you from being hurt or disappointed again. Your heart in its non-hardened state is vulnerable. Indeed, there will be times when your faith and love will be tested. It will happen and it will not always be an easy test. If you want to maintain intimacy, you must not allow anything to harden your heart. When we offer 100% of our heart to God, we keep open the doors for God's promises to be fulfilled in our lives and the power of His kingdom works on our behalf.

You are now aware that unconfessed sin will harden your heart. Since you are examining yourself, consider a few other things that can slowly harden your heart and ease you away from intimacy with God. God told us in Exodus 20:3-4, *You shall have no other gods before me. You shall not make for yourself an idol in the form of anything in heaven above or on the earth beneath or in the waters below.*

To Christians in this modern world, this may seem like an odd phrase to repeat when most people no longer appear to worship graven images. However, understanding the truth of this passage is important today. The list of what we can worship or make into an idol is pretty exhaustive. Jesus clarified this concept when Satan tempted Him to worship him (Satan) instead of God. Jesus said to him, *away from me, Satan! For it is written: "Worship the Lord your God and serve Him only,"* (Matthew 4:10). Satan was asking Jesus to turn away from God, put His (Jesus) trust and faith in Satan, and serve in his kingdom.

Who Has Your Heart?

Only Satan worshipers openly admit to putting their faith and trust in the devil. However, when we put our faith and trust in the kingdom of this world, instead of in God, we are trusting in the devil's kingdom. This is a dangerous trap. Satan was not asking Jesus just to worship him, but to serve him as well. Jesus said, "NO!" to both. When we put our faith and trust in our money or in the things we earned by our own efforts, we shift our trust from God and His Kingdom onto the kingdom of this world. Some may think they are not in danger of struggling with this problem because they do not have a lot of money in which to put their trust. This is not a matter of money, but instead it is about where or in what/whom we place our trust. The Bible says greed (whether you have money or not) is idolatry (Colossians 3:5).

Jesus told us, *For where your treasure is, there your heart will be also*, (Matthew 6:21). Though you are a spirit being, you do operate and live on an everyday, human earthly level. You will give your time and attention to the things you value or treasure the most. We sometimes give priority to things that are not in God's perfect plan for our life. When we do this, the heart slowly turns and focuses on the things of this world instead of God. Material things are not bad. He knew you would need them. He provided them for you, and He even called them good (Genesis 1). However, ask yourself, "Is my heart in pursuit of God and serving Him through serving others, or is my heart only serving and taking care of its own self?"

Remember, love is not self-seeking, (1 Corinthians 13:5). When you are in lack or hurt, you will seek relief first, as you should. You can best serve others when you are whole. Before you got into this condition, were you living for God and serving others, or were you living for yourself? Was your focus all about you, your needs and your life or was it bigger than your world alone? When you are walking in agreement with God's nature, you will be living for Him and thinking of others before you live for yourself. Think about it for a minute and know the answer in your heart.

Would your schedule (where you spend your time) and your finances (where you spend your money) confirm your answer? Why or why not? If your focus is not aligned with God's purpose for your life, then repeat this prayer from your heart:

Father, I confess that I have not put all my trust and faith in You. I also have been (say the ones that apply) self-serving, selfish, self-centered, greedy, trusting in myself and what I can produce. I have trusted in my wealth, my income, or have been trusting in the things of this world instead of You. That is idolatry and I repent in Jesus' name. Father, forgive me for this sin. I give You all my heart and will serve You alone from this day forth in Jesus' name. Father, I thank You for your forgiveness and Your love. Amen.

Paul gave us this instruction that can keep your heart focused: *Since, then, you have been raised with Christ, set your hearts on things above, where Christ is seated at the right hand of God. Set your minds on the things above, not on earthly things* (Colossians 3:1-2).

There is a simple test to see if your plans resemble God's purpose for your life. When faced with any decisions in your future, ask yourself these two questions: "Will it serve others or only me? And will it bring glory to God?" Also, we are cautioned to weigh our decisions on the scale of whether or not we have the Peace of God. The Bible confirms this: *Do not be anxious about anything, but in everything, by prayer and petition, with thanksgiving, present your requests to God. And the peace of God, which transcends all understanding, will guard your hearts and your minds in Christ Jesus* (Philippians 4:6-7).

There is also another deception that can lead to the hardening of your heart. You may be carrying the cares of this life and circumstances that you cannot change on your own shoulders. This is not God's plan for you. The Bible says to cast *all your care upon Him, for He cares for you*, (1 Peter 5:7 NKJV). Disrupted sleep is a common sign that you are carrying these burdens on your own (Proverbs 3:24). Another symptom is recurring neck and shoulder problems that disappear after you release these burdens to God and repent for disobeying God in this area.

When you take on these responsibilities, worries and fears, you are cooperating with the enemy of your soul who robs joy and peace from your life (John 10:10). You can pick up these worries because you have a belief, or fear, that God is not dealing with them properly. In your heart, you may believe God should have taken care of your problem in your timing or in your preferred way. We can easily trust in our own ability to get the job done in our timing. This thinking is based on doubt and fear. It reveals that you simply are not putting all your trust in God. There are so many circumstances in our lives that can overwhelm us, and we were never designed to carry the weight of things we cannot change. Examples of these concerns could be our finances, health, spouse, or any number of other issues (Luke 12:22-23). We are to take them to God in supplication. Philippians 4:6 NKJV states, *be anxious for nothing, but in everything by prayer and supplication, with thanksgiving, let your requests be made known to God.*

Picking up the worries and cares of others can also lead to the hardening of your heart. Mothers often carry the burdens of their children after they have left home. Yes, you are to pray for your children and those whom you love and give them wise counsel. However, you are not made to solely carry their concerns or struggles. That is God's job, His responsibility. God gave you children to raise (Proverbs 22:6). You are only stewards over them in this process and you are never to take ownership of them or their problems. Your children are the Lord's and the problems they have are His. We can and should pray for them but not carry their burdens.

Scripture repeatedly says you are not to worry about people or things. *Therefore, I say to you, do not worry about your life, what you will eat or what you will drink, nor about your body, what you will put on. Is life not more than food and the body more than clothing? Look at the birds of the air, for they neither sow nor reap nor gather into barns, yet your heavenly Father feeds them. Are you not of more value than they?* (Matthew 6:25-26 NKJV). *And do not seek what you should eat or what you should drink, nor have an anxious mind. For all these things the nations of the world seek after, and your Father knows that you need these things. But seek the kingdom of God, and all these things shall be added to you. Do not fear, little flock, for it is your Father's good pleasure to give you the kingdom,* (Luke 12:29-32).

When you place your faith in fear, doubt, and unbelief, you are aligning with the purposes of the enemy of your soul. In some way, you do not trust God is capable of moving on your behalf, even when He is willing to do it for others. Whenever you put your faith in these things, you conflict with His purpose for your life, and you will bear the fruit of it. This belief alone, can limit God in your life. You simply need to repent for disobedience and lack of faith in

Who Has Your Heart?

Him, and cast your "care' on Him, allowing Him to care for you (1 Peter 5:7). He will meet you where you are and begin restoration.

When you pick up problems you are not meant to carry, there is a rule of thumb for you to follow. Anything you cannot take to the cross (personal repentance, forgiveness etc.), you should take to the Father in prayer and then not worry further about it. Trust in Him.

This simple but effective prayer will free you from these burdens. Remember, the Bible says to *cast your cares upon Jesus because He cares for you*, (1 Peter 5:7). If this applies to you, pray this prayer from your heart:

Father, I have been carrying the burdens of my circumstances and relationships. I ask You to forgive me for disobedience by worrying and not trusting in You. I now choose to lay those things I cannot change at Your altar. Father, I lay my spouse at Your altar. I lay my children at Your altar. I lay my job and my finances at Your altar. I lay (the circumstances you cannot change) at Your altar. You are my supply, and You alone can move in my circumstances. I give these to You and trust you with them in Jesus' name. Father, I thank You for caring for me. Amen.

Scripture References:

Put to death, therefore, whatever belongs to your earthly nature: sexual immorality, impurity, lust, evil desires, and greed, which is idolatry.

(Colossians 3:5)

LIVING FULLY FREE

It does not dishonor others, it is not self-seeking, it is not easily angered, it keeps no record of wrongs.

(1 Corinthians 13:5)

When you lie down, you will not be afraid: when you lie down, your sleep will be sweet.

(Proverbs 3:24)

The thief comes only to steal and kill and destroy. I have come that they may have life and have it to the full.

(John 10:10)

Then Jesus said to his disciples: "Therefore I tell you, do not worry about your life, what you will eat; or about your body, what you will wear. For life is more than food, and the body more than clothes."

(Luke 12:22, 23)

Start children off on the way they should go, and even when they are old, they will not turn from it.

(Proverbs 22:6)

Cast all your anxiety on him because he cares for you.

(1 Peter 5:7)

CHAPTER 7

TRUTHS OF THE KINGDOM

And now these three remain: faith, hope, and love. But the greatest of these is love (1 Corinthians 13:13).

Chapter 13 of 1 Corinthians plainly says when prophecies, tongues, and knowledge pass away, or disappear, the truths of faith, hope and love will remain. It also qualifies love to be the greatest of these attributes. These three forces are life changing, and when they are imparted into our lives, we are changed in miraculous ways. As these forces move through us, the Kingdom of God advances mightily.

Christians may not have the revelation of these three basic truths of the Kingdom of God, although they may believe they do. Part of the problem is the increased emphasis the Church has given to faith instead of love. Another issue is with the interpretation of these truths by people whose original thinking came from, or at the very least has been filtered by, the world.

This contaminated thinking needs to change. I remember taking the lid off some freshly made vanilla ice cream when I was a young child and seeing how pure white it looked. Later in life, I experienced the sun reflecting off a mountain of fresh fallen snow and my perception of what the color white actually was changed. If the Word of God says "white" and you see "ivory," everything else is slightly discolored or distorted from that point on and will not be 100% pure. So, what part of your thinking is not the truth? How will you know until you experience the Truth? We ask you to consider the perspective presented here with an inquiring and receptive heart.

If you have been hurt, broken, trapped, or bound for some time, it is probably because of a misunderstanding of one or all these life-giving truths. Even a small misconception in one of these areas could lead to an error in our belief systems. We will identify these truths, show you how to obtain them, how to grow because of them, as well as what is in opposition to them. Knowing the opposites of these truths will help you identify any deceptions you may currently believe or encounter in the future. We will deal with the basics of these truths to correct any foundational misconceptions. Understanding these truths can strengthen your relationship with God and others and empower you through the storms of life (Matthew 7:24-27).

FAITH

Now faith is the substance of things hoped for, the evidence of things not seen (Hebrews 11:1 NKJV).

If you have been a Christian for any length of time, you have heard this verse repeated many times as the definition of faith. Even though this is an immensely powerful statement, it is not the definition of faith. This is, instead, a "characteristic" of faith.

A definition of a word will always be able to replace that word without changing its meaning, but a characteristic of the word will not accurately replace the word's meaning when used in a sentence. An example would be best demonstrated with the word "flower." One characteristic of a flower is "a demonstration of God's splendor." However, the definition of a flower according to most dictionaries is "a colored, sometimes scented, part of a plant that contains its reproductive organs."

If you use this characteristic in the following sentence, it will not paint an accurate picture.

The boy picked "the demonstration of God's splendor" and gave it to his mom.

Now, let us read it with the definition of a flower and we believe you will get the idea.

The boy picked the colored, sometimes scented part of a plant that contains its reproductive organs and gave it to his mom.

Although the second sentence is not very poetic, it does paint a more accurate picture of what happened. By contrast, the first sentence is open to multiple interpretations that can lead to confusion or a distorted reality.

So, if Hebrews 11:1 is not the definition of Faith, then what is? It can be found in Hebrews 11:6, *And without faith it is impossible to please God, because anyone who comes to him must believe that He exists and that He rewards those who earnestly seek him.* Faith is simply "Believing." Faith in God is believing "He Is, and that He will do what He says." Before you dismiss this approach, consider a popular scripture, and apply both the characteristic and the definition, as we did with the previous example. Which statement makes sense?

You are all sons of God through faith in Christ Jesus, (Galatians 3:26). Does it make more sense if you read it as *You are all sons of God through the substance of things hoped for, the evidence of things not seen in Christ Jesus?* Or is it clearer as *You are all sons of God through believing in Christ Jesus, and He rewards those who seek Him?*

The characteristic of faith as described in Hebrews 11:1 is the fulfilled nature of faith. We will explain. One of our daughters believed it was the Lord's plan for her life to attend a special Bible school in Sydney, Australia. She, however, had to believe for the funds required to pay for her tuition. The day came when she miraculously had the check in her hand to pay the school in full. That check <u>was</u> the "substance," the proof of what she had hoped for, and was the "evidence" of what she had not yet seen. It was the fulfillment of her faith.

Faith always has a focal point, and it is not faith unless it does. Faith does not just believe that something is, but also believes in its function. Hebrews 11:6 states that we must first believe that God exists (a focal point) and secondly, believe He rewards those who earnestly seek Him. This means you believe He can do what the Bible says He can do. It is not enough only to believe that God exists. That is not Kingdom faith. You might believe there is a God, but even the demons know that. The Bible confirms this in James 2:19, *You believe that there is one God. Good! Even the demons believe that and shudder.*

You are directed to put your faith (belief) in Jesus (John 2:11), in God (Mark 11:22), in His blood (Romans 3:25), in His ability and in the power of God (Colossians 2:12). However, there are other things you can choose to put your faith in (believe) that bring about less than desired results. For instance: your money, your career, your own abilities, or any number of other things which are based on the kingdom of this world instead of the Kingdom of God. It is not a matter of having faith, because everyone has faith, but it is a matter of where, what, or in whom you place your faith that makes the difference. It is about your focal point.

**You already have faith;
it was given to you by God.**

When the disciples were in the boat, afraid they were about to sink, Jesus asked them, *Where is your faith?* (Luke 8:25). He was not asking them if they had faith. He already knew they had faith. He was asking them in whose kingdom they had placed their faith. Did they believe in Him and His Kingdom, or did they believe in the world, the enemy's kingdom? Applying faith to (believing in) the kingdom of this world often traps good believers. By placing their faith in their own abilities and the world's sources of supply, they can leave God and His promises out of the equation.

If, as the Bible says, you must have faith (believe), how do you receive that faith? *For by the grace given me I say to every one of you, do not think of yourself more highly than you ought, but rather think of yourself with sober judgment, in accordance with the <u>measure of faith</u> God has given you* (Romans 12:3).

The Word states that you already have faith. It was given to you by God.

If you are sitting down at this moment, you are using a form of faith. When you sat down in the chair, did you pick it up first to confirm the legs were strong? Did you gently sit down, slowly placing the full weight of your body on it? Were you extra careful before you leaned back and relaxed? Or did you just sit down? If you just sat down, you exercised *faith* in that chair to support you. Over time, chairs have proven themselves faithful, safe places to sit. You are confident a chair will perform its function. Faith is no more complicated than that.

What would you do if you were driving at night and a car with dark, tinted windows pulled alongside you, then the stranger driving the car told you to pull over because he had money to give to you? If you were operating in wisdom and common sense, there is little or no chance you would stop your car. Instead, you would drive away, and fast. However, if you are driving down the street at night and a good friend asks you to pull over because he has something to give you, chances are you will stop. Why? Your friend has already proven he is faithful, that he can be trusted.

The foundations of our faith, or trust, are determined by our life experiences and what we have been taught through our relationships with others. Your parents told you the teachers at school could be trusted. Because you trust your parents, you trusted your teachers, or maybe you had to get to know your teacher's character first. Either way, if that experience caused you to believe that they were trustworthy, your faith in teachers grew.

There is a principle of the Kingdom of God at work here.

Christians who go through trials are taught to hold on to the principles and promises of God. As one principle proves to be trustworthy, you will stand on (believe in) another. Step by step, you will have a more secure faith in God because God proves to you that He is always faithful, even when we are not. The Bible tells us *even if we are faithless, He will remain faithful, for He cannot disown Himself* (2 Timothy 2:13).

How do you increase the faith God has given you? The disciples asked this very question in Luke 17:5-6, *The apostles said to the Lord, "Increase our faith!" Jesus answered their question in the next verse, if you have faith as small as a mustard seed, you can say to this mulberry tree, "Be uprooted and planted in the sea," and it will obey you.* Jesus' answer was quite simple and yet can be puzzling if you do not understand another principle of God.

The disciples understood Jesus' answer because He had already explained the parable of the seed to them (Luke 13:19), also recorded in more detail in Matthew 13:31-39. They understood that their faith grew because their hearts were not calloused (Matthew 13:15). In this way, they were able to hear the truth in the words of Jesus, who was the Word of God (John 1:14).

In Romans, the Bible tells you how your faith increases. Consequently, faith comes from hearing the message, and the message is heard through the Word of Christ (Romans 10:17). The Word of God comes from His Kingdom and is about His Kingdom, which is why it is called the Good News. When you grasp the Living Word of God, you become more aware of the truth of God's existence in your life. You then become more entrenched in His Kingdom. As you count on, trust, and believe in its principles, your faith becomes stronger as a by-product. It's not about the size of your faith, but about in whom you place your trust and faith.

The opposite of faith is doubt and unbelief. If you have doubt or unbelief, you are not walking in Kingdom faith. *Jesus replied, "I tell you the truth, if you have faith and do not doubt"* (Matthew 21:21). *Later Jesus appeared to the Eleven as they were eating, he rebuked them for their lack of faith and their stubborn refusal to believe,* (Mark 16:14). It is important to identify the opposites of faith so you can determine if you are walking in faith or walking in something that opposes faith. All believers have had to wrestle with doubt and unbelief at some point on their journey with the Lord. However, if these are recurring issues, they can be a sign or symptom of another problem that will be addressed in the next few chapters.

If you are struggling with doubt or unbelief, be honest with yourself and God about the situation. Call on Jesus, the Author and Perfecter of our faith (Hebrews 12:2), just like the father of the epileptic boy did in Mark 9:24, *Immediately the boy's father exclaimed, "I do believe, help me overcome my unbelief!"* Jesus helped him and the boy was instantly healed. He will do the same for you as well.

Faith is not complicated or difficult to understand. Faith simply believes. For believers, having "faith" means we have determined in our hearts that we believe God is who He says He is, that He can and will do what He has promised to do, and that we trust in that belief. The part of this process that most people find difficult is the maturing of our faith to the point that we are confident and secure in what we believe. To reach a level of total confidence and security in what you believe, you must determine in your heart <u>that God is who He says He is</u>. As

Paul firmly confessed in 2 Timothy 1:12b, *Yet I am not ashamed, because <u>I know</u> whom I have believed, and <u>am convinced</u> that He is able to guard what I have entrusted to Him for that day.*

People of great faith understand God's principles and use them. This is best seen in Matthew 8:5-11. *When Jesus had entered Capernaum, a centurion came to him, asking for help. "Lord," he said, "My servant lies at home paralyzed and in terrible suffering." Jesus said to him, "I will go and heal him." The centurion replied, "Lord, I do not deserve to have You come under my roof but just say the word, and my servant will be healed. For I, myself am a man under authority, with soldiers under me. I tell this one, "Go," and he goes; and that one, "Come," and he comes. I say to my servant, "Do this," and he does it. When Jesus heard this, He was astonished and said to those following Him, "I tell you the truth, I have not found anyone in Israel with such great faith."*

The centurion knew this principle of God and it was credited to him as faith. The centurion knew his servant would be healed by Jesus' Word. That is faith.

HOPE

God's definition of "hope" in His Word is not the same as the definition commonly used in the world. If you accept the world's definition of hope, you will misuse this important truth. The dictionary defines the world's "hope" as a wish or desire, something that somebody wants to possess, to do, to have occur, or to be true."

This hope or "wishful thinking" from the world is not the hope as referenced in the Bible. Hope as a Truth of God is a "confident expectancy" based on the fulfillment of God's Kingdom on earth, which includes our promised hope of resurrection and ultimate placement within that Kingdom. Even though hope is certain and sure, it does not have a defined timeline. It is not a fleeting wish or desire; it is an anchor (Hebrew 6:19). It is centered in Christ Jesus who is our hope (1 Timothy 1:1). And it is found in God who is the God of hope (Romans 15:13). Hope, like faith, has a focal point. Our hope is in God (1 Peter 1:21), it is in our Lord Jesus Christ (1 Thessalonians 1:3), and of course, in the resurrection from the dead (Acts 23:6).

Faith, hope, and love are spiritual truths which work together to accomplish what they are directed to do. They exist independently of each other and can be identified by their characteristics but do not work on their own.

For instance, you will find hope in both faith and love. In the letter to the Hebrews, the Bible explains that hope is in faith, *now faith is being sure of what we hope for and certain of what we do not see,* (Hebrews 11:1). 1 Corinthians 13:7 further confirms that hope is in love, *Love always protects, always trusts, always hopes, always perseveres.* Therefore, you can see that hope is at work in both faith and love.

So how do you receive hope? Not knowing this answer has caused pain to many believers. Unfortunately, hope is the least taught of these three truths, and there are Christians who are not sure of its source. The Bible tells us where our hope comes from in Paul's letter to the Romans, *not only so, but we also rejoice in our sufferings, because we know that suffering produces perseverance; perseverance, character; and character, hope,* (Romans 5:3a).

Hope develops through trials and tribulations where your faith and love are tested. When you maintain a godly character through your trials and persevere in the truths that you already believe, hope becomes part of your identity. Hope is a byproduct of the testing of our faith. It is part of the maturity mentioned in James 1:2-4, *Consider it pure joy, my brothers, whenever you face trials of many kinds, because you know that the testing of your faith develops perseverance. Perseverance must finish its work so that you may be mature and complete, not lacking anything.*

Your godly character is maintained by not wavering from the instruction you receive from the Word of God. The Bible confirms this in Romans 15:4, *For everything that was written in the past was written to teach us, so that through endurance and the encouragement of the Scriptures we might have hope.*

Hope is developed through trials and tribulations.

The opposite of hope is hopelessness. Hopelessness is more prevalent in the Church than you might realize. It is a slow death that has no relief in sight, and it is the precursor to depression and suicide. Hopelessness is caused through both trials and tribulations. Yes, you did read that correctly and it is not a misprint. <u>Both hope and hopelessness come from the same place: trials, and tribulations.</u>

What is the difference between the two outcomes? Hope is produced by applying your faith and God's love while holding onto His truths through your trials. Getting through your trial successfully both produces and increases your hope. People who are hopeless have either not applied faith or love properly during their trial, or they did not understand faith and love to start with. Any combination of these errors can contribute to hopelessness. This is explained in more detail in the next chapter.

Remember, there is hope in faith and there is hope in love. Paul tells us about this association in his letter to the Colossians. *We always thank God, the Father of our Lord Jesus Christ, when we pray for you, because we have heard of your faith in Christ Jesus and of the love you have for all the saints, the faith and love that spring from the hope that is stored up for you in heaven and that you have already heard about in the word of truth, the gospel,* (Colossians 1:3-6). Remember, all these truths work together to accomplish God's will. Paul confirms this in Galatians 5:6, *The only thing that counts is faith expressing itself through love.*

Consider the following testimony:

Charlene was the only Christian working at a small county bank. She was not comfortable with the atmosphere there and had been praying for it to change. After she had been working at the bank for two years, a sum of money came up missing from the bank's vault. A coworker who oversaw the vault, accused Charlene of stealing the money. Charlene was one of the employees who went into the vault daily. However, because of the timing of the loss, she became the only suspect and quickly became the center of attention. An investigation ensued that involved the police and banking authorities. Even though her aggressive coworker slandered her on a regular basis, Charlene never returned an ill word. On several occasions, this coworker raised her voice, called her names, and pressured her to confess and quit lying about the theft.

The persecution, which went on for three months, included

Charlene's picture appearing in the local newspaper with an article mentioning that she was under investigation. To make things worse, after the article was published, her children were also ridiculed at school. It did not seem long before some of Charlene's friends abandoned her as well. Even though the bank found no hard evidence against her during the long investigation, they quietly gave Charlene the opportunity to resign. However, Charlene believed she was supposed to stay. Even though she no longer had duties managing cash, she worked diligently every day at whatever was put before her.

During this time of trial, Charlene's only hope was in Jesus. She knew if she stood on His teaching and remained steadfast in what she believed, she would get through it, if not be totally exonerated. She admitted the waiting and standing in faith was not easy. Indeed, it was often extremely hard to endure.

After what seemed like an endless ordeal, the money was found. An employee of the transport company had made an error in a cash exchange. He was terrified that he would lose his job. Rather than accept the responsibility for his actions, he had quietly waited for someone at the bank to contact his company so he could act surprised when they found the mistake. Charlene's accuser was responsible for confirming there was not an error by the transport company, but she was so convinced of Charlene's guilt, she never followed up on the alternate possibility.

After the transport company finally came forward with the truth, Charlene was approached by her coworker once again. In a cold sarcastic voice, Charlene's accuser quickly said, "Sorry, big mistake." and then turned and walked away. Charlene followed the coworker into her office and closed the door behind them.

Her co-worker's eyes got as big as saucers and fear covered her face as she backed into her desk getting ready for the blast she felt was coming.

Charlene paused for a moment, looked her straight in the eyes, and then said; "I love you and I forgive you for everything you said and did to me." The co-worker stood there for a moment as Charlene's words sunk in. Her fear turned to shock, which then melted away into deep conviction. Her heart was pierced and she began to cry.

After several minutes of crying, her coworker said, "I don't know what you have, but I need to have it." Charlene confessed that her strength and love came only from God. Because of her testimony, Charlene's coworker came to the Lord. Charlene's accuser then led another employee to the Lord the next day. By the end of the week, other bank employees had also accepted Christ!

The whole atmosphere of the bank was changed because the Kingdom of our God overtook the kingdom of this world using the truths of God through a believer. God had answered Charlene's prayer. Everything Charlene lost was restored, which included a substantial raise in both her position at the bank and her income. That is hope.

LOVE

Love is the most misunderstood of these three truths. It may surprise you to know that not all the truths of God are created equal. In addition, some truths of God only bring life when they are built upon other truths from the Word of God. *But the word of the LORD was to them, "Precept upon precept, precept upon precept, Line upon line, line upon line* (Isaiah 28:13 NKJV).

Different truths from the Word of God are built on each other, with love as the foundation of them all. *But the greatest of these is love,* (1 Corinthians 13:13). Love as talked about in the Bible, is not even close to what the world calls love. The world uses the word "love" to describe feelings for everything from ice cream to automobiles and, of course, do not forget puppies. Everybody loves puppies.

Truths from the Word of God are built on each other. Love is the foundation of them all.

The power of the word "love" has been so cheapened that it really has no consistent meaning today. It means different things to different people depending on how they feel about something at that moment. People claim they love a particular item one day but may not feel the same about it the next. We are inundated with the world's view of love from an early age through books, television, movies, and the secular media. Switching from the world's view to the Bible's view of love can be difficult for a believer and requires a radical change of thinking. This is what the Bible is referring to in Romans 12:2, *Do not conform any longer to the pattern of this world, but be transformed by the renewing of your mind.*

The Bible was not originally written in English. During translation, some words from the original text did not have an exact English equivalent. Several words in the original text of the Bible were translated as the English word "love" even though they each have a completely different meaning.

When used in reference to people, the word love is often used in an emotional sense. In the original text of the Bible, the word "phileo" resembles a type of love that means to "have an ardent affection or feeling for." Though it is very real, this type of love is characterized as impulsive love that can vary with any change of emotion. "Phileo love" is self-centered and influenced by man's own nature. Because this 'I' centered love can be found in the world, some teach that this love is not godly.

Actually, "phileo love" is a natural and healthy love between Christians (Ephesians 4:22-24). Our God has emotions and is the Author of "phileo love" in its pure form. This love is used in the Bible in reference to family relationships including husband and wife or brotherly love between close friends. God showed "phileo love" both to his Son (John 5:20) and to us, His children (John 16:27). "Phileo love" is not the same love that is a foundational truth of the Kingdom. However, "Phileo love" does exist along with it as a truth within God's Kingdom.

There is a more powerful type of love used in the original text of the Bible. It is an intimate affection centered in our will and not from our emotions. "Agape" is the type of love that the Kingdom of God is built upon. This may seem a strange concept to some. However, it is understandable to those who have experienced it and can now see things from God's perspective (Ephesians 4:23-24). "Agape love" does not change with our feelings. This Love, as described in the Bible, has no emotion in it. Because Charlene had "agape love" for her co-worker, it did not change with her circumstances. Charlene expressed "agape love" when she told her accuser that she loved her. "Agape love" does not come from within us, but instead, flows through us from an outside source. It comes from God, poured out from Him, through us, and into others (1 John 4:19).

"Agape love" is the least understood of these two types of love. The definition of "agape love" is found in 1 Corinthians 13:4-8, *Love is patient, love is kind. It does not envy, it does not boast, it is not proud. It is not rude, it is not self-seeking, it is not easily angered, it keeps no record of wrongs. Love does not delight in evil but rejoices with the truth. It always protects, always trusts, always hopes, always perseveres. Love never fails.*

It is necessary to know this definition because it is the foundation of all truths. Repeat this passage, meditate on it, declare it aloud until you know the truth of it in your heart.

How do you get this type of love? "Agape love" is available to every born-again believer because it comes from God by His Holy Spirit. *And hope does not disappoint us, because God has poured out his love into our hearts by the Holy Spirit, whom he has given us* (Romans 5:5). God gives this love to us in such a way that it becomes an experience rather than mere knowledge.

There is a significant difference between knowledge and experience. When I (Michael) was a young boy, I knew about the temperature "hot." I could spell "hot" and, on more than one occasion, I had to ease myself into a "hot" bathtub of water. Therefore, I believed I knew all about "hot." I still remember the day my mother made a batch of cookies when I found out something new about "hot." My mother was an extremely good cook. (This fact has nothing to do with the story, but I threw it in because it may well be a truth of God.)

After taking the cookies out of the oven, she put them on the back burner of the electric stove to cool and turned on the front burner to fry some chicken. She then left the room for just a moment to answer a phone call. At this point, I smelled the cookies and went into the kitchen to help myself to a treat. Reaching for one, I felt an odd cold sensation across my hand and heard a sizzling sound that I knew could not be good. At that moment, the cold tingle turned into one thousand daggers. I jerked my hand back, but it was slightly stuck.

When I separated my hand from the hot coil, the dark rings that resembled the burner of the stove were burned into my flesh. I could smell the burnt tissue, I heard the sizzle, I could feel the daggers stabbing my fingers, and the whole neighborhood heard me scream as I experienced a new degree of "hot." Running back into the kitchen, my mother experienced "hot" with me. She instantly grabbed a block of cold butter from the refrigerator and slapped it into my hand. The butter melted quickly, but I do not remember anything in my young life that felt as good as that cold butter. Years later, this unforgettable experience is still a part of me.

This experience became part of my being, and I am convinced to this day that neither death nor life, neither angels nor demons, neither the present nor the future, nor any powers, neither height nor depth, nor anything else in all creation, can separate me from what I know about "hot"! It is my sincere belief that I will escape the lake of fire on Judgment Day by the grace of God, so my experience with "hot" will never again be equaled or surpassed.

The Apostle Paul prayed for us to know this "agape love" by experience. *To know this love that surpasses knowledge - that you may be filled to the measure of all the fullness of God* (Ephesians 3:19).

The word "know" in this verse is the exact same word that Mary, the mother of Jesus, used when she was explaining to the angel of God why she could not be pregnant. *Then Mary said to the angel, "How can this be, since I do not "know" a man?* (Luke 1:34 NKJV). In this case, the word "know" means to have an intimate personal encounter. After Paul had his encounter with love, he made this statement. *For I am convinced that neither death nor life, neither angels nor demons, neither the present nor the future, nor any powers, neither height nor depth, nor anything else in all creation, will be able to separate us from the love of God that is in Christ Jesus our Lord* (Romans 8:38-39).

There is another significant difference between emotional love and the love of God. Telling someone, "I love you more than ever" or "My love grows stronger for you every day" is common in an emotionally based love relationship. This is an example of a "Phileo" love that comes from our own being. The love that originates from us can change in intensity or fade over time, but the "agape" love of God never changes. Unlike the world's love, the love of God already exists in its full measure within His Kingdom. There is not more or less of it at one time or another. It was in the beginning, and it will be in the end, no matter what we do.

However, it is a fact that people experience an increase in "agape love" as stated in 2 Thessalonians 1:3, *and the love every one of you has for each other is increasing.* This may sound like a contradiction, but it is not.

Remember, the love of God does not come <u>from</u> us but instead goes <u>through</u> us. Living in God's Kingdom with His Truth and within His plan for our life, we experience more of what already exists all around us. As more of His love flows through us, we become more sensitive and aware of it. God's love increases within us because of one of the most powerful truths of the Kingdom: **God is love**. This love is not in His nature, it is His nature. The Bible tells us; *Whoever does not love does not know God, because God is love,* (1 John 4:8). Whenever you love others with His love, you are reflecting His nature and allowing His love to flow through you to another.

So, how do you increase in love? You experience more of it by giving love to one another. You do not have to hunt for it or work for it. Your capacity to love increases exponentially every time you give it away. It also becomes increasingly easier to give it away again. This open-handed, open-hearted kind of love is a forceful tool to advance God's kingdom.

God lives in the born-again believer, and the more you love another, the more complete you become in His love. John confirms this. *Dear friends, since God so loved us, we also ought to love one another. No one has ever seen God; but if we love one another, God lives in us, and his love is made complete in us,* (1 John 4:11-12).

Love is most fruitful when it is given to those who have not done anything to earn it. In other words, blessings come when we share our love without demanding anything in return. When we require something in return, the exchange becomes a business arrangement, a transaction, not love. If we only love those who love us back, we are acting like people of the world, not like God. Jesus tells us in Luke 6:32-33, *If you love those who love you, what credit is that to you? Even "sinners" love those who love them. And if you do good to those who are good to you, what credit is that to you? Even "sinners" do that.*

There is a powerful principle of God in "agape love" that is always at work, but rarely mentioned. The Bible reveals this to you in 1 Corinthians 13:8, *Love never fails*. When you operate in this love as directed by the Spirit of God, His love will always accomplish what it intended to do. <u>Love Never Fails</u>! It cannot.

God is Love and He never fails.

Why? Because <u>God is Love, and God never fails</u>. Even though "agape" love does not demand anything in return, something will always be returned, because love will not fail. Love never fails! It cannot fail because <u>He cannot fail</u>. Remember, your circumstances and experiences do not have the power to change God. No matter what the circumstances in your life, nothing can change the fact that Love never fails.

Like faith and hope, love has a focal point. All believers understand that our focus should be on God. Matthew 22:37-38 tells us, *Love the Lord your God with all your heart and with all your soul and with all your mind. This is the first and greatest commandment.*

Believers often miss another focal point of equal importance, not because they do not know about it, but because they do not understand its truth. The Word of God says the second commandment is "LIKE" the first. It is the same as the first, except it is seen from a different perspective. Jesus confirmed this in Matthew 22:39, *"And the second is like it: 'Love your neighbor as yourself.'"* In Mark 12:31, Jesus explains the importance of these two statements. *There is no commandment greater than these.*

These two statements are like two sides of the same coin. Even though a coin has two different "faces," looking at one side or the other does not change its value. A United States quarter is worth twenty-five cents whether you look at the side with the eagle or the side with the head. Using this analogy and applying it to the above scripture reference, the second commandment is just as important as the first. They are the same in intensity and purpose.

Some Christians believe that God should get top priority on the hierarchy of your "love scale," and others should come in at a close second. God absolutely should get your love, but others should receive just as much of it. The love you are commanded to show others is His love flowing through you. By allowing His love to flow freely through you, you are reflecting His nature and character in yourself.

Paul told us the importance of this in Galatians 5:14. *The entire law is summed up in a single command: Love your neighbor as yourself.* Jesus tells us what will happen to everyone upon his return in Matthew 25:31-46. Within those verses, He makes a sobering remark: *I tell you the truth, whatever you did for one of the least of these brothers of Mine, you did for Me,* (Matthew 25:40). People fill God's heart, so they should fill ours as well. Read that sentence again. You may have misunderstood this Truth. The misunderstanding of this Truth is responsible for much of the pain and fear in our world.

At times, it appears easier to love God than to love our neighbors. We can be hurt when our neighbors (family, friends) do things that cause distance in their relationships with us. If we are giving them our love and they do nothing in return, we can feel the hurt and pain of rejection. In those moments we must remember that it is not only our love we are to give them, but His. It is possible to have God's heart for our neighbors when we ask Him to reveal His love for them to us. This comes best by actively praying for them and asking for His heart towards them. When we do, He gives us eyes to see them as He sees them. Our hearts will begin to burn with a love for them that we could not have previously imagined. The result is nothing less than amazing.

What is the opposite of love? Most people reply, "Hate." But hate is an emotion. Remember: "agape love" is not an emotion. "Agape" love's true opposite will not be an emotion either. Some teach that the opposite of love is doubt and unbelief. Even though faith, hope and love work together, doubt and unbelief are opposites of faith, not of love.

In truth, the force opposing love is fear. The Bible tells us, *there is no fear in love. But perfect love drives out fear* (1 John 4:18). Even though they are opposites, love and fear are not equals. Nothing equals the Love of God! His love drives out fear. Fear in a believer's life is a flashing neon sign announcing that there is an absence of love. Before you start qualifying phobias or wonder if your fear of loud noises is because of a lack of love, let us explain. We are only talking about fears associated with the outcome of your future.

People walking in the true love of God do not worry about what the future will bring. Jesus cautioned us; *Therefore, do not worry about tomorrow, for tomorrow will worry about itself. Each day has enough trouble of its own*, (Matthew 6:34). Do not confuse worry about the future with concern for today's challenges. Reflect on the trials God has brought you through in the past. Why do you thank Him? What has He done for you, your family or loved ones? Do not worry, He will do it again. He never changes. Love never fails!

It is possible for Christians to lose connection with God's love. They might have once walked in it daily, but now intimacy with Him seems to have disappeared. The Bible tells us in John 15:10, *If you obey my commands, you will remain in my love.* If this love, this intimacy is lost, you did not obey His commands, and you may be living contrary to His Word. It could be something as simple as putting your faith in the wrong place, not loving others as He called you to do. You might also be dealing with a sin for which you have not repented and received forgiveness. Your heart may have hardened over time, and you can no longer hear (Him) as you once did.

We are always surprised when we meet Christians who know they are doing wrong, yet they believe that God's silence is somehow His approval about their situation. Nothing could be further from the truth or more dangerous (Psalms 50:16-21). It can be caused by one of the reasons stated above. However, remember that even though sin is a separator, the separation we sometimes experience could be caused by the sins of others committed against us. If that is the case, forgiveness is necessary. If it is your sin, repentance is necessary. If, however, the separation could be caused by a misuse of faith, hope, or love, you will find help in the prayer that follows.

Finally, it is difficult to discuss love without including these powerful scriptures. 1 John 4:7-10, *Dear friends, let us love one another, for love comes from God. Everyone who loves has been born of God and knows God. Whoever does not love does not know God, because God is love. This is how God showed his love among us: He sent his one and only Son into the world that we might live through him. This is love, not that we loved God, but that he loved us and sent his Son as an atoning sacrifice for our sins.* That is love.

If you have not walked in these truths and have not applied your faith, hope, and love during your trial, it is time to change your direction and do it now. Repeat the following prayer from your heart:

Father, I have allowed doubt and unbelief to influence my life, and I repent for it now. Doubt and unbelief are not of You, and I refuse to follow them any longer. I will put my faith in You and Your Word, and I will follow Your instructions alone. Father, I have allowed hopelessness into my life by not using the love and faith You have given me. I repent. I will apply them in this situation and every other one from this day on. Finally, Father, I have not loved my neighbors as much as myself and I repent. I will love them as You direct me to do. Father, this is sin, and I ask you to forgive me this sin. I ask that you reveal to me Your love for them, in Jesus' name. Thank you, Father! Amen.

If correction has come because of the instruction you just received, then "Thank God!" Follow Paul's lead, *but one thing I do: Forgetting what is behind and straining toward what is ahead, I press on toward the goal to win the prize for which God has called me heavenward in Christ Jesus* (Philippians 3:13-14). Understanding these truths will make seeing and walking in the Kingdom of God much easier and much more rewarding. These simple truths are the foundation to your advancement in the Kingdom of God. When you "live" them, you become like the One who made you. You will reflect the Author of <u>all</u> Truth to others as stated in 2 Corinthians 3:18, *And we, who with unveiled faces all reflect the Lord's glory, are being transformed into His likeness with ever-increasing glory, which comes from the Lord, who is the Spirit.*

Scripture References:

Therefore, everyone who hears these words of mine and puts them into practice is like a wise man who built his house on the rock. The rain came down, the streams rose, and the winds blew and beat against that house; yet it did not fall, because it had its foundation on the rock. But everyone who hears these words of mine and does not put them into practice is like a foolish man who built his house on sand. The rain came down, the streams rose, and the winds blew and beat against that house, and it fell with a great crash.

(Matthew 7:24-27)

This, the first of his miraculous signs, Jesus performed at Cana in Galilee. He thus revealed his glory, and his disciples put their faith in him.

(John 2:11)

"Have faith in God," Jesus answered.

(Mark 11:22)

God presented Him as a sacrifice of atonement, through faith in his blood. He did this to demonstrate his justice, because in his forbearance he had left the sins committed beforehand unpunished.

(Romans 3:25)

Having been buried with Him in baptism, in which you were also raised with Him through your faith in the working of God, who raised Him from the dead.

(Colossians 2:12)

It is like a mustard seed, which a man took and planted in his garden. It grew and became a tree, and the birds of the air perched in its branches.

(Luke 13:19)

He told them another parable: "The kingdom of heaven is like a mustard seed, which a man took and planted in his field. Though it is the smallest of all seeds, yet when it grows, it is the largest of garden plants and becomes a tree, so that the birds come and perch in its branches." He told them still another parable: "The kingdom of heaven is like yeast that a woman took and mixed into about sixty pounds of flour until it worked all through the dough." Jesus spoke all these things to the crowd in parable; He did not say anything to them without using a parable. So was fulfilled what was spoken through the prophet: "I will open my mouth in parables, I will utter things hidden since the creation of the world." Then he left the crowd and went into the house. His disciples came to Him and said, "Explain to us the parable of the weeds in the field." He answered, "The one who sowed the good seed is the Son of Man. The field is the world, and the good seed stands for the people of the kingdom. The weeds are the people of the evil one, and the enemy who sows them is the devil. The harvest is the end of the age, and the harvesters are angels."

(Matthew 13:31-39)

For this people's heart has become calloused; they hardly hear with their ears, and they have closed their eyes. Otherwise, they might see with their eyes, hear with their ears, understand with their hearts and turn, and I would heal them."

(Matthew 13:15)

The Word became flesh and made his dwelling among us. We have seen his glory, the glory of the One and Only, who came from the Father, full of grace and truth.

(John 1:14)

Consequently, faith comes from hearing the message, and the message is heard through the word about Christ.

(Romans 10:17)

Fix our eyes on Jesus, the author and perfecter of our faith, who for the joy set before Him endured the cross, scorning its shame, and sat down at the right hand of the throne of God.

(Hebrews 12: 2)

Truths of the Kingdom

We have this hope as an anchor for the soul, firm and secure. It enters the inner sanctuary behind the curtain.

(Hebrews 6:19)

Paul, an apostle of Christ Jesus by the command of God our Savior and of Christ Jesus our hope.

(1 Timothy 1:1)

May the God of hope fill you with all joy and peace as you trust in him, so that you may overflow with hope by the power of the Holy Spirit.

(Romans 15:13)

Through him you believe in God, who raised him from the dead and glorified him, and so your faith and hope are in God.

(1 Peter 1:21)

We continually remember before our God and Father your work produced by faith, your labor prompted by love, and your endurance inspired by hope in our Lord Jesus Christ.

(Thessalonians 1:3)

Then Paul, knowing that some of them were Sadducees and the other Pharisees, called out in the Sanhedrin, "My brothers, I am a Pharisee, the son of a Pharisee.
I stand on trial because of my hope in the resurrection of the dead."

(Acts 23:6)

LIVING FULLY FREE

You were taught, with regard to your former way of life, to put off your old self, which is being corrupted by its deceitful desires; to be made new in the attitude of your minds; and to put on the new self, created to be like
God in true righteousness and holiness.

(Ephesians 4:22-24)

For the Father loves the Son and shows him all he does. Yes, to your amazement He will show Him even greater things than these.

(John 5:20)

No, the Father Himself loves you because you have loved me and have believed that I came from God.

(John 16:27)

We love because He first loved us.

(1 John 4:19)

When the Son of Man comes in his glory, and all the angels with Him, He will sit on His glorious throne. All the nations will be gathered before Him, and He will separate the people one from another as a shepherd separates the sheep from the goats. He will put the sheep on His right and the goats on his left. Then the King will say to those on His right," Come, you who are blessed by my Father; take your inheritance, the Kingdom prepared for you since the creation of the world. For I was hungry and you gave me something to eat, I was thirsty and You gave me something to drink, I was a stranger and you invited me in, I needed clothes and you clothed Me, I was sick and you looked after Me, I was in prison and you came to visit me. Then the righteous will answer Him, "Lord, when did we see you hungry and feed you, or thirsty and give you something to drink? When did we see you a stranger and invite you in? or needing clothes and clothe you? When did we see you sick or in prison and go to visit you? The King will reply, "Truly I tell you whatever you did for one of the least of these brothers and sisters of mine, you did for me." Then he will say to those on His left, "Depart from Me, you who are cursed, into the eternal fire prepared for the devil and his angels. For I was hungry and you gave me nothing to eat, I was thirsty and you gave me nothing to drink, I was a stranger and you did not invite Me in, I needed clothes and you did not clothe Me, I was sick and in prison and you did not look after me." They also will answer, "Lord, when did we see You hungry or thirsty or a stranger or needing clothes or sick or in prison, and did not help You?" He will reply, "Truly I tell you, whatever you did not do for one of the least of these, you did not do for Me." Then they will go away to eternal punishment, but the righteous to eternal life."

(Matthew 25:31-46)

But to the wicked person, God says: "What right have you to recite My laws or take My covenant on your lips? You hate My instruction and cast My words behind you. When you see a thief, you join with him; you throw in your lot with adulterers. You use your mouth for evil and harness your tongue to deceit. You sit and testify against your brother and slander your own mother's son. When you did these things and I kept silent, you thought I was exactly like you. But I now arraign you and set my accusations before you."

(Psalms 50:16-21)

CHAPTER 8

TRIALS OF LIFE

We have identified a theme that is common to anyone who has experienced a wounded or broken heart: the hurt usually occurs while enduring a trial or going through a traumatic event. The type of event we are referencing is not minor. Instead, we are talking about those severe trials that can stretch on indefinitely, like a chronic illness or years of oppression. People going through painful experiences can slip into hopelessness because, to them, the trial becomes an endless tribulation. There are those who have suffered for so long that they have even prayed for death as a way out of the pain and desperation. Feeling defeated or dead inside, they plod through the motions of life without peace, joy, or strength.

Jim left for work frustrated, as he had done many times before. Kathy was left to contend with their two children and the day's ever-increasing problems. She had been trying to talk to Jim about the issues she had been struggling with but was unsuccessful in her communication with him. It was as if Jim had filters over his ears causing her words to be distorted to him. No matter how hard she tried, he did not understand what she was saying. Thinking he was providing an answer to Kathy's problems, Jim counseled Kathy on how to "fix" the problems she was experiencing.

Frustrated, but still hoping to get through to Jim, she would explain her feelings again the next day. Each attempt ended with Jim still unable to hear her. Kathy grew more distant and angry. Jim only grew more upset that she was not applying his solutions, which he was sure would solve the problems. The situation continued to grow worse until neither one of them was willing to talk about their issues.

The people they turned to for advice were going through similar problems and had no lasting solutions. Days turned into weeks and weeks turned into years, and nothing ever seemed to change. The unending chores of the home, the demands of the children and the stress of her unanswered marital problems led Kathy into a hopelessness that eventually set the groundwork for her to fall into a deep depression. She felt surrounded by hopelessness. It was when she was in this condition that we met Kathy.

After sharing with her how to walk in the truths of God, and leading her in a few simple prayers, she had a strength and peace that she never thought possible. We went our separate ways and heard from her months later. She was experiencing His joy and peace. She told us how God had touched Jim, and they were experiencing new life together. She reported the atmosphere in their home had changed as if a cloud had been lifted. The children were experiencing a newfound joy as well. Her neighbors commented on the peace they felt when they were visiting, and it was something they wanted for their own homes. The Kingdom of our Lord overtook the kingdom of this world and something miraculous happened.

Trials of Life

The Bible tells us in James 1:2, *Consider it pure joy, my brothers, whenever you face trials of many kinds.* Why would James, the brother of Jesus, make such a bold and seemingly contradictory statement? Paul said something similar in Romans 5:3, *we also rejoice in our sufferings.* Finally, Peter repeated the same thing, *"Dear friends, do not be surprised at the painful trial you are suffering, as though something strange were happening to you. But rejoice,"* (1 Peter 4:12-13). This whole concept may seem strange. It is not like you see a line of people ready to sign up for the "pain and suffering committee" at church. However, there is a truth in this, a truth which is commonly missed and not often taught.

Paul said in Acts 14:22, *We must go through many hardships to enter the kingdom of God.* Cyndi and I were taught that the Christian life should be glorious, and trials only happen when you or someone around you do something wrong. Leaders who are teaching about this glorious life in God have gone through many trials and hardships themselves, which is a fact they may have omitted in their lessons. Listeners feel as if there is something wrong with them because their lives are not perfect. Some do not ask for help because they fear they may be condemned for not being able to "overcome" their situation and live the "victorious" life. Because of this teaching and others like it, many Christians silently endure these hardships alone and suffer needlessly.

God is not the author of your trials.

God is not the author of your trials (James 1:13). However, you are fighting in a battle for who will have dominion in your life. These trials are inevitable until that issue is settled (1 John 2:15- 16). Through these trials, God's dominion over your life is proven and established. Believers, who have Jesus in their hearts, will go through many trials until the dominion of God's Kingdom becomes the fortress of their Christian life. Kingdom means "king's domain where the King has dominion."

In this process, some of God's truths may be lost or even misunderstood. The reason for this is some leaders do not instruct believers that trials are a healthy and normal part of our Christian life until maturity is reached. It is stated clearly in James 1:2-4, *Consider it pure joy, my brothers, whenever you face trials of many kinds, because you know that the testing of your faith develops perseverance. Perseverance must finish its work so that you may be mature and complete, not lacking anything.*

God is in control of everything believers go through, including our trials, as confirmed in Romans 8:28, *And we know that in all things God works for the good of those who love Him, who have been called according to His purpose.* God will never allow us to endure a trial greater than we can bear if we keep our eyes on Him. The Word confirms this in 1 Corinthians 10:13, *And God is faithful; He will not let you be tempted beyond what you can bear. But when you are tempted, He will also provide a way out so that you can stand up under it.*

Another way to read this is that you are already equipped to pass the test, or He would not have allowed you to go through it. To get through any trial, you must walk through it holding fast to your faith, trusting in Him and His ability to see you through. When you do, the promises of God will manifest in your life.

If you do not understand the purpose of a trial, you are on your own to figure out what to do next as well as question why it happened in the first place. Contrary to some beliefs, trials do not show God the condition of your heart. He already knows it. Nothing is hidden from Him (Acts 15:8). Trials reveal to <u>you</u> what is in your heart and offer you the opportunity to grow in faith and love through the circumstances. Knowing these Kingdom Truths by experience will manifest God's nature and character in your heart, and you will be empowered to advance His Kingdom.

Adversity will often reveal a man to himself. During times of trial, beliefs and attitudes hidden deep within our hearts rise to the surface and are exposed for us, and occasionally the entire world to see. This "picture of the heart" is not always what you believe it would be. Of course, this is more comfort to you after you have gone through a trial than while you are in the middle of one. Remember, when you squeeze grapes, you get grape juice. When you are in a trial, the essence within your heart comes to the surface, both good and bad.

Adversity will often reveal a man to himself.

When Jesus was telling His disciples about His death and ultimate resurrection, Peter made a boastful statement to the Lord in Luke 22:33-34. *But he replied, "Lord, I am ready to go*

with you to prison and to death." Jesus answered, *"I tell you, Peter, before the rooster crows today, you will deny three times that you know Me."* Peter was astonished at Jesus' reply. Peter completely believed that he would never deny his Lord, but Jesus knew what was hidden in Peter's heart. We all know the story. Peter denied Jesus three times before morning.

Jesus made an interesting comment just one verse before this great trial in Peter's life occurred, *"Simon, Simon, Satan has asked to sift you as wheat. But I have prayed for you, Simon, that your faith may not fail. And when you have turned back, <u>strengthen your brothers</u>,* (Luke 22:31-32). Jesus knew that not only would Peter make it through this trial (and see what was in his own heart) but also that the revelation he received through it would make him stronger. He would be so much stronger, in fact, that he would be able to strengthen his brothers during their trials. This trial revealed to Peter that a part of his heart needed to change.

When you go through trials and hold on to your faith and love, <u>you are stronger for it</u>. You are then able to encourage others through similar situations. Through this refining process, God places riches in your heart and removes the useless things. Those jewels of life (His attributes) that God cherishes come to the surface and you are changed. The negative aspects of your old nature are discarded. Afterwards, the river of living water flows freely through you as you reflect God's nature.

This refining process is recorded in Job 28:1-11:

> *There is a mine for silver, and a place where gold is refined.*
> *Iron is taken from the earth, and copper is smelted from ore.*

Man puts an end to the darkness,
He searches the farthest recesses,
for ore in the blackest darkness.
Far from where people dwell, he cuts a shaft,
in places forgotten by the foot of man.
Far from men he dangles and sways.
The earth, from which food comes, is transformed below as by fire.
Sapphires come from its rocks, and its dust contains nuggets of gold.
No bird of prey knows that hidden path, no falcon's eye has seen it.
Proud beasts do not set foot on it, and no lion prowls there.
Man's hand assaults the flinty rock,
and lays bare the roots of the mountains.
He tunnels through the rock. His eyes see all its treasures.
He searches the sources of the rivers,
and brings hidden things to light.

The enemy (bird of prey, proud beast, lion / Satan) does not have access to this process. Only God does. Just like Job, you may feel vulnerable and alone, and you may not understand why God allowed you to go through another trial. God Himself is the overseer of the process that changes you into His image. He protects you during that process, and you are changed (made richer) through your trial. God does not cause the trial. However, He does use it for your good.

According to scripture, no one knows your heart except for God. This is confirmed in Hebrews 4:13, *Nothing in all creation is hidden from God's sight. Everything is uncovered and laid bare before the eyes of Him to Whom we must give account.* The things you surround yourself with reflect what is in your heart. Your environment will always reflect who you are inside. Your home and friends reveal a picture of your heart's condition. Sometimes it is obvious in the colors you choose, the things you collect, the artwork you display, or the movies, books, or games you have in your home. Have you ever walked into someone's home and felt an overwhelming sense of peace and welcome? They will have worked diligently to create that inviting atmosphere, and it is a direct reflection of the person or people living there.

Of course, sometimes we encounter the opposite. As you walk into a home, you are immediately overwhelmed with chaos and feel unsettled both during your visit and after you leave. Peaceful homes are generally clean and comfortable, while chaotic homes can reflect total disorder. We have yet to find a home where both conditions exist at the same time without conflict. But having your home in perfect order also does not mean that your heart is in order. It is possible to make everything around you look "clean and neat" while everything inside you is in complete turmoil. Some "neat freaks" searching for peace believe that if everything around them looks perfect, it will somehow also bring peace to their heart. Unfortunately, cleaning up and having control over your living space does not mean that your heart is at peace. People in this condition are often left feeling frustrated and empty in a clean house. Conversely, changes for the worse in someone's home environment during a trial are usually a tell-tale sign of the stress and chaos they feel internally.

There is knowledge that is realized only during your times of need. When you go through trials, you will discover whether your "head knowledge" (your thinking, like Peter before he denied Jesus) has reached your heart and become what you believe. If you only have "head knowledge," your opinions or beliefs can be changed by a more persuasive argument. If that knowledge has been rooted in your heart and becomes part of who you are (your faith), nothing and no one will be able to take it from you.

God is certainly known as a Healer to those He has healed. He is known as a Deliverer to those He has delivered. He is known as Supplier to those He has supplied. He is known as a Comforter to those He comforted, and He is known as Savior to those He has saved. Reading about and acknowledging that He is all these things is simply "head knowledge". When you have experienced Him in any of these ways (Supplier, Healer, Savior, etc.), you grow in the knowledge of the Lord in both who He is and what He can do. By extension, your faith grows.

Referring to Job's story, once God had finally answered all of Job's complaints (chapters 38-41), Job acknowledges that he had only <u>heard</u> of God before his trial, (Job 42:5) but now he had <u>seen</u> (experienced) Him for himself. Firsthand knowledge of God's attributes came when Job encountered Him during a life-altering trial. That experience impacted him in such a profound way that, for the rest of his life, Job would never be able to be separated from what he learned. He learned that God is faithful, and He will come through as He always has for those who believe in Him.

So, why do some people "fail" the test when the trials come? People who are not currently experiencing victory through their trials may recognize themselves in one of the following examples:

1. Perhaps you have tried to get through your trials utilizing key beliefs or scriptures you have heard or read

about, but because you have not yet personally experienced the revelation of those truths for yourself, the beliefs or scriptures appear ineffective. You may have heard the testimony of others who endured a similar trial using those same scriptures or truths from God, but you are questioning if He will do it for you.

2. Or maybe you have gone through a trial attempting to "act out" what you believe is the best thing to do in the situation. You will have tried to solve the problem by utilizing your own resources or previous experiences. But, when those resources were exhausted, you were forced to endure the trial until its completion. Your efforts may have seemed to end in failure. At that point, you may have made a notation to never repeat the same mistake or get in the same circumstances again. You may have said statements like, "I will never let my heart get that close to anyone again," or "I will never trust like that again", or "That's the last time I will ever" (you fill in the blank). The list could go on and on. You may have even said a few or all the statements yourself. At this point, your heart has become hardened.

In the first of these two scenarios, the person is acting as the Pharisees did. The Pharisees stood on the scriptures but could not hear the message of the Kingdom that Jesus preached. They had no revelation of the truth of the scriptures they believed they knew so well. The Pharisees knew the Word of God and could debate it effectively, but they could not see it as truth, even when Truth (Jesus) stood in front of them.

The Word without the revelation of truth is empty and powerless.

The Word without the revelation of the truth is empty and powerless. It becomes words written on a page, memorized and repeated, without lasting fruit or life. It can even be used to challenge the true purposes of God. This is what happened when Satan used the Word of God to test Jesus in the desert (Matthew 4:1-10). Satan may still use this tactic today to keep men's hearts captive when they do not know the truth of God's Word.

The Pharisees heard the testimony of those whom Jesus healed but they allowed doubt and unbelief to keep them from receiving the truth. Some Pharisees who could not deny the truth of a miracle occurring even went as far as to explain that the miracle must have come from some other source than God. Just like the Pharisees, we can allow doubt and unbelief to keep us from having victory, too, if we hear the testimony of what God did for others and do not believe He will do the same for us.

When you try to act out what you believe is the "right thing" to do based on your own understanding, you may be behaving like the people of the world trapped within the kingdom of this world. In this way, you are trying to use your own logic, reason, and resources (your own abilities and strength) to resolve your trials. If that is unsuccessful, you write it off as simply "learning from your mistakes."

LIVING FULLY FREE

Unfortunately, what you learn does not bring life to you. In fact, it can even take away from it. As discouragement sets in, your heart hardens. This kind of perceived "faith failure" may leave you believing a lie that you are a second-rate Christian, and that God did not come through for you. The enemy can use this lie against you. Exhausted, weary, frustrated, and usually feeling abandoned, you may believe that if you had just prayed more, read more, or did fill-in-the-blank more, things would have turned out differently. Although doing any of these things might be useful in theory, this thinking is still "I centered." No matter how noble your intentions are, you will still end up with the same unfulfilled results. You will come to realize that you responded to that trial just like the rest of the world (the lost) does with self-reliance. You were not following God's plan but yours.

If you are going through your trials using either one of these scenarios, you are bound to repeat them and may have to go around that mountain one more time. This may even be more than your second trip. If you have been one of those "frequent travelers" around the proverbial mountain, there is a better way. It is time to get off that merry-go-round and walk through these trials the way God intended. Going through God's way does not mean that you will not have problems in the future. It also does not mean that worldly-minded people will never persecute you. The Bible tells us this will eventually happen in 2 Timothy 3:12-13, *In fact, everyone who wants to live a godly life in Christ Jesus will be persecuted.* These ongoing trials will be for righteousness' sake and may not always be because of your own actions.

The good news is you will find you have a peace amid your stormy trial that you never had before. You will realize that you have a sense of strength inside that you did not have before. You will begin to know you are not alone. You will come through your trials with revelation and greater wisdom from God and His Kingdom. You will also have a contentment you could not have imagined amid the stormy battle.

This Kingdom (king's domain) already exists, but only those who are born again can see it or experience it. Jesus confirms this in John 3:3, *In reply Jesus declared, "I tell you the truth, no one can see the kingdom of God unless he is born again."* All believers are aware of this Kingdom, but, unfortunately, not all walk in its fullness. Jesus told the Pharisees in Luke 11:20 NKJV, *"But if I cast out demons with the finger of God, surely the kingdom of God has come upon you."*

The Kingdom of God exists in parallel to the kingdom of this world.

The Kingdom of God exists in parallel to the kingdom of this world, and the fruit of God's Kingdom is available to all believers now. It is just a step away from believers who do not choose to walk in it. Believing this Kingdom exists or not has no effect on it. Like gravity, Kingdom principles always work even if you are not aware of them. You do have a choice, though. You can be a Christian and still choose to identify with the kingdom of this world instead of heavenly realities. However, we have found it true that you cannot walk in both earthly and heavenly realities without conflict. Thankfully, the option is available for you to fully choose God's Kingdom and live in ever-increasing victory day by day.

Although all believers should walk in the fullness of God's domain, you cannot walk in it without going through some hardships. If your experiences have not brought about the fullness of this Kingdom in your own life, do not start looking for more hardships and trials. Also, do not allow condemnation to tell you that you are not worthy of this wonderful life because of something you did, or are currently doing wrong. Instead, hear this simple truth.

Before we go any further, it is most important to point out that either God directs your path and works all things for good for those who love Him and are called upon His purposes (Romans 8:28), or He does not. You get to choose if you will believe this truth or not.

If you are crediting Satan for your trial in any way, you do not have the total belief that God oversees your life. Sin is most likely the cause of your trial and remember it does not always have to be sin that originated with you. Trials, like cancer, are not God's plan for your life, and yes, the enemy comes to kill, steal, and destroy (John 10:10). However, continuing to give him credit for things only empowers him. He is not the One who is going to get you through it. So, do not ever mention the devil's name and give him glory, even if the glory is for negative effect. You can easily become Satan-conscious and there is no strength in that.

God is working in us to correct things that need to change

and strengthen those things that need to be stronger in our lives. He confirms this in Hebrews 12:7, *Endure hardship as discipline; God is treating you as sons. For what son is not disciplined by his father?* This discipline means "correction through instruction" and does not mean punishment. Christians who believe that God is somehow punishing them have a distorted perspective of who God is and how He operates in the believer's lives.

As a believer, you have already been qualified to live in God's Kingdom, according to Colossians 1:12-13, *giving thanks to the Father, who has qualified you to share in the inheritance of the saints in the kingdom of light. For he has rescued us from the dominion of darkness and brought us into the kingdom of the Son he loves.*

We talked about why many of us have gone through, or are going through, a trial, even ones not of our own making. It should be evident now that hope ultimately comes from coming through your trials. (Romans 5:3-5). However, experience teaches us that hopelessness can also come from the same trial and produce disastrous results. How do we change the outcome of our test? The answer is simple: by applying courage. The definition of the world's courage is a "strength that faces pain in the face." Many of us have applied this worldly type of courage through our trial until our strength ran out. We are then left calling on the Lord in desperation or even blaming Him for His lack of attention to our needs. At this point, we may feel powerless or even broken.

"Powerless" and "broken" is the starting point where we begin to recognize what really lives in our own hearts. You may want to read that again. This is where true heart change begins. Like when Peter denied Jesus for the third time (Matthew 26:69-75), it is from this place that we begin to understand what it means to depend on His courage.

His courage is the application of Faith and Love during our trial. This courage is not from us but is manifested through us. These powerful forces of faith and love will empower the Hope you need to get through every trial, every time.

**How do you know if you are using
your courage or His?**

So, how do you know if you are using your courage or His? The answer is found in who you see as your enemy? Is it the person or persons on the other side of your trial the enemy? That is a sign of a lack of love, and you need His Love in this situation. Did you know we are instructed to bless from our hearts those who persecute us (Romans 12:14)? This may be difficult when you believe an injustice has been done against you and you are still suffering as the result of it. God is against injustice (Leviticus 19:15), but he does not hate those that have committed this sin. He loves them, do you? Remember, trials reveal what can be hidden in your heart.

When we doubt whether we will get through the trial without being severely wounded or if we will even survive it, believing we will be worse off, that is a sign of a lack of faith. We need His faith to empower us in this situation. Remember, *God works all things for the good of those who love Him and are called according to His purpose*, Romans 8:28. Believing this is the opposite of believing the trial will end in disaster. This is faith. The application of this faith is explained in the previous Faith, Hope and Love chapter (Truths of the Kingdom). Please reread it until it is in your heart. It could easily be the beginning of the end of the trial you are currently facing.

When you operate by the principles of God's kingdom, you will advance through your trials into victory. If you choose to operate by the principles of this world, you will keep repeating your trials until you know and experience these Truths.

Believers who choose to become an active part of the advancing Kingdom of God, experience the life that is promised in His Word. When Jesus returns, life in your glorified body will be infinitely better, but life in God starts the day Jesus enters your heart. You do not have to wait for some other appointed time to know fulfillment in God.

If we did have to wait for that fulfillment, His Word would not be Good News. It would be only a Good Promise. In John 16:33, Jesus told us, *"I have told you these things, so that in me you may have peace. In this world you will have trouble. But take heart! I have overcome the world."* He is the Victor! When He lives in your heart, you are a victor too!

If you have misunderstood the trials in your life or have blamed God for them, repeat this prayer from your heart.

> *Father, I have not considered it pure joy when I have gone through various trials and have even become angry and frustrated through them. I repent for any words I said such as: I would never trust, never love, never give my heart again or never (fill in the blank). Father, I have made the people*

on the other side of this trial the enemy. This is sin. I repent and ask for Your Heart towards them.

Father, I have given the devil credit for this trial as if You were not the author and perfecter of my faith. I repent and refuse to even mention His name.

Father, I repent for these words and ask you to Forgive me for them. I will put my trust in You through this trial. I will give You thanks in everything from this day forth. Father, I thank You that You said "You will never leave me or forsake me and that You will lead me to maturity in You. In Jesus name, Amen.

There is a weapon that has the power to change the outcome of almost every trial. <u>Reflect</u> on the trials God has brought you through in the past. <u>Remember</u> what He did for you. <u>Say them aloud</u> to others and watch what happens in your life. Each victory is a <u>testimony</u> of the advancement of God's kingdom. This practice of <u>remembering and declaring</u> what He has done in your past will strengthen you through every trial. He will do it again!

Finally, let us look at your trial from a Kingdom perspective. It is understood that all born again believers will live through eternity in Heaven. Free from all hindrances including pain, fear, doubt, and sorrow, giving God praise in Heaven will come as naturally as breathing does here on earth. All of heaven will be joining you in that chorus. However, you will never, in all your existence throughout eternity, be able to offer a greater sacrifice of praise than when you are here on earth going through a trial

(Hebrews 13:15). Think about that for a moment. At a time and place where you are at your lowest, you can choose to give Him honor and praise. It truly is a sacrifice of praise. One offered from the lowest place in your heart, where unlike Heaven, you are not surrounded by His Glory.

Scripture References:

When tempted, no one should say, "God is tempting me." For God cannot be tempted by evil, nor does he tempt anyone.
(James 1:13)

Do not love the world or anything in the world. If anyone loves the world, love for the Father is not in them. For everything in the world – the lust of the flesh, the lust of the eyes, and the pride of life – comes not from the Father but from the world.
(1 John 2:15,16)

God, who knows the heart, showed that he accepted them by giving the Holy Spirit to them, just as He did to us.
(Acts 15:8)

My ears had heard of you but now my eyes have seen you.
(Job 42:5)

Then Jesus was led by the Spirit into the desert to be tempted by the devil. After fasting forty days and forty nights, He was hungry. The tempter came to Him and said, "If you are the Son of God, tell these stones to become bread."

Jesus answered, "It is written: 'Man does not live on bread alone, but
on every word that comes from the mouth of God.'"

Then the devil took him to the holy city and had Him stand on the highest point of the temple. "If you are the Son of God," he said, "throw yourself down.
For it is written: 'He will command his angels concerning you, and they will lift you up in their hands, so that you will not strike your foot against a stone.'" Jesus answered him, "It is also written: 'Do not put the Lord your God to the test.'"

Again, the devil took Him to a very high mountain and showed Him all the kingdoms of the world and their splendor. "All this I will give you," he said, "if you will bow down and worship me." Jesus said to him, "Away from me, Satan! For it is written: 'Worship the Lord your God and serve Him only'"

(Matthew 4:1-10)

And we know that in all things God works for the good of those who love Him, who have been called according to His purpose.

(Romans 8:28)

"The thief comes only to steal and kill and destroy; I have come that they may have life and have it to the full."

(John 10:10)

Not only so, but we also glory in our sufferings, because we know that suffering produces perseverance; perseverance, character;

Trials of Life

and character hope. And hope does not put us to shame, because God's love has been poured out into our hearts through the Holy Spirit, who has been given to us.

(Romans 5:3-5)

Now Peter was sitting out in the courtyard, and a servant girl came to him. "You also were with Jesus of Galilee," she said. But he denied it before them all. "I don't know what you're talking about," he said. Then he went out to the gateway, where another servant girl saw him and said to the people there, "This fellow was with Jesus of Nazareth." He denied it again, with an oath: "I don't know the man!" After a little while, those standing there went up to Peter and said, "Surely you are one of them; your accent gives you away." Then he began to call down curses, and he swore to them, "I don't know the man!" Immediately a rooster crowed. Then Peter remembered the word Jesus had spoken; "Before the rooster crows, you will disown Me three times." And he went outside and wept bitterly.

(Matthew 26:69-75)

Bless those who persecute you; bless and do not curse.

(Romans 12:14)

"Do not pervert justice; do not show partiality to the poor or favoritism to the great but judge your neighbor fairly.

(Leviticus 19:15)

Through Jesus, therefore, let us continually offer to God a sacrifice of praise—the fruit of lips that openly profess his name.

(Hebrews 13:15)

CHAPTER 9

THE POWER OF WORDS

Switching focus a bit, let us do a small exercise together. Please read the following paragraph below aloud:

> Hidden within the pages of this book is an elephant. It is a large African elephant with big floppy ears. It has the misfortune of being a bright circus pink in color. Because of this wild color, this elephant really stands out in front of the large green trees that are located behind it. On its body are plenty of large purple polka dots, and sitting on top of this monstrosity of an animal is a monkey with a bellman's cap on his head.

Do you know where you can find this animal? It is not hidden within the pages of this book. However, it is where you can clearly see it. Where is it, you ask? It is vividly alive in your mind's eye, in your head, and it was put there by words.

Words are one of the most powerful things on earth. God created the earth by speaking it into existence as stated in

Genesis 1:9, And God said, *"Let the water under the sky be gathered to one place, and let dry ground appear." And it was so.*

The chair you are sitting in while reading this book was first spoken about before it was created. Someone originally had the vision for it and told someone else about it, explaining in detail its design, color, shape, and size until the other person could see it for themselves. You are sitting in the result of that conversation. The building you are in was first spoken about before it was made. Our examples of this could go on and on, with endless possibilities. The point is: there is no limit to the power of our words. They are a creative force and lay a foundation for incredible endeavors, good things that bring joy, and life. Equally, they can also be used to harm, tear down, destroy and even kill.

In Proverbs 18:21 it states boldly, *The tongue has the power of life and death, and those who love it will eat its fruit.* Jesus confirmed the power of our words and our responsibility to use them wisely in Matthew 12:36, *But I tell you that men will have to give account on the Day of Judgment for every careless word they have spoken.* Explaining further, He goes on to tell us of their importance in the next verse, Matthew 12:37, *For by your words you will be acquitted, and by your words you will be condemned.*

**For by your words you will be acquitted,
and by your words you will be condemned.**

The Power of Words

If our words have such a vital role in our acquittal or condemnation on the Day of Judgment, then at any given time we should be able to judge ourselves by a simple method of measurement. Our words could fall into one of two categories. One category is words of life, words that are thankful, uplifting, constructive, encouraging and faith-filled (creative in nature). The other category is words of death, words that spread griping and complaining, are discouraging, and laced with doubt and fear (destructive in nature). By examining the words from our mouth, we are able to measure whether we are spreading life or death to ourselves and others.

Using this type of example to explain the power of your words, you could say that your words are a measuring stick for your acquittal or condemnation on the Day of Judgment. This being the case, ask yourself, "What about my words being measured is so important?" The answer is quite simple, yet extremely sobering. Words are the measuring stick, barometer, or the evidence of what is in your heart.

Jesus confirms this in Matthew 12:34-35, *For out of the overflow of the heart the mouth speaks. The good man brings good things out of the good stored up in him, and the evil man brings evil things out of the evil stored up in him.*

Our words are a direct reflection of the life and death which is hidden deep within our heart. In another reference, Jesus explains to the disciples in Mark 7:20-23, *What comes out of a man is what makes him "unclean." For from within, out of men's hearts, come evil thoughts, sexual immorality, theft, murder, adultery, greed, malice, deceit, lewdness, envy, slander, arrogance, and folly. All these evils come from inside and make a man unclean.*

LIVING FULLY FREE

Having the knowledge of the power of our words, we are cautioned to keep a tight rein on our tongues (James 3). When things are going well, you may be able to keep your tongue in check. However, what happens when you are under pressure? Remember, that if you squeeze grapes, you get grape juice, and if you squeeze an orange, you get orange juice. You can only get out of something what was in it to begin with. What comes out of you when you are under pressure is what was already in your heart. We can all mask our hearts for a season and know how to "act" in normal circumstances, but eventually, pressure will cause what is in our hearts to come out of our mouths. To think otherwise would mean that you are deceiving yourself and believing a lie.

Now is a suitable time to reflect on your heart by looking at the words coming out of your mouth. If you are in heavy traffic, having conflict in relationships, or are just having a difficult day (pressure), are you able to overcome those pressures by being thankful for the things around you or participating in an activity like listening to uplifting music? If the answer to that question is no, ask yourself if, instead, you are prone to surrendering to pressure by complaining and arguing with people in other cars that cannot even hear you. Perhaps you are tempted to go as far as using your car horn as an extension of your voice. When you are at work and your boss or key client is argumentative and complaining about issues that are not of your making (pressure), are you at peace, using soft words in response?

Proverbs 15:1 says, *A gentle answer turns away wrath, but a harsh word stirs up anger.* When the person you conflict with walks away, are you murmuring under your breath or even openly complaining to others about them? When you get home and find things you expected to be done by your family have not been done (pressure), do you regroup your thoughts? Or do you raise your voice and react negatively, expressing your feelings so others can share in your disappointment?

We are not suggesting that it is wrong to feel emotions or have times when you get upset. The truth is that God has already given us His peace so that our hearts can prosper through any of the pressures and trials of life (John 14:27). When the pressures come, things do not go as you planned or hoped and there is utter chaos and turmoil all around, you can still choose to keep your thoughts in check and maintain a tight rein on your tongue. Your words and attitude should remain consistent. If you are not living in that place now, then it is a sign that something may need to change.

The goal is not to have our words of life win out over our words of death, but to have no words of destruction at all. If God inhabits our praises (Psalm 22:3), what or who inhabits our complaints?

If God inhabits our praises, what or who inhabits our complaints?

To caution you, we are not pointing this out so that you can start making plans for how to exercise more "self-control" when it comes to what you say. We are not suggesting that you should simply change your words, and this will solve the problem. Everyone can say whatever he or she chooses and present a temporary, false picture of peace. We have all done this at some time or another.

"Policing" your words is not unhealthy. However, it is similar to treating the symptoms of a problem and not dealing with the root cause. For instance, think about how silly it would be to only change your dirty clothes when what you really need is a shower. In this way, it is actually more important to change things within your heart so that you can forever change the words that come out of your mouth.

By now, it should be clear that our words are the signpost of the attitudes of our hearts. Let us look at what the Word states about this in James 3:9-11, *With the tongue we praise our Lord and Father, and with it we curse men, who have been made in God's likeness. Out of the same mouth come praise and cursing. My brothers, this should not be.* James is making the point that these types of actions show us (and everyone around us) that it is time for a change (of the heart).

Most people are unaware that what they are saying could be considered a curse unless cuss words were spoken. So, we will look at some examples of what that would look like. In the next chapter we will explain the process of how to avoid speaking curses altogether.

We all know someone who appears critical and judgmental, and it seems to just be in their nature. They condemn those around them with their words. Oftentimes, these same people are the ones who may hold "grudges" and appear to be unwilling to forgive when someone has hurt or offended them.

**Our words are the signpost
of the attitudes of our heart.**

The Bible deals with all these symptoms in one Scripture in the New Testament. Strangely enough, this Scripture is repeated quite often during offering teachings in many churches. It would be rare for even a new Christian not to have heard it used in church at least once, if not more. We all know the passage in Luke 6:38, *Give and it will be given to you. A good measure, pressed down, shaken together, and running over, will be poured into your lap. For with the measure you use, it will be measured to you.*

Though this is a powerful truth of the Bible, it was not written about money. While it is a principle of God that will always work, to use it solely for teaching on giving is to take it out of its original context.

To understand what this passage is referring to, you must look at the entire scripture to capture its true meaning. *Do not judge and you will not be judged. Do not condemn, and you will not be condemned. Forgive, and you will be forgiven. Give and it will be given to you. A good measure, pressed down, shaken together, and running over, will be poured into your lap. For with the measure you use, it will be measured to you,* Luke 6:37,38.

Let us look at the problem of judging and condemning others. First, understand that you are called to judge the actions of our Christian brothers and sisters (as well as yourself) as right or wrong according to the Word of God. That would be calling sin, sin. However, you cannot judge the motives or intent of the heart of your brothers and sisters without bringing judgment on yourself.

You are judged as you judge others.

Paul tells us in 1 Corinthians 4:5, *Therefore judge nothing before the appointed time; wait till the Lord comes. He will bring to light what is hidden in darkness and will expose the motives of men's hearts. At that time each will receive his praise from God.* If you see another believer whose actions would be sin according to the Word of God, you are directed on how to manage it in Matthew 18:15-17. You are not to slander the one who sinned, but according to Galatians 6:1, we are to instead correct them gently. You are also to pray for them according to 1 John 5:16. Anything else may cause you to fall under judgment yourself and may be the reason for the struggles within your own life.

The Bible confirms this in Romans 2:1-3, *You, therefore, have no excuse, you who pass judgment on someone else, for at whatever point you judge the other, you are condemning yourself, because you who pass judgment do the same things. Now we know that God's judgment against those who do such things is based on truth. So, when you, a mere man, pass judgment on them and yet do the same things, do you think you will escape God's judgment?*

People judge others through the eyes of their own heart. It is not uncommon for the things that make you the angriest to be a problem that actually lives within you. However, Jesus addressed this issue in Matthew 7:3-5, *Why do you look at the speck of sawdust in your brother's eye and pay no attention to the plank in your own eye? How can you say to your brother, "Let me take the speck out of your eye," when all the time there is a plank in your own eye? You hypocrite, first take the plank out of your own eye, and then you will see clearly to remove the speck from your brother's eye.*

We need to point out that we are not talking about the travesties of injustice where innocent people get hurt because of other peoples' sins. Being upset about injustices means that we have God's own nature within us. The Bible is full of references where God gets angry about injustice. Instead, we are discussing times when you not only judge other's actions as right or wrong but also judge the motives and perceived character flaws that produced those actions.

The Bible instructs us in Titus 1:15, *To the pure, all things are pure, but to those who are corrupted and do not believe, nothing is pure. In fact, both their minds and consciences are corrupted.* Judgment and condemnation creep out of our hearts and onto others when the attitudes we carry, which are hidden inside of us, come out of our mouths in the form of spoken words.

When you speak ill of other people, you are allowing your words against them to be used against you instead. When the children of Israel were complaining in the desert, God told them He was going to do to them that which He had heard them speak (Numbers 14:28). Ephesians 5:19-20 instructs you to Speak *to one another with psalms, hymns, and spiritual songs. Sing and make music in your heart to the Lord, always giving thanks to God the Father for everything, in the name of our Lord Jesus Christ.* When you act contrary to God's Word, you will not reflect His nature, and you will reap negative results.

The Bible also tells us, *do not be deceived, God is not mocked; for whatever a man sows, that he will also reap,* (Galatians 6:7 NKJV.) When you are using words that are equal to speaking a curse over other people, you will reap curses in return as others speak badly about you. This does not mean that what you said about the other person was inaccurate, but if it does not help resolve the problem or line up with the teachings of Jesus, then what is the purpose of speaking it? You will reap the fruit of those negative words in your own life (Proverbs 18:20-21) Be careful not to join forces with the accuser of the brethren (Revelation 12:10).

There is a trap that even the best of people have fallen into at some time in their life, and that trap is gossip. We are cautioned about its danger in the Word of God (Romans 1:29). Many Christians gossip while trying to disguise it with a comment such as, "We need to pray for this person." They proceed to give the details of the shortcomings of the one who needs "prayer." Quite often, this laundry list of things is simply hearsay. This "list" does not need to be discussed with someone who does not have anything to do with the situation or is not involved in its resolution.

We are still surprised by the number of churchgoing people who, over the years, attempted to tell us of all the shortcomings of their churches and pastors when we first arrived as a guest of their congregation. They would not allow us in the door until they had stated all the details of the situation. This is simply a sin, and the fruit of that sin is judgment. This attitude of judgement does not reflect the nature and character of God.

The Power of Words

We need to understand the connection between the attitudes of our hearts, the words that we speak, and the effect of those words on what we reap as consequences of our actions. Have you ever felt like you were walking under a heavy cloud, but you could not figure out why? No matter what you did, nothing seemed to go right! You knew God was around, but He did not seem to be there for you at that time. Your prayers did not seem to go past the ceiling, and that is if you even had the strength to pray at all. You were aware that something was wrong. However, you may have had no idea of what was causing it or what you could do to resolve the problem.

Although some people today do not admit the existence of curses, the Bible confirms they do, indeed, exist. Believers may know curses exist, yet many of them do not believe that curses can apply to Christians. The belief that Christians cannot be walking under a curse is a lie. While the blessings of God are taught in every Christian circle, the fact that curses apply to our disobedience is rarely discussed.

Before we can go further, it is important to point out that the curses we are referring to are simply the absence of the blessings of God. When we walk within the kingdom of this world, we are open to every evil in it. When we walk with Jesus and obey His teachings, we grow and reflect His nature and character. When we operate in both kingdoms, there will be conflict, and this conflict is not a blessing but a curse (the absence of blessings).

The New Testament does not contain a lengthy list of "do not do—or else" commands. It contains words of life. However, within the New Testament, things are listed which bring death as a direct result of choosing not to follow the truth within God's Word.

It is easy to be caught up in lists of dos and don'ts. If you get caught in that cycle, you may have missed the messages of Jesus. Being bound to a list of do's and don'ts is based on a form of the truth but has missed the true message of Christ (2 Timothy 3:5). This is a trap of religion in its ugliest form because you are now concentrating your efforts on perfecting your outward actions and not on cultivating the inward condition of your heart. This binds you up in the letter of the law, which is characterized by lists of "do this and do not do that," instead of focusing on empowering you to be set free.

Getting caught up in being concerned with your outward appearance, while trying to hide your inward condition, is what Jesus cautioned the Pharisees about in Matthew 23:25-26, *Woe to you, teachers of the law and Pharisees, you hypocrites! You clean the outside of the cup and dish, but inside they are full of greed and self-indulgence. Blind Pharisee! First clean the inside of the cup and dish, and then the outside will also be clean.*

Make no mistake: your actions will follow your heart, and not the other way around. Changing your actions to line up with the Word of God, just to get the blessings of God, is a type of legalism. This will take you away from the message of the cross. Changes need to take place in your heart first and then your subsequent words and actions will follow. A saying we have found to be true is, "You cannot change your heart, and God <u>will not</u> change your mind. But, if you will change your thoughts or your mind, God will change your heart."

After you have repented and God has changed your heart,

The Power of Words

Scripture tells you that you now have a responsibility to renew your thinking so that it reflects His. The only thing that you can change is your mind, your way of thinking. Completing this process will result in the changing of your actions. The "do not do list," along with its curses, is there so you can recognize any ungodly beliefs you have and correct your thinking accordingly. This is covered completely in the next chapter.

A Christian family that was having problems in every area of their lives came to their pastor for counseling. It was difficult for the pastor to even start dealing with the truths needed to resolve their disputes, as the family members would break into loud arguments out of their frustrations of not being heard. This grew progressively louder every time an issue was discussed. Their words were often filled with hurt and bitterness and offered no atmosphere of healing or unity.

Unable even to reach the genuine issues because of the intense arguments, the pastor gave this family an assignment for one month. He had them all agree that for 30 days they would sing every word they said to each other and not talk under any circumstances. The teenagers were the most reluctant to participate, but the whole family agreed that something had to change, so they were willing to do it. The pastor told them that even if they were communicating to each other over the phone they would have to sing their words and could not talk. This caused even greater embarrassment when the father was at work or the teenagers were on their cell phones in front of their friends, but they remained faithful and did it anyway.

What happened to the family by following this plan was amazing. It turned out that they could not successfully raise their voice in arguments and sing at the same time, no matter how hard they tried. They could do one or the other, but not both, and the loud arguing simply ended. They began to communicate from their hearts, which is where most songs come from, and they were able to hear each other for the first time. They were able to understand the way their own words hurt each other, and this exercise allowed them to compare how they treated each other when they were speaking versus singing. They all repented for the hurtful words and actions that caused their separation and pain. Now with a tender heart towards one another, they were able to easily deal with and resolve the issues. This simple exercise changed their lives forever.

Now, we are not suggesting that this is an "end all" solution to every situation, or that it is the only way to correct all family problems. We are merely pointing out the fruit of speaking from the heart and the importance of providing an atmosphere for heartfelt communication. Trying to listen more than be heard is truly a characteristic of the love of God (James 1:19). When you apply the teachings of Jesus in this area, miraculous things happen.

Before you decide that this is the answer for your whole family, please take this to prayer. If, after prayer, you still believe this method is for you, we suggest trying it in your own life for 30 days first, before you decide to offer it as a solution to others. With a changed heart, you can then offer help to others (Matthew 7:3-5).

I (Michael) was born in England and lived in Europe for many of my childhood years. In my early teens, we made a move back to my family's original home in the middle of South

Carolina, in what is commonly called the Deep South. I found myself having some difficulty understanding what some people were saying. I realized I had to listen very closely to my new friends, because they had a very deep and defined southern accent. This was in drastic contrast to the accent I had become accustomed to hearing in Europe. When visiting friends' homes, I was not surprised to find that their parents had an even more pronounced accent.

**We are the product of our environment
and the training we have received, or lack of it.**

We are products of our environment and the training we have received, or the lack of it. Our upbringing will be reflected in our words later in life, just like our accents. People can usually tell where you are from simply by your accent. In the same line of reasoning, if you came from a home where there was complaining, arguing, and yelling you will find that you grew up understanding that these things are somehow OK. You may believe that they are permissible in your everyday activities, or at least allowable under certain conditions. When you discover that these products of your home environment are not acceptable in society, you are faced with the opportunity to overcome them. It is important to mention this now, because even after a change of heart, some habits may still need to be broken. This is an easy process but may take some retraining.

For the purposes of our discussion here, we will be talking

about unhealthy habits, not good ones. Habits are learned behaviors or responses we have acquired through our life experiences. Habits can be changed, but we are responsible to make the course corrections necessary to correct or stop a habit when it is harmful. Here are a few examples and explanations of how others managed them.

I (Michael) grew up in a Christian home and I was taught Christian values. However, I chose to go a different direction as a young adult (not my wisest moment). Hanging around with the wrong crowd, it did not take long for me to cuss as they did. I never picked up the strongest cuss language, but any of my new terminology would have been quite offensive to anyone in my family.

As you can imagine, one day I found myself in a conversation with someone, in front of my mother, when I almost said a cuss word. As the first word that was going to come out of my mouth was forming on my lips, I was somehow able to catch myself and put another word in its place. My mom looked at me as if she clearly heard the word I was going to say, and her disapproval showed on her face. Without her mentioning one word to me, conviction hit me like a semi-truck. It was at that moment I made the decision that I would never cuss again.

I would love to tell you that there was an instantaneous change in my language that reflected my heart. However, that was not the case. I had been casually cussing for a while and it had become a bad habit. I made a conscious effort to choose replacement terminology. It took weeks of stopping mid-sentence, or quickly repenting right after I did cuss, before the change fully came. I had repented for my actions and God had brought the change in my heart. Nevertheless, I had to change my thinking and exercise some self-control over my tongue.

I could not tell you how many weeks it took before I realized what had taken place. I still remember the day I was doing some carpentry work at home, and I was diverted for just a second. The hammer in my hand had missed the nail and with full force hit my thumb. It took the thumbnail off completely and it was a mess. To my surprise I did not even think of a cuss word, when before one would have automatically come out of my mouth.

I knew the habit was broken and it was forever gone. I am not suggesting that you use a hammer to help you break habits, but I do want to encourage you with the knowledge that learned habits will take some time to break. Studies have shown that, after we determine to make habit changes, it takes about six weeks or longer of consistent choices to change old habits and create new ones. Have we seen people change habits instantly and not need to go through this process? Absolutely! However, for most of us, time and consistency are required to break the habit.

Katherine did not grow up in a Christian home and had a mother and grandmother that complained about everything. Nothing was ever good enough for either Katherine's mom or her grandmother. This seemed especially true about anything that Katherine did, even if it was in service to the two of them. They were critical and disapproving and rarely found anything good to say. Instead, they would instantly tell her what they did not like about whatever she had done.

Katherine's belief system was built around the words she had heard about herself all her life. As a result of hearing those negative words over and over, she believed them all. Her self-esteem was low at best. She was even convinced that she was unlovable and did not really deserve the love she was now receiving from her husband. Katherine had met him years after leaving home, but the voices from her past were still hounding her. Unfortunately, those lies had found their way into Katherine's marriage to the point that she and her husband were in marriage counselling. Nothing seemed to help, even when she did everything the counselor had told her to do.

After some basic instruction and prayer with us, Katherine experienced an understanding of the truth, and her heart was healed. She contacted us weeks later and told us of the amazing changes that had taken place. She was a completely different person inside. She felt a love she had not experienced before. She was closer to her husband and her friends than she ever thought possible. She said there was only one problem: she was still complaining about things, even though, in her heart, she did not want to. She did not understand why this complaining attitude was persisting in her heart when so many other things had changed dramatically.

We explained the power that unhealthy habits have in our lives and why we need to break them. We then gave her a simple exercise that would change her thinking and solve the problem. We instructed her that, every time she caught herself complaining, she should find three good things to say about the situation first. We stressed the importance of doing that and of saying them <u>aloud</u>. When she was stuck in traffic and found herself complaining by habit, we advised her to immediately repent and find three things to be thankful for. We told her to thank God for even having a car, or to express gratefulness because the sky was so beautiful, or that she even passed her driver's test to start with. We heard from her a few months later, and she said she was free of complaints. She spoke of how her life had changed and that she no longer responded to life's difficulties with complaints, even under the greatest of pressure. The habit was broken. The kingdom of our God advanced in her.

ONLY THE TRUTH!

The Word says in Matthew 5:37, *Simply let your "Yes" be "Yes" and your "No," "No." Anything beyond this comes from the evil one.* It seems silly to tell a Christian that it is wrong to lie. However, influences from the world have produced terminology such as "soft lies" or "white lies" that Christians have used in reference to their own words.

I was called to the home of a member of my church to help him deal with a problem he was having with his teenage son. It turned out that his son was lying and stealing, and the father did not know what to do about the problem.

We were back in his study when I noticed the father had valuable items on his desk with his company's logo. I asked him if they were awards of some kind. He explained to me that the company understood that their employees took home this company property and that all the employees did it. Laying that aside, we were in mid-conversation about his son's problem when his wife stuck her head in the door and said he had a phone call. Without thinking, he blurted out in an annoyed voice, "Tell them I am not at home" and turned to me to continue our conversation. He truly seemed unaware of what he was doing. I told him that I may have found what I believed to be the source of his son's problem. Excited that I could help, he exclaimed, "Great! What is it?"

I will present two more scriptures before we take this matter to prayer. The first is 1 Corinthians 4:12-13, *We work hard with our own hands. When we are cursed, we bless; when we are persecuted, we endure it; when we are slandered, we answer kindly......* The second is 1 Peter 3:9, *Do not repay evil with evil or insult with insult, but with blessing, because to this you were called so that you may inherit a blessing.* It is time for the blessing.

If you are feeling conviction that you are one of the people just described, take a moment, and repeat a simple prayer of repentance for the words that you have been speaking.

When you repent, God makes the changes in your heart. You still have the responsibility to renew your mind, to change the way you think, or even what you think, because of the truths you see in His Word. What you believe will determine how you act. If this applies to you, then repeat this prayer from your heart:

"Father, Your Word tells me to say things that edify, to build up, that correct in love or confirm. Words of condemnation, lies, slander, and gossip or accusation are not of You. People have said words for and against me that were sin. I choose to forgive them for this sin and release them from it. Father, bless them in Jesus' name.

"I have said words about (name of person you spoke badly about) that did not edify, and did not correct, and did not confirm. I have allowed judgment and condemnation in my heart towards others. They are sin and I choose to

repent. Forgive me for this sin. I will only say words that bless (name of person you spoke badly about) from this day forth. I take responsibility for those words and renounce them in the name of Jesus. Father, I thank You for your healing and forgiveness. Amen."

You may feel a difference in your heart after you sincerely say this prayer. You will have also effectively neutralized the power of any words spoken against you by others. Those who have repented for their own inappropriate words will be released from judgment according to God's Word.

Scripture References:

Peace, I leave with you; my peace I give you.
I do not give to you as the world gives.
Do not let your hearts be troubled and do not be afraid.
(John 14:27)

But You are holy,
Enthroned in the praises of Israel.
(Psalm 22:3 NKJV)

If your brother sins against you, go, and show him his fault, just between the two of you.
If he listens to you, you have won your brother over. But if he will not listen, take one or two others along, so that 'every matter may be established by the testimony of two or three

witnesses.' If he refuses to listen to them, tell it to the church; and if he refuses to listen even to the church, treat him as you would a pagan or a tax collector.

(Matthew 18:15-17)

Brothers, if someone is caught in a sin,
You who are spiritual should restore him gently. But watch yourself, or you also may be tempted.

(Galatians 6:1)

If anyone sees his brother commit a sin that does not lead to death, he should pray, and God will give him life. I refer to those whose sin does not lead to death. There is a sin that leads to death. I am not saying that he should pray about that.

(l John 5:16)

So, tell them, "As surely as I live, declares the LORD, I will do to you the very things I heard you say."

(Numbers 14:28)

From the fruit of their mouth a person's stomach is filled; with the harvest of their lips they are satisfied. The tongue has the power of life and death, and those who love it will eat its fruit.

(Proverbs 18:20-21)

Then I heard a loud voice in heaven say:
"Now have come the salvation and the power
and the kingdom of our God,
and the authority of his Messiah.

The Power of Words

For the accuser of our brothers and sisters, who accuses them before our God Day and night, has been hurled down."

(Revelation 12:10)

They have become filled with every kind of wickedness, evil, greed, and depravity. They are full of envy, murder, strife, deceit, and malice. They are gossips.

(Romans 1:29)

Having a form of godliness but denying its power. Have nothing to do with them.

(2 Timothy 3:5)

My dear brothers, take note of this: Everyone should be quick to listen, slow to speak and slow to become angry.

(James 1:19)

Why do you look at the speck of sawdust in your brother's eye and pay no attention to the plank in your own eye? How can you say to your brother, "Let me take the speck out of your eye," when all the time there is a plank in your own eye? You hypocrite, first take the plank out of your own eye, and then you will see clearly to remove the speck from your brother's eye.

(Matthew 7:3-5)

CHAPTER 10

THE POWER OF THOUGHTS

This chapter repeats many "Truths" from many of the previous chapters. This is with purpose. We believe that other than salvation and with that, forgiveness, the renewing of your mind is the most important part of this book. Everything written in this book so far is purposed for that endeavor.

You need to know, by experience, the nature and character of God. It is developed and empowered through your regenerated mind. Ephesians 4:22-24 says, *you were taught, with regard to your former way of life, to put off your old self, which is being corrupted by its deceitful desires, to be made new in the attitude of your minds, and to put on the new self, created to be like God in true righteousness and holiness.* Do not get this confused, or out of order. Righteousness and holiness come from a renewed mind, not the other way around. The latter is a "works" mentality. It is a trap into which many have fallen.

Your mind will become the mind of Christ (1 Corinthians 2:16). It is not a metaphor but the actual reality in which you can live and have your being. Take note that we did not say the mind of Jesus, but of Christ. Christ is the anointing of God and the Anointed One. In 2 Corinthians 10:5 the Apostle Paul says: *We demolish arguments and every pretension that sets itself up against the knowledge of God, and we take captive every thought to make it obedient to Christ.* With this mindset, you can see His Kingdom in everything and advance it mightily while you are developing in the nature and character of God. There is no greater fulfillment for your life.

When Michael and I were first married, it was not uncommon for us to have misunderstandings. We learned to work them out over time, but it was a challenging road. At first, "Mr. Fix-it" did not understand the emotional investment our arguments created for me. And let us just say, at that time, his listening skills were less than perfect. It was when we were in this stage of our lives that we had an argument that outdid all the ones before. When the dust settled, we acknowledged that our hearts were for each other and made a choice to forgive one another and reconcile.

Now, I'm not sure how you would handle such intense emotional moments, but for me, not letting the feelings be all I could think about the rest of the day was easier said than done. As I went about my day something happened later that morning that taught me one of the most valuable lessons of my life. I was driving in the car and found myself at a long stop light and as I waited, the "video" of our argument began to play in my head. I sat there and relived the whole argument over again. But this time I thought about the things I wish I had said in response to his quips. I was arguing aloud with myself, which looked silly to my kids and the strangers in the car next to me.

With tears now streaming down my cheeks, I suddenly

realized what was happening to me and made the decision to change the channel that was playing in my head. Just like grabbing the remote control and changing the program on the TV, I made a conscious decision to change my thinking and continued driving. I would love to say that was the end of it, but sometime later, it was back. However, this time, I said aloud "NO" and I was able to control my thoughts before that video fully played out. This required a conscious <u>effort</u> on my part. I <u>had</u> to change my thinking to align with the truth. Philippians 4:8 says, *Finally, brothers and sisters, whatever is true, whatever is noble, whatever is right, whatever is pure, whatever is lovely, whatever is admirable—if anything is excellent or praiseworthy—think about such things.* Once we had repented and put the situation to rest, when that video tried to replay in my head, I simply took those thoughts captive and chose to think on the positive things that had come from that situation. I had successfully changed my thinking.

Unlike the rest of this book, where we talk about how simple it is to be healed and restored, this takes an ongoing effort on your part. You will discover more about Him and His truths with every breath you take. In doing so, you will recognize and replace the deceptions of the enemy with the truth of God's Word. These conscious decisions on our part allow us to discern God's will and <u>experience</u> His good and perfect plan for our lives. Romans 12:2 says, *Do not conform to the pattern of this world, but be transformed by the renewing of your mind. Then you will be able to test and approve what God's will is—his good, pleasing, and perfect will.*

A desire for, and a yielding to, the relationship with God

always produces a more fulfilled life. As we have stated before, if you do not know the nature and character of God, you will by default give Him your own. The good news is that you will not be alone on this journey of a renewed mind. The Lord will be with you in this process of discovery because it was His plan for you from the beginning. (Jeremiah 29:11)

In the beginning when God created everything, He hovered over the formless, empty darkness (Gen 1:1,2) and "brooded" over it if you will, considering all that He was to create. The possibilities were infinite. What did he think would make it a beautiful and wonderful place to live? What was necessary to sustain life and what would He create just for joy's sake? Every detail had meaning. Then, He spoke, and things were hurled into existence. Genesis 1:3 says *God spoke and said, "Let there be light,' and there was light."* It had begun.

Our thoughts are seeds that contain life!

Everything that exists starts as a thought. <u>Our thoughts are seeds that contain life and the DNA of what that life can become.</u> When we have thoughts, good or bad, we choose their value by determining whether to agree with or reject them. The reason this choice is important is because we empower (give life to) whatever we choose to agree with. Once these ideas are empowered, they will take root in our hearts, growing and producing crops (a harvest). There is a principle in nature: like only produces like. Apple seed, apple tree, apples. Orange seed, orange tree, oranges. You get the idea. Fruit that has grown in the garden of our hearts will be evident through the words of our mouth. What you feed will grow. What you starve will die. It is that simple. Jesus confirms this in Matthew 12:34-35, *For out of the overflow of the heart the mouth speaks. The good man brings good things out of the good stored up in him, and the evil man brings evil things out of the evil stored up in him.*

Why are our thoughts so important? Why did God command us to renew our minds after we were given a new heart? Because, *as a man thinks, so he is* (Prov 23:7 NKJ). This passage is not about your passive thought life that can be persuaded to change by hearing a better argument. It is about what you know (in your heart) to be true no matter the argument. It has been said that "a man with an experience is never at the mercy of a man with an opinion." You are the culmination of your interpretation of your life experiences, both good and bad. Your old thinking will be self-evident as an unfruitful heart in search of what is missing.

Why did God not just renew our minds for us? He did take out our stoney heart and give us a heart of flesh. Surely, He could have just touched our brains and changed our thoughts too? Right? However, He would then have superseded something He valued in us from the beginning. Something He deemed important to our identity, our own minds. Because our thoughts come from our minds, that is controlled by <u>our</u> own (free) will. It is our choice (Joshua 24:15).

God gave us the power to choose. He always gives you a choice. It is important to Him that you are a willing participant in this relationship and not just a forced subject. We get to choose. Why? Because He has designed everything so that we realize the consequences of our choices (Hebrews 11:6). He goes to great lengths to make sure our right to make a choice is always there.

In the garden, God gave Adam and Eve a choice to own up to and take responsibility for what they had done. Honesty would have set them up to receive forgiveness and maintain the relationship with their Father who loved them. Instead of taking ownership of their choices, they boldly proclaimed it was *not me,* pointing fingers at anyone else but themselves. Adam took it even further, ultimately blaming God, and in that choice, they lost their opportunity for reconciliation. Their choice not only had destructive consequences for their lives but eventually for all mankind. As we learned from Adam and Eve: our choices rarely affect only us. Like a pebble thrown into a glassy pond, the ripple effect is a reality. The people around us and ultimately God's Kingdom will always be affected by our choices whether we are aware of it or not.

When we meditate on a belief we empower it to travel into our hearts as a seed full of DNA that becomes what we believe. When we believe that which is rooted, growing, and producing a crop deep in our hearts, it drives us to act according to that belief. The belief becomes a part of us in a way that cannot be so easily persuaded to change, leading to a life that reflects those precepts.

Most Christians believe that God is real and that the stories in the bible actually happened. However, we are surprised at the number of Christians believers who know that God can do what He said He would do, yet they just do not believe He will do it for <u>them</u>. They believe that there is something different or wrong with them and so God will not fulfill His truths in their lives until they fix, overcome, correct, or change something in or about themselves.

These same people profess a love for God and have testimonies of how their lives changed after they accepted Him as Savor. However, they do not believe God's Word is true for them because they, themselves are somehow flawed. This is a LIE!

Many have had this limiting belief (that they are different) for as long as they can remember. In addition, some of their life's situations have been interpreted to support their belief that there is something wrong, even dark, about them that will keep God from moving on their behalf. This belief may have been born from declarations or accusations from others that they have absorbed into their hearts as truth. They see a part of themselves as defective, damaged, or imperfect, so they inherently believe that is how God sees them. This is a LIE!

This belief becomes so ingrained in them, that they repeat it aloud as a declaration to themselves and others. Once this happens, a stronghold, which is a belief system set against God's purposes, is created and the struggle begins. This stronghold is then reinforced by the failings in life's experiences that confirm its existence. Some even get to the point where they surrender to this belief and think, "It is who I am."

While we were writing this chapter, we encountered many people who had built this type of stronghold in their lives. Here are just a few stories:

Toni believed there was something "inherently wrong" with her and that is why she found it hard to move forward in her christian walk. She believed the lie that something inside of her could keep God from moving on her behalf, and that belief alone was a self-fulfilling prophecy.

Toni was the victim of inappropriate touching when she was a child and was later groped by a neighbor's teenage son. When Toni was a young woman, she was sexually active with several partners. She had since met her husband and came to know Christ. Afterwards, her life changed dramatically for the good. However, she knew something was wrong. Intimacy was difficult to achieve and even harder to maintain.

Toni had repented for her ungodly lifestyle and truly forgiven the boys and young men who sexually abused her. However, she was unable to get over the belief that she was defective, damaged, or imperfect. She believed there was something wrong with her or she would never have been victimized in the first place. Over the years she agreed with this belief, creating a stronghold that would keep her bound. She would often state the fact of it aloud.

Bobby grew up in what some might call a legalistic Christian home. His parents cared for him and his sister and taught them biblical values. However, behind closed doors, his parents' love seemed to be conditional and tied to his and his sister's obedience. They were loved as long as they were perfect. Since Bobby was the older of the two, he seemed to be the one who was targeted as the example. Any deviation from what was expected brought both words of condemnation followed by apathy until he complied. In addition, he was taught that God would treat him the same way unless he obeyed His every word.

Bobby struggled in life because he carried this standard of perfection and all of his friends turned out to be less than perfect, and he just could not find the perfect girl. Bobby's career led him to the other end of the United States, far away from his hometown. At a new church there, Bobby heard the Truth of God's love, and He was never the same again. His life in Christ took on a whole new meaning. Perfectionism was gone and he felt a freedom he had never experienced before. However, Bobby still felt there was something missing inside and was always searching for a way to correct it. Bobby read Christian books, attended Christian conferences and worship services. He was looking everywhere he knew to fix what was missing. He finally resigned himself to thinking that this was the Christian life and hoped it would not be like this in heaven.

Olivia grew up in a home where she was the mistake that her parents never wanted. It was obvious. She struggled to achieve their acceptance, and no matter what she did, she never ever got it. Later, as a teenager, she rebelled against the world as she knew it. She had become the problem child her parents declared her to be. It was in college that someone introduced her to Christ, and the love of God changed her in ways she could never have imagined. She found a church home that became the family she never had. In addition, God eventually restored her relationship with her mother and father and healing took place.

She was able to forgive them and to share a love she had never felt before. However, there was something missing in Olivia's walk with Christ that seemed to be a battle. She struggled when reading the Word of God and the revelation of it did not seem to flow for her as it did for others in her Bible group. She understood the Word but found it hard to believe that it was written for her. She knew in her heart there was something different about her but could not identify it. She had developed a habit of repenting for her rebellious lifestyle that was now long over, believing she must have missed some sin that was keeping her from intimacy with God. She often stated that she was unable to reach that level of intimacy she saw in others and was forever in search of the sin that was holding her back.

In each one of these situations, they had surrendered their lives to Christ and the old man had died like it says in Romans 6:6, *knowing this, that our old self was crucified with Him, in order that our body of sin might be done away with, so that we would no longer be slaves to sin.* They repented, their old lifestyle was over, and they had forgiven those who had harmed them and walked through many changes that brought good fruit into their lives and in the lives of others. However, even many years into their Christian walk they still believed there was something flawed about them that was keeping them from getting close to God. They were absolutely right.

Oddly enough, the thing that kept them bound was the belief that there was something wrong (flawed, defective, damaged, or imperfect) with themselves. *As a man believes, so is he.* That belief alone was responsible for the separation they felt. It was a belief they agreed with and even stated aloud at various times in their lives. They were each believing a lie.

This lie is a common effective tactic of the enemy of our souls. *When he (the Devil) lies, he speaks his native language, for he is a liar and the father of lies,* (John 8:44b). Many of us have fallen for this deception at one time or another until we are able to discern the Truths of God. However, some beliefs are so ingrained in us we need to be shown the truth in a way we have never seen it before. So how did they get free of what they believed in their hearts that was ultimately a lie?

After King David (a man after God's own heart) had taken Bathsheba (another man's wife) and ultimately had her husband (Uriah) killed (2 Samuel 11-12), Nathan the prophet told David a story that David could relate to. The story Nathan told was not about David, but David was able to see himself in it and see the truth of his situation he could not see before.

When we are ministering to people who are struggling with this issue, we ask the person to identify someone they love or a good friend about their age. Or better yet, a child they know who is near the age they were when they first began believing there was something wrong with them. We then ask them a simple question: if this other person/child went through what they had gone through and then repented for it, should they still believe that there was something flawed about themselves? They all answer with a resounding "No."

Then we ask, "If your loved one believed they were defective, damaged or imperfect, would they be believing the truth about themselves or a lie?" They all respond with, "A lie." We then ask, "Are you believing the truth or a lie when you believe there is something wrong with you?" They see the truth and respond, "I am believing a lie." We have them repeat aloud, "I am believing a lie" or "it was a lie" many, many times until the truth of that statement sinks into their heart. You can see it happen before your eyes. Freedom is that easy. Why does it often require them to repeat "it was a lie" as many as twenty times? It is because they agreed with the lie many, many times over the years.

How does that work? Toni had sincerely forgiven those that had hurt/abused her as a child and a young adult. However, she still had the belief that something was wrong with her and that is why she fell victim to others. She had believed this ever since the neighbor's teenage son visited her on several occasions. How did we know when this belief started? We asked her. Here is the statement Toni declared that set her free:

Toni said she was eight years old when the neighbor's son first groped her. We asked if she knew of a child that was around eight years old, and she told us that her favorite niece had just turned nine. We then asked her, "If your niece was sexually assaulted and believed it happened because there was something wrong with her, would she be believing the truth or a lie?" She responded, "a lie." We asked her, "Are you sure?" Toni stated, "I am positive."

Then we asked her, "What if your niece was your age now and still believed that there was something wrong with her and that is why the assault happened. Would she still be believing the truth or a lie?" Again, Toni stated, "She would be believing a lie." The truth really started to set in when we inquired, "Toni, are you believing the truth or a lie?" She said, "I have been believing a lie." We had her repeat that statement a dozen times or more until it really sank into her heart. You could see the change in her when it did. Then she declared, "The truth is that I am the righteousness of God in Christ Jesus!"

Toni has already confirmed the amazing change in her intimacy with God and the renewed love she has for herself, one she had not known before. Bobby and Oliva have similar

The Power of Thoughts

testimonies. What brought about this change in their lives? They changed their thinking to line up with the Truth.

THE POWER OF NEGATIVE THOUGHT

When you begin to ponder certain thoughts repeatedly, either good or bad, they become like powerful magnets, attracted to one another and they bond together. They create a structure, a fortress, which becomes a stronghold (a belief system) in your life. When you build these structures with patterns of thinking that do not align with God's nature, you provide an inhabitance, a dwelling place, that the enemy can propagate his deceptions. From there, he will wreak all manner of havoc in our lives using our own beliefs. <u>Your negative thoughts</u> created a place for the adversary of our faith to interact with you.

Romans 8:5,6 says, *Those who are dominated by the sinful nature THINK about sinful things, but those who are controlled by the Holy Spirit THINK about things that please the Spirit.* If your sinful nature controls your mind, there is death. But if the Holy Spirit controls your mind, there is life and peace. It is simple, black, and white. These opposing realities will always cause conflict in both your heart and mind. You cannot have both without conflict. Either life or death. Good or bad. Blessing or curse. Abundance or lack. Love or fear or a war between the two.

If God inhabits my praises, who might want to inhabit my negativity and complaints?

Stop and think about that for a minute. YOU created a place for the enemy to have a stronghold within you by meditating on thoughts that were not in line with God's character or nature. If God inhabits our praises, who might want to inhabit our negativity and complaints? The good news is that you created the fortress, so <u>you</u> have the power and authority to demolish it! Repent for your wrong way of thinking. Expose the enemies hiding place and serve him with an eviction notice. You chose the line of thinking, so recognize your thoughts and start making different choices. Replace your negative thoughts with thoughts of good things, lovely things, pure things as scripture tells us. Philippians 4:8 says, *And now, dear brothers and sisters, one final thing. Fix our thoughts on what is true, and honorable, and right, and pure, and lovely, and admirable. Think about things that are excellent and worthy of praise.*

You cannot make this change by thinking "I will no longer have negative thoughts." But what you can do is take each negative thought captive and change it to align with God's truth. Second Corinthians 10:5 says, *We demolish arguments and every pretension that sets itself up against the knowledge of God, and we take captive every thought to make it obedient to Christ.* This will not happen naturally until you have trained yourself to do so. It requires an effort with a reward far exceeding the work.

Thoughts that come against the knowledge of who God is, His nature and character, are obviously not of Him. They are meant to undermine and distract us from His design and plan and derail us from His purposes. This is why it is important that we get very acquainted with who He is. We need to know His nature and character so well that when destructive thoughts come, we can immediately judge where they are from and make a quick choice about whether to agree with or reject them.

Think about it like this. I (Cyndi) am intimately acquainted with my children. I know how they look, that little speck in their eye, the freckles on their noses, the shape of their faces and the color of their hair. I know their mannerisms, the sound of their unique laughter. I recognize their voices without ever having to see their faces. No one, and I do mean NO ONE, could ever try and substitute one of my children with someone else's child and get me to accept that it is them.

I am never going to believe that a stranger is my child. I cannot be fooled because I know them. In the same way, we need to be intimately acquainted with our Father God so that we instinctively know His character and nature. We must know how He acts, looks and what His voice sounds like so that we will not be fooled by a counterfeit or fake (John 10:27). Fortunately for us, He did not leave us to figure out who He is on our own. He gave us a detailed account that reveals who He is. It is called the Word of God, the Bible, and we can discover amazing things about Him within its pages.

To align your thinking with the truth, you must begin the journey of acknowledging when a belief does not line up to His character and nature. The Word of God is the standard we are to follow. Where you have been believing lies, replace them with the truth of God. Did you know repentance means to change the way you think? That happens when you renew your minds, your thoughts, and your beliefs. You realign your way of thinking

LIVING FULLY FREE

back to His way of thinking. You align with His purposes, His desires, His ways, and His plans. When you do this, it changes everything!

When you alter your mindset and empower the right way of thinking, it brings revolutionary change to your life from the inside out. You will begin to experience the fruit of your thought life. (the same way empowering the wrong thoughts do). Where before you might have felt uneasy or anxious, without peace or joy, now you begin to experience all the fruits of the spirit. Galatians 5:22-23 says, *But the fruit of the Spirit is love, joy, peace, forbearance, kindness, goodness, faithfulness, gentleness, and self-control. Against such things there is no law.*

Your eyes now start to see things from a completely unique perspective. Perspective shifts are paradigm shifts. The way you see things matters. When you have eyes to see God's Kingdom, your world is forever changed. Your vision is now forever changed; you have a new perspective. Ask yourself if the picture you have of yourself is the real image. Are you seeing all that is there? We see things through the lens of our belief system. This is why it is important to renew our minds to His way of thinking and His way of seeing things.

You have been given all authority and all power over your mind, your thoughts and your choices. We are commanded to renew our minds, our way of thinking. So, take hold of the responsibility of controlling the thoughts that you allow to reside in your mind. Do some gardening and pull out the weeds, even destroy some structures if needed, but make way for His thoughts, His ideas, His way of thinking and watch the miraculous changes that come with those choices. If there are thought patterns that you know need to change, then simply repeat this prayer from your heart:

Father, I have not taken authority over my mind and thoughts as you commanded. I have not taken every thought captive and even repeated out loud thoughts that contradicted your nature and character. I take ownership for these actions and ask for Your forgiveness; I renounce my words that did not line up with your truth. Lord, I will take responsibility for my thoughts and my words from this day forward. Thank you for a new beginning, in Jesus' name, Amen!

Scripture References

For whom hath known the mind of the Lord, that he may instruct him? But we have the mind of Christ. For "Who can know the Lord's thoughts? Who knows enough to teach him?" But we understand these things, for we have the mind of Christ.

(1 Corinthians 2:16)

*"For I know the plans I have for you," declares the L*ORD*, "Plans to prosper you and not to harm you, plans to give you hope and a future."*

(Jeremiah 29:11)

In the beginning God created the heavens and the earth. Now the earth was formless and empty, darkness was over the surface of the deep, and the Spirit of God was hovering over the waters.

(Genesis 1:1,2)

But if serving the Lord seems undesirable to you, then choose for yourselves this day whom you will serve, whether the gods your ancestors served beyond the Euphrates, or the gods of the Amorites in whose land you are living. But as for me and my household we will serve the Lord.

(Joshua 24:15)

And without faith it is impossible to please God, because anyone who comes to Him must believe that He exists and that He rewards those who earnestly seek Him.

(Hebrew 11:6)

My sheep listen to My voice; I know them, and they follow me.

(John 10:27)

CHAPTER 11

TRUTH ABOUT COVENANTS

To better understand God's nature and recognize when you are walking in agreement with Him, you need to understand the value of covenants. It is one of the foundational truths of the Bible. Our God is a God of covenants with His people. A covenant is an agreement between two parties that involves promises to one another. It is different from a legal contract or an agreement because a covenant has no ending date and is binding until death. The covenants that God initiated were with a family or nation to last forever, such as with David (2 Chronicles 21:7).

God has made covenants with His people from the time of Adam to the New Covenant (New Testament), not of law but of promise by grace with believers today. The covenants with Adam and David promise the Messiah would be born through His chosen people (Genesis 3:15). God's covenant with Noah promises to withhold judgment on nature during the salvation of men (Genesis 8:21-22; 2 Peter 3:7-15). Because of Abraham's faith, God made a covenant promise to bless Abraham's descendants.

LIVING FULLY FREE

In the Old Testament, the people of Israel, at Mount Sinai, confirmed their covenant with God by making oaths or promises, but they failed to keep their word and broke covenant with God (Exodus 24:3). They later renewed their promises, re-establishing their covenant with God (2 Kings 23:3). Unlike people, God does not break His promises (covenants) for any reason, under any circumstance.

There is a difference between the covenants of Law (Old Covenant) and the covenants of Promise (New Covenant) spoken about by Paul in Galatians 4:24-26. These "two covenants," one originating from Mount Sinai, the other from the Jerusalem above, describe the difference between being a slave and being free. The Old Covenant was one of law, which is characterized by impossible restrictions no man could follow. To live under the law is a type of bondage. To live in the New Covenant is to live in freedom through the Holy Spirit because of Jesus' shed blood. The New Covenant is a promise with grace.

Jesus' death ushered in the New Covenant—a better way—by which we are now justified by the grace and mercy of God rather than by our own human attempts to keep the rules and regulations of the law. The Old Covenant is about external things, (do this, do not do that) and the Holy Spirit was only around for a season or an event. The New Covenant is all about the heart and the opportunity for the Holy Spirit to live _in_ you and _through_ you, not just visit you. Our Savior and Redeemer, Jesus Himself, sits at the right hand of the Father as the Mediator of this better covenant (Hebrews 9:15).

There are three covenants that God calls Holy: the Old Covenant, the New Covenant, and the Marriage Covenant.

The Old Covenant and the New Covenant are between man and God. The Marriage Covenant is between husband and wife.

Three Covenants are called Holy: The Old Covenant, the New Covenant and the Marriage Covenant

Each of these binding covenants is confirmed with a "sign of the covenant" on man's part. These signs of the covenant have one thing in common. They are marked by blood. The sign of the Old Covenant is circumcision (Genesis 17:11, Acts 7:8); the sign of the New Covenant is the cup of the covenant, the blood of Jesus (Matthew 26:28, 1 Corinthians 11:25); and the sign of the Marriage Covenant is intercourse (Genesis 2:24, Matthew 19:5).

It is important to point out the Old Covenant is still in effect with its impossible laws, restrictions, rules, and regulations for those who choose to live in it. Pay attention to His laws and instructions of the Old Covenant which include: the Ten Commandments, God's promises of blessings and curses in Deuteronomy, the prophecies of the coming Messiah, words of wisdom and love, and His covenants with His people which will stand for eternity. This includes over six hundred rules, regulations, and laws you must keep. However, there is a new and better covenant.

The New Covenant is based on the life, death, and resurrection of Jesus Christ. This covenant, as found in Jeremiah, promised to fulfill what the Old Covenant was unable to accomplish.

LIVING FULLY FREE

"The time is coming," declares the LORD, "when I will make a new covenant with the house of Israel and with the house of Judah. It will not be like the covenant I made with their forefathers when I took them by the hand to lead them out of Egypt, because they broke my covenant, though I was a husband to them," declares the LORD.

"This is the covenant I will make with the house of Israel after that time;" declares the LORD. "I will put my law in their minds and write it on their hearts. I will be their God, and they will be my people. No longer will a man teach his neighbor, or a man his brother, saying, 'Know the LORD'; because they will all know me, from the least of them to the greatest," declares the LORD. "For I will forgive their wickedness and will remember their sins no more" (Jeremiah 31:31-34).

In this New Covenant, God declares a better knowledge of the Lord, a new forgiveness so our sins are no longer associated with us, and an awareness of God's purposes and laws written in our hearts. Because of this knowledge, it suggests that there is a new level of submission required for man. He desires us to follow His purposes and walk in unity with Him. This New Covenant offers us the only avenue in which to accomplish this—it is the wellspring of life.

Salvation offered through this covenant is not a one-time event with only the promise of life everlasting. It is marked by the giving of your heart to God and by the fulfillment of the covenant every day of your life until you are with Him in heaven. It is a lifelong journey with a commitment equal to it, not a one-time statement of faith and then life as usual. This is not a covenant of law, but of love. We follow Him because of this love.

God will write His Word on your heart.

Jesus says, *If you love me, you will obey what I command*, (John 14:15). Jesus goes on to tell us how important this is to our lives. *As the Father has loved me, so have I loved you. Now remain in my love. If you obey my commands, you will remain in my love, just as I have obeyed my Father's commands and remain in His love. I have told you this so that my joy may be in you and that your joy may be complete*, John 15:9-11. This is further confirmed in 1 John 5:3, *This is love for God: to obey His commands. And His commands are not burdensome.*

God will write His Word on your heart. To follow those words is to follow His Spirit and walk in unity with Jesus. 1 John 2:5-6 states, *But if anyone obeys His Word, God's love is truly made complete in Him. This is how we know we are in Him: Whoever claims to live in Him must walk as Jesus did.* This New Covenant is a life commitment and requires a completely new walk. If this is your perspective, you will fare well. However, if it is not, now is the time to repent. Commit to this New Covenant. Great will be your reward in this lifetime and in the life to come.

There are many good books on how to live the Christian life, but primarily, we recommend the Bible. It will confirm your walk and make your joy complete when you follow its truths. You should establish a firm foundation in the Word, understanding it, so you will be able to walk your life of faith on solid ground.

The marriage covenant is defined in Matthew 19:4,6,

"Haven't you read, that at the beginning the Creator made them male and female," and said, *"For this reason a man will leave his father and mother and be united to his wife, and the two will become one flesh? So, they are no longer two, but one. Therefore, what God has joined together, let man not separate."*

The union of the two people produces one flesh. Not one soul or one spirit. It is a fallacy to believe that you can become one soul or one spirit with someone else. Having a common love for someone or even a love for each other can unite two people together (in total agreement) but they never become one spirit. They can even be one *in* the Spirit (of God), but they are never one spirit. This common love can knit the two individual souls together through love, but they cannot become one soul.

The sign of the marriage covenant is Sexual intercourse when the two become one flesh. Until a few centuries ago, many cultures followed the old Hebrew tradition practiced during the times of the Old Testament. On the morning after the wedding, the bloodied sheets from their wedding bed were displayed to the family members to confirm sexual intercourse had taken place, the marriage was established, and the woman had been a virgin when given to the man. When intercourse took place, the couple was considered married. This holds true for those who are not Jewish as well. Jesus told the Samaritan woman in John 4:18, *The fact is, you have had five husbands, and the man you now have is not your husband.*

The Bible sternly cautions us not to join ourselves with anyone other than our spouse. This is confirmed in 1 Corinthians 6:16, *Do you not know that he who unites himself with a prostitute is one with her in body? For it is said, "The two will become one flesh."*

When you have sexual intercourse with someone, you become one with him or her. You have entered into a covenant with them by performing the sign of the Marriage Covenant whether you were aware of it or not.

Therefore, when you have intercourse with another person, you have participated in the sign of the marriage covenant. You have entered into a covenant with that person whether you said the usual vows or not. No longer individuals, the two of you are one flesh (Mark 10:8). This is God's divine purpose for those who are married. To those that are not officially married, this union means more than you might first realize.

When you become one flesh by having intercourse with another, not only are you allowing any bacteria or pathogens (such as sexually transmitted diseases) to share your body, but you are inviting whatever else is residing in them on a spiritual level to share your body also. This can be scary but also sobering.

People describe a profound change in their lives after having sex outside of marriage.

People describe a profound change in their lives after having sex outside of marriage. Sleeplessness, bad dreams, fears, anxieties, negative thoughts, or physical symptoms like tightness in the chest or tension in the stomach. This is commonplace in people who are sexually involved with someone other than their spouse. Unhealthy attributes in others can move into those who participate in sexual intercourse outside of the Marriage Covenant.

LIVING FULLY FREE

Jason started having nightmares not long after his sexual relationship started with his new girlfriend. Later, he found out she was into the occult. Beth, one of the sweetest girls you could ever meet, realized her road rage started shortly after she had sex with an old boyfriend who had serious anger issues. Olivia's thoughts of suicide started just weeks after having sexual relations with her boss, who was fighting the same war within himself.

There are many other examples such as these. When you join yourself to someone other than your spouse, you open the door for your own flesh to be attacked with whatever is in the one you joined with. Sexual intercourse outside of the Marriage Covenant produces an unholy covenant and the fruit of it does not produce life. Instead, it can bring destruction. It can continue to affect your life until you take ownership and repent.

In an age where sexual promiscuity is rampant, even in the church, this subject is not given enough attention to educate those suffering the effects of it. The Bible warns us in Hosea 4:6, *My people are destroyed from lack of knowledge.* Sex is not bad; sex is a good and healthy part of a marriage relationship. Because the value of the sexual union has been distorted and cheapened by the world's view, many believe intercourse has nothing to do with a marriage covenant.

If you accept this view, you fall into the same deception. Hollywood and the world's media are working diligently to promote this deception. Though Christians do not agree with their destructive agendas, they may compromise you if you consistently view their "entertainment" as an interpretation of what is acceptable. As these lies from the enemy are poured into your life like slime, you can become desensitized to the truth. Luke 11:34

Truth About Covenants

says, *Your eye is like a lamp that provides light for your body. When your eye is healthy, your whole body is filled with light. But when it's unhealthy, your body is filled with darkness.*

The Bible tells us, *Religion that God our Father accepts as pure and faultless is this: to look after orphans and widows in their distress and to <u>keep oneself from being polluted by the world,</u>* (James 1:27). Christians who successfully remain separated from the world's pollution, live more joyful, prosperous lives.

If shutting off the TV, forgoing movies or internet programming is not an option for you, consider a "fast." Take time away from the world's ideas and entertainment for an appointed time. Seek what He would have you watch, listen to, or read. Re-evaluate the source of your entertainment. It will be an eye-opening experience. Pushing the "on" button is so easy, allowing the world's media to occupy your mind and distract you from the pressures and concerns of the day. It can draw you away from the true source of peace, God.

If you have had sexual intercourse with anyone outside of marriage, you <u>have</u> performed the sign of the marriage covenant. You have established an unholy covenant with that person and could be reaping destructive attributes from it. To be free, you need to renounce that covenant, using their name when you can. If this applies to you, repeat the following prayer aloud from your heart.

If you cannot remember the person's name, repeat this prayer saying, "the person I am thinking about," God knows who they are.

Father, I renounce the ungodly covenant I made when I participated in sexual intercourse with (name of the person). I repent and I will not continue in it. It was a sin. Place this sin on the cross, separate it from me, and forgive me for it, in Jesus' name. Thank you, Father, that this covenant is dissolved. Amen.

For some, this prayer may be difficult to say from the heart because not only did they give their bodies to this person but gave their heart as well. For these people it is necessary for you to take your heart back by a declaration. A part of you will always be missing if you have given your heart to someone with whom you have had sexual intercourse, who is no longer involved in your life. When you are able to take back your heart, repeat this statement aloud.

I choose to take back my heart from (name of person). It is no longer theirs.

It is not uncommon for some people who are currently married to say this statement about past loves who still occupy a place in their hearts and minds. Some even play out greener grass scenarios with these past loves when intimacy within their own marriage is lacking. This is dangerous ground. Take back your heart and give it to the one that deserves it.

ADULTERY

When talking about the marriage covenant, it is necessary to discuss adultery. Everyone is aware that adultery is wrong. One of the ten commandments in Exodus 20:14 states, *you shall not commit adultery.* People who have a complete understanding of the marriage covenant rarely commit adultery. Most people who have committed adultery either have been ignorant of covenant or have fallen into the trap of sin they have justified in their heart. However, those in an adulterous relationship know there is no peace. If you have committed adultery, understand that is sin and it can easily be removed from you and placed on the cross of Jesus Christ (John 8:2-11). However, until you repent, you will have a battle going on inside of you.

Repentance for adultery is different from other sins that are not covenant related. Not only is adultery a sin against God (Genesis 39:9), but it is also a sin against your covenant partner because the marriage bed has been defiled. In Hebrews 13:4 the Bible says, *Marriage should be honored by all, and the marriage bed kept pure, for God will judge the adulterer and all the sexually immoral.* The Bible also tells us: *Flee from sexual immorality. All other sins a man commits are outside his body, but he who sins sexually sins against his own body*, 1 Corinthians 6:18. When two people marry, they enter into a covenant with each other and become "one flesh." The guilty person has sinned against their partner and needs to approach that partner for forgiveness for this sin as well.

Some believe confession of the sin of adultery to your pastor or friend is enough. They reason that God will forgive you, which is true. He does forgive you when you repent, however, is the sin of adultery truly dealt with until you have asked forgiveness from the one against whom you have sinned?

When Jesus taught on the mountainside, He said something interesting, *Therefore, if you are offering your gift at the altar and there remember that your brother has something against you, leave your gift there in front of the altar. First go and be reconciled to your brother; then come and offer your gift,* (Matthew 5:23-24). Isn't it interesting that He said if <u>you</u> remember that there is something between you and your brother? You will remember things you have done against your brother that could be considered an offense. In these cases, Jesus instructs you to go directly to the one you have sinned against and reconcile your relationship. If it were not necessary to go to your brother for reconciliation, He could have said, *If you remember there is something between you and your brother, confess it to Me and be forgiven.* This would be so much easier, wouldn't it? However, He wants you to reconcile with your brother, your partner, and your God.

Some people still battle with an adulterous affair they committed years before. They have confessed it to their pastor or best friend and have repented. They have changed and are no longer acting the same way, however, they never discussed it with their covenant partner. Tormented by guilt and condemnation, they fear they will be exposed. The intimacy they once shared with their spouse is not the same as it once was. Usually, they find it difficult if not impossible to be at peace in their hearts, causing many anxieties and problems.

Until they humble themselves and go to the one that they have sinned against, the marriage bed remains defiled even if the act of adultery is not ongoing. In addition, until they have removed the offense that stands between them, they are not restored into a relationship of oneness. They have deceived their spouses and betrayed their trust. They have exposed their bodies and relationship to any number of spiritual, not to mention possible physical, ailments through their adulterous affair. The enemy will use guilt and fear to keep the marriage partner bound until the sin is confessed and removed from the relationship.

Those with unconfessed adultery are living with a secret, ticking bomb that could explode at any time. The enemy of their souls uses the fear of exposure like a dark shadow looming over their shoulder. If he gets an opportunity to extort you with this knowledge, he will. You are now susceptible to a terrible realm of fear. Remember, fear is the adversary of love.

One day, God will judge your secrets, and your life will be exposed (Romans 2:16). But praise God, He has shown you a way to end the battle of fear and torment. Confess your sin to the one you sinned against, your covenant partner, and remove the enemy's access to your life.

Your initial reaction to approaching your spouse may have been a loud resounding "NO WAY!" Take a deep breath. It will all be okay. Fear has kept you from confessing this sin. People often rationalize, "I don't want to hurt my spouse even further" or "If I tell them, they will leave me."

This type of justification and reasoning are only a form of self-preservation. These statements are all about you and have nothing to do with your spouse. Confession to your spouse will have to take place in God's timing and with the grace of the Holy Spirit. When restoration of the marriage is done for the right reasons, things may seem to get worse for a while. However, the truth always brings healing and life.

When the guilty partner goes to their spouse with a heart that is yearning to restore the relationship and intimacy, there is no limit to what God can do. Going to them in the right spirit makes an enormous difference in the outcome. Before you go to your partner to confess this sin, make sure you are doing it for the right reasons and with the right attitude.

LIVING FULLY FREE

You will have to be patient while you and your spouse work through this issue. God will be amid your discussion, bringing His heart of love and His Spirit of restoration to the relationship, if you are yielded to Him. He is always faithful, and as the Word says in Ephesians 3:20, *He is able to do immeasurably more than all we ask or imagine, according to His power that is at work within us.*

This sin may be destroying you spiritually and physically and getting it off your chest for relief might be a priority for your life. You may want to get out of the trap of the ongoing adulterous relationship but are unable to break it off. You may be willing to confess your sin to your spouse as a way of ending the relationship. Stop and consider your spouse first. You can do even more damage to your relationship if you do not first consider your spouse during this process. Do not avoid telling them, but examine the "who, what, when, and where" with your pastor or prayer partner before you begin. Listen to their counsel and move in accordance with wisdom, not your feelings. The "heart" or "spirit" or "attitude" in which you approach your spouse will determine the outcome. If any of this describes you, repeat this prayer from your heart:

> *"Father, forgive me for the sin of adultery. I repent and ask for forgiveness. I renounce the covenant I made with (person with whom you committed adultery). It was a sin. Please take this sin from me, put it on the cross of Jesus Christ and separate it from me, in Jesus' Name. Father, I choose to honor the covenant with my spouse, and I thank You for healing and restoring my marriage. Amen."*

UNGODLY COVENANTS

The Bible cautions us not to go into covenant with unbelievers (2 Corinthians 6:14). However, what happens if you were not born again when you were married or married a non-believer? What if you married someone for security, money, or out of fear that you would never get married? Your relationship has undoubtedly not been fulfilled based on these decisions. How do you manage these problems?

To understand the answer to your problem, you need first to understand the answer to David's problem. Was it God's plan for King David to kill Uriah the Hittite and take Uriah's wife, Bathsheba, for himself? Of course not. *But the thing David had done displeased the LORD*, (2 Samuel 11:27). God, however, did bless the marriage. Our Savior, the Lord Jesus, was eventually born through their union and bloodline. What happened to bring about God's blessing?

When David was confronted with his sin, he took responsibility for his actions, repented for his sin and honored God from that day forth (1 Kings 15:5).

If your relationship with your spouse was initiated with ungodliness or out of rebellion, greed, or fear, do what David did. Accept ownership of your actions, repent for your sin, and honor your covenant with your spouse and the Lord. God will honor the Marriage Covenant <u>you choose</u> to honor. Watch for wonderful changes in your relationship when you respect and honor your marriage covenant.

There are people reading this that are not married and are in an ungodly relationship, and you know it. Adding a marriage certificate does not make it holy. You are living like the child who prayed for a bicycle and had not received it. So, they stole one and asked God for forgiveness.

If your spouse is an unbeliever, follow the words of Paul in 1 Corinthians 7:12-16, *If any brother has a wife who is not a believer and she is willing to live with him, he must not divorce her. And if a woman has a husband who is not a believer and he is willing to live with her, she must not divorce him. For the unbelieving husband has been sanctified through his wife, and the unbelieving wife has been sanctified through her believing husband. Otherwise, your children would be unclean, but as it is, they are holy. But if the unbeliever leaves, let him do so. A believing man or woman is not bound in such circumstances; God has called us to live in peace. How do you know, wife, whether you will save your husband? Or, how do you know, husband, whether you will save your wife?*

To an unbelieving spouse, your actions speak much louder than your words. Especially if you are using scripture as a weapon. The devil did that in the desert with Jesus (Matthew 4:1-4). Allow your actions, not your words, to be your witness for Christ. Regardless of their actions or unbelief, honor your covenant with them. In everything be led by the Spirit (Romans 8:14).

DIVORCE

Finally, what do you do if you have been divorced? Divorce is <u>not</u> an unforgivable sin. It should be avoided whenever possible because God hates divorce (Malachi 2:16). However, God does not hate people who have been divorced. He hates sin, but He loves people. There are only two actions recorded in the Bible that could cause the marriage covenant to be broken. One is marital unfaithfulness (Matthew 19:9) and the other is the death of a spouse (1 Corinthians 7:39). When you gave your life to the Lord, you should have renounced all other covenants that would be in opposition to Jesus being the Lord of your life. If you are divorced and remarried, you need to renounce all other covenants in opposition to your union.

Some married people cannot seem to shake thoughts about a past partner. Feeling guilty over these secret thoughts, people can feel pulled to return to their previous partner or wonder what life would be like with them. These thoughts are in opposition to your marriage covenant. They will harm the quality and intimacy in your marriage. They are poisons that will seep into every area of your marriage. If left unattended, they can eventually destroy your current relationship.

The answer to this problem is quite simple. First, you must renounce any previous covenants that you have entered that are in opposition to your marriage covenant. Secondly, you need to take every thought about a past partner captive and stop dwelling on thoughts about them, eliminate it according to the Word (2 Corinthians 10:5). Your contentment in this relationship depends on it.

SOUL TIES

In direct opposition to covenant, a dangerous teaching has spread through some parts of the church. It is the teaching about breaking or renouncing soul ties. The term "soul ties" cannot be found in the Bible. It is used by well-meaning Christians who have improperly taken it from the Old Testament story of Jonathan and David. *Now when he had finished speaking to Saul, the soul of Jonathan was knit to the soul of David, and Jonathan loved him as his own soul,* (1 Samuel 18:1 NIV).

Those who teach this concept believe a "soul tie" is an emotional, mental, or "spiritual" bondage to others, whether good or bad. They are still missing the point and leading some astray. This passage is an expression of the oneness of hearts and love between friends and is not some mystical binding of their souls. Jonathan and David did not make a "soul tie" that could be broken or renounced with a change of opinion or whim. They made a covenant. There is a significant difference. *Now when he had finished speaking to Saul, the soul of Jonathan was knit to the soul of David, and Jonathan loved him as his own soul. Saul took him that day and would not let him go home to his father's house anymore. Then Jonathan and David made a covenant because he loved him as his own soul,* (l Samuel 18:1- 3 NKJV). They made another covenant as well. *So, the two of them made a covenant before the LORD. And David stayed in the woods, and Jonathan went to his own house,* (l Samuel 23:18 NKJV).

Jonathan and David made a covenant.

People who believe that dealing with "soul ties" as a solution for healing instead of addressing covenants are only treating a symptom—the emotional and mental bond. They are not dealing with the root issue of the covenant itself. We agree that there can be mental and emotional bonds in a covenant and use the marriage covenant as an example of that. However, there is a danger in thinking that addressing "soul ties," instead of covenant, is the answer or the root of ungodly relationships. "Soul ties" can easily become the central focus of our attention and we can get sidetracked. Have you ever played a carnival game called Whack-A-Mole? In the game, you use a mallet to try and hit a target as it keeps popping up from different holes at random intervals. That is what it is like when you are only treating the symptom of a problem instead of the root cause of it. In making "soul ties" the concern, these people (and we used to be one of them) miss the bigger picture of the impact of a covenant relationship. The whole idea of covenant is replaced with "soul ties," and that is the deception.

Another false concept of "soul ties" is that this mystical binding "just happens" because of our love or partnership with someone else. It would be as if "soul ties" have little or nothing to do with our own actions or will and can randomly happen at any time even if we are opposed to it. This is simply not true and was not the case with Jonathan and David. They had a great love for each other and decided, or chose, to enter into a covenant with one another. It did not just happen because they loved one another. It also could not be broken or revoked by anyone other than Jonathan or David.

Those who renounce or "break soul ties off" of others believe that they have the power to declare this mystical binding (mental and emotional) of someone else's relationship to be over. This is foolishness. They usually do not understand that repentance is necessary, and because of this fact, it is rarely addressed. Only the individuals that make a covenant have the authority to renounce or break it. If you have given your heart to someone who should not have it, you need to repent and take your heart back. If you joined in a covenant with someone that you should not have, simply repent, and renounce the covenant. When you renounce the covenant and repent, the "strings" or attachments that exist no longer have any grounds or right to remain.

If you have an unhealthy relationship because of sin or entering into an ungodly attachment, repent, forgive, or act in accordance with the scriptures about the relationship. You do not have to renounce a "soul tie". Our question is this: if renouncing soul ties were the method that would bring total healing, would not Jesus or Paul have mentioned or somehow referenced it in their teachings? We cannot emphasize this strongly enough because we have seen lives devastated by well-meaning people who have made "soul ties" their focus instead of repentance, covenants, or the clear truths of God's Word.

A line is crossed by some of those who practice breaking or renouncing "soul ties" off others. They are attempting to supersede the authority of someone else's will. They believe that they can "break this" or "renounce that" on behalf of someone else. This is wrong! This point also cannot be stressed strongly enough. We do not have authority over someone else's will to break or renounce a covenant into which they have entered. We cannot renounce or break someone else's covenant in their place or on their behalf. Even if it is done with good intentions or with their permission. This is not something you can do any more than you can accept salvation on behalf of someone else.

Only the one who is in the covenant can declare their position towards it. We did not make the covenant for them, and we cannot break it for them. Once they have repented or renounced the covenant, we can join in agreement with them,

Truth About Covenants

making a declaration based on their words, that the covenant is over! This is a completely different concept and is so powerful. Those who break or renounce the "soul ties" of others do not have authority to do so and are on dangerous ground. When people try to supersede someone else's will, they are mimicking witchcraft.

If you have been mistakenly doing this type of ministry, it is easy to regroup, repent and begin to see the lasting fruit and healing that Jesus talked about. You simply ask God for His forgiveness and repent. Take time to study in the Word about covenants so that you know the scriptures for yourself and can effectively minister to those in need. Remember that God always brings healing when we come to Him with a humble heart and are willing to take responsibility for our actions. You have a choice either to hang onto your belief despite what the Word of God says, or to abandon your belief for the truth in the Word.

We are cautioned in the Word that no one should be yoked with an unbeliever (2 Corinthians 6:14). This is a matter of the heart and not about legalism. Follow the leading of the Spirit of God and listen before you go into covenant with anyone. If you know in your spirit that you have any ungodly covenants in your life, then repeat this prayer from your heart:

Father, I renounce the ungodly covenant I made with (name of person) in Jesus' Name. I repent of this sin in Jesus' Name. Forgive me this sin and place it on the cross of Jesus. I confirm the covenant I have with you and my spouse. I thank you Father for Your healing and freedom. Amen.

LIVING FULLY FREE

Scripture References

Nevertheless, because of the covenant the LORD had made with David, the LORD was not willing to destroy the house of David. He had promised to maintain a lamp for him and his descendants forever.

(2 Chronicles 21:7)

And I will put enmity between you and the woman, and between your offspring and hers; he will crush your head, and you will strike his heel.

(Genesis 3:15)

The LORD smelled the pleasing aroma and said in his heart: "Never again will I curse the ground because of man, even though every inclination of his heart is evil from childhood. And never again will I destroy all living creatures, as I have done. So long as the earth endures, seedtime and harvest cold and heat, summer and winter, day and night will never cease."

(Genesis 8:21-22)

By the same word, the present heavens and earth are reserved for fire, being kept for the day of judgment and destruction of ungodly men. But do not forget this one thing, dear friends: With the Lord a day is like a thousand years, and a thousand years are like a day. The Lord is not slow in keeping his promise, as some understand slow ness. He is patient with you, not wanting anyone to perish, but everyone to come to repentance. But the day of the Lord will come like a thief.

Truth About Covenants

The heavens will disappear with a roar. The elements will be destroyed by fire, and the earth and everything in it will be laid bare. Since everything will be destroyed in this way, what kind of people ought you to be? You ought to live holy and godly lives as you look forward to the day of God and speed its coming. That day will bring about the destruction of the heavens by fire,
and the elements will melt in the heat. But in keeping with His promise, we are looking forward to a new heaven and a new earth, the home of righteousness. So then, dear friends, since you are looking forward to this, make every effort to be found spotless, blameless and at peace with Him. Bear in mind that our Lord's patience means salvation, just as our dear brother Paul also wrote to you.
with the wisdom that God gave him.

(Peter 3:7-15)

When Moses went and told the people all the Lord's words and laws, they responded with one voice, "Everything the LORD has said we will do.

(Exodus 24:3)

The king stood by the pillar and renewed the covenant in the presence of the LORD to follow the LORD.
and keep his commands, regulations, and decrees with all his heart and
all his soul, thus confirming the words of the covenant written.
in this book. Then all the people pledged themselves to the covenant.

(Kings 23:3)

LIVING FULLY FREE

These things are being taken figuratively: The woman represent two covenants. One covenant is from Mount Sinai and bears children who are to be slaves: This is Hagar. Now Hagar stands for Mount Sinai in Arabia and corresponds to the present city of Jerusalem, because she is in slavery with her children. But the Jerusalem that is above is free, and she is our mother.

(Galatians 44:24-26)

For this reason, Christ is the mediator of a new covenant, that those who are called may receive the promised eternal inheritance - now that he has died as a ransom to set them free from the sins committed under the first covenant.

(Hebrews 9:15)

You are to undergo circumcision, and it will be the sign of the covenant between me and you.

(Genesis 17:11)

Then he gave Abraham the covenant of circumcision. And Abraham became the father of Isaac and circumcised him eight days after his birth. Later Isaac became the father of Jacob, and Jacob became the father of the twelve patriarchs.

(Acts 7:8)

This is my blood of the covenant, which is poured out for many for the forgiveness of sins.

(Matthew 26:28)

In the same way, after supper he took the cup, saying, "This cup is the new covenant in my blood; do this, whenever you drink it, in remembrance of me."

(1 Corinthians 11:25)

For this reason, a man will leave his father and mother and be united to his wife, and they will become one flesh.

(Genesis 2:24)

And said, 'For this reason a man will leave his father and mother and
be *united to his* wife, *and the two will* become one *flesh.*

(Matthew 19:5)

And the two will become one *flesh. So, they are no longer two, but* one.

(Mark 10:8)

At dawn he appeared again in the temple courts, where all the people gathered around him, and he sat down to teach them.
The teachers of the law and the Pharisees brought in a woman caught in adultery.
They made her stand before the group and said to Jesus, "Teacher, this woman was caught in the act of adultery. In the Law Moses commanded us to stone such women.
Now what do you say?" They were using this question as a trap, in order to have a basis for accusing him. But Jesus bent down and started to write on the ground with his finger.

LIVING FULLY FREE

When they kept on questioning him, he straightened up and said to them,
"If any one of you is without sin, let him be the first to throw a stone at her." Again, he stooped down and wrote on the ground. At this, those who heard began to go away one at a time, the older ones first, until only Jesus was left, with the woman still standing there. Jesus straightened up and asked her, "Woman, where are they? Has no one condemned you?"
"No one, sir" she said. "Then neither do I condemn you," Jesus declared. "Go now and leave *your life of sin."*

(John 8:2-11)

No one is greater in this house than I am. My master has withheld nothing from me except you because you are his wife. How then could I do such a wicked thing
and sin against God?

(Genesis 39:9)

This will take place on the day when God judges men's secrets through Jesus Christ, as my gospel declares.

(Romans 2:16)

Do not be yoked together with unbelievers. For what do righteousness and wickedness have in common? Or what fellowship can light have with darkness?

(2 Corinthians 6:14)

For David had done what was right in the eyes of the LORD and had not failed to keep any of the Lord's commands all the days of his life except in the case of Uriah the Hittite.

(1 Kings 15:5)

Then Jesus was led by the Spirit into the wilderness to be tempted by the devil. After fasting forty days and forty nights, he was hungry. The tempter came to him and said, "If you are the Son of God, tell these stones to become bread." Jesus answered, "It is written: 'Man shall not live on bread alone, but on every word that comes from the mouth of God.'"

(Matthew 4:1-4)

Because those who are led by the Spirit of God are sons of God.

(Romans 8:14)

"The man who hates and divorces his wife," says the Lord, the God of Israel, "does violence to the one he should protect," says the Lord Almighty. So be on your guard, and do not be unfaithful.

(Malachi 2:16)

I tell you that anyone who divorces his wife, except for marital unfaithfulness, and marries another woman commits adultery.

(Matthew 19:9)

LIVING FULLY FREE

A woman is bound to her husband as long as he lives. But if her husband dies, she is free to marry anyone she wishes, but he must belong to the Lord.

(1 Corinthians 7:39)

We demolish arguments and every pretension that sets itself up against the knowledge
of God, and we take captive every thought to make it obedient to Christ.

(2 Corinthians 10:5)

Do not be yoked together with unbelievers.

(2 Corinthians 6:14)

CHAPTER 12

TRUTH ABOUT DELIVERANCE AND STRONGHOLDS

A friend went through the United States Treasury Department's counterfeit training to learn how to spot counterfeit currency. He told us it was an intense school with long hours of study. After graduation, all the students could spot any counterfeit US currency. We asked our friend just how many counterfeit bills they saw during the classes? He informed us that he only saw one, which was displayed on the wall. It was one of the first counterfeit bills ever discovered, a hand drawn bill from the early 1800's, framed and hanging at the classroom entrance.

In wonder, we asked how you could learn to spot counterfeit bills if you never saw one? He told us that they could have studied all the counterfeit bills that were in circulation, but he would just have had to return to school every time a new counterfeit was made. The way they learned about counterfeit currency was to only study real currency and learn it so well that anything that did not match up with it was easily recognized.

You can take the time to learn everything about demons and the god of this world, but, instead, we encourage you to spend your time and effort learning about who God is. Then you will easily spot anything contrary to His nature and character (counterfeit). It is with this in mind that we examine the next subject.

It is important to be knowledgeable of Satan and his demons, but it is a serious error to live with a Satan consciousness, to be Satan-minded. We are not to be ignorant of his devices (2 Corinthians 2:11). However, we are to be always aware of God, who directs our steps (Psalms 37:23), and to keep our thoughts in line with our future in Christ (Colossians 3:2). Although Satan has been cast down from heaven to earth, (Isaiah 14:12) and he is the enemy of our souls, we are not to recognize him as an equal to God or to in any way give Satan glory. Satan is a created being and only comparable to the angel Michael. God has no equal or rival (Isaiah 46:5). Why give any time or thought to the enemy? We only need to keep our thoughts on the Lord (Hebrews 3:1).

Giving Satan glory is what men are doing when they credit him with anything they believe he has helped bring about in their lives. No one would think to honor Satan for anything good that has happened in their life. However, when we credit him with the terrible things we are going through, we are still giving him honor, even if it is for negative effects. We do not intend to honor Satan for anything as he is not worthy of any glory or honor. He is a created being, and it will only take one angel to put him away at the appointed time. *And I saw an angel coming down out of heaven, having the key to the Abyss and holding in his hand a great chain. He seized the dragon, that ancient serpent, who is the devil, or Satan, and bound him for a thousand years,* (Revelation 20:1-2). The Bible also assures us that Satan will later be thrown into the lake of fire (Revelation 20:10).

When we met Carl, he was struggling in about every area of his life and had been for many years. It seemed that, with each passing year, things got worse for him instead of better. He was having health issues, his finances were in peril, and his relationship with his wife and family was strained. Even praying and worshipping had become just exercises to him. Carl had lost his strength, and he knew it. As he was dealing with this spiral, Carl was an active elder in his church and taught each week in the adult Bible study. After a brief interview, it was easy to see what his problem was: Carl was giving Satan credit for every problem in his life.

To Carl, Satan was the cause of what had gone wrong in his business. He eventually credited Satan with all the issues within his family, and finally, with his health. He often verbalized this fact to those who would listen. When he met with us, he lamented about how hard the fight was to advance the Kingdom of God. He believed he was making headway for the Lord, and that was the reason he was under this continual attack. Carl was living a life contrary to what Jesus promised, because Carl was giving Satan credit for everything that appeared wrong in his life.

It is true that the enemy of our souls will come against us. He tempted Jesus (Matthew 4:1), prompted Judas to betray Jesus (John 13:2) and stopped Paul from entering Thessalonica (1 Thes. 2:18). However, the Bible tells us that God would never leave us nor forsake us (Hebrew 13:5). In addition, Jesus told us that His burden for us was light (Matthew 11:30). I asked Carl if his life as a Christian was always this hard? He informed me that it had only been like this for the past three years. He told us he had gone through a particular financial problem in his business, and he believed Satan was the cause of it. He said that was the first time he could remember crediting Satan with anything.

We explained to Carl that every time he gave credit to Satan for something detrimental that was happening in his life, he empowered Satan. In addition, he gave him glory, even if it was just for the pain he inflicted. Even if the enemy is working in our lives, we are directed to give thanks to God in everything. *Give thanks in all circumstances, for this is God's will for you in Christ Jesus,* (1 Thessalonians 5:18).

Carl realized his life had taken a turn for the worse right after he started crediting Satan for the events in his life. Carl repented and decided to credit God for directing his steps from that day forward. He decided not to mention the enemies name again in reference to his circumstances or give him credit for anything.

We met with Carl three months later and he looked like a different man, full of life and energy. He informed us that everything in his life turned around and only mentioned Satan's name in reference to the Bible. He said he had accomplished more for the Kingdom of God in the last three months than he had done in the previous three years. When the enemy attacks us we will become stronger, but when he distracts us, we become weaker.

When the enemy attacks us we will become stronger, but when he distracts us, we become weaker.

When I (Michael) was young, I went to a tent revival one spring in a farming community deep in the South. As the meeting began, a huge storm swept in and began hitting the tent with heavy rain. The evangelist loudly announced that the devil was trying to stop the meeting. With that, about a third of the people got up and left. What the evangelist did not know was it had not rained in that area for the past six weeks, and the farmers had been praying for rain, so they did not lose their crops. He was giving credit to the enemy for something that was an answer to prayer for the farmers.

In a similar vein, we should discuss another practice that is fairly commonplace in the church: believers who address the devil during their prayers. Nowhere in Scripture is Satan addressed during a prayer to God. If you have been saying prayers to God and in the same breath coming against the devil, please evaluate why you are doing this. You will not find this model of prayer in the Word of God. There is ungodly fruit in the lives of those who do this. God will deliver us from the evil one if we ask Him (Matthew 6:13).

Although Satan is in opposition to God, he is in no way equal to God.

Although Satan is in opposition to God, he is in no way equal to God. A simple analogy to put this in perspective can be done with a book of matches. Take a match out of the pack and light it. This lit match will represent Satan, and it can burn you. In comparison, our God is the Sun. Any questions?

If you want to displace the darkness in your life, it is done by replacing it with light. If you go into a dark room, you can come against the darkness and even yell for it to leave, but it will not become light. If you want to do away with the darkness, turn on the light! This works in the life of every believer. *When Jesus spoke again to the people, He said, "I am the light of the world. Whoever follows me will never walk in darkness but will have the light of life,"* (John 8:12).

Every time you come into agreement with the enemy's plan for your life, you empower him. This is especially true through your thought patterns. The Bible tells us in 2 Corinthians 10:5, *to take captive every thought to make it obedient to Christ.* You also empower Satan when you credit him with anything or call his name in reference to something negative that happens. It gives him glory for who he is. If you have been giving Satan credit for the issues of your life, now is the time to repent. If this applies to you then repeat this prayer from your heart:

Father, I repent for giving Satan glory. This is a sin, and I ask you to forgive me for it. I will no longer give him credit for anything, but will always give thanks to You, in Jesus' Name. Father, I thank You for restoring me in every area of my life. Amen.

DELIVERANCE

Deliverance is one of the most controversial subjects in the church, but it should not be. There are two extremes in the school of thought surrounding deliverance from demons. The first is believing that demons exist behind every rock or bush and that we are in a constant battle for supremacy over them. The second is believing demons are just made up by ignorant people in order to "spiritually" explain mental and emotional illness. We will avoid these two ditches altogether and look to the Word of God for the answers. The Bible is clear about the subject: demons did and do exist (Mark 5:12;16:9). One third of the face-to-face ministry of Jesus recorded in the Bible included driving out demons from hurting people. We need to know what that means to us today.

What is a demon? It is an unclean spirit that does not have a body, and it is looking for one in which to operate and function. They are called *unclean spirits* (Matt 10: l, Mark 6:7), *wicked (or evil) spirits* (Luke 7:21), and *deceiving spirits* (1 Timothy 4:1). They were cast down to earth with Satan, the prince of demons (Matthew 12:24). Jesus referred to these demons as snakes and scorpions in Scripture (Luke 10:19).

Some teach that a demon cannot reside in a Christian, but we have found that to be untrue. A demon is a spirit without a body looking to inhabit one. Do Christians have bodies? Of course. It is necessary, however, to point out that a curse cannot effectively operate without a cause, and a demon would qualify as a curse (Proverbs 26:2).

Others teach that a demon can only oppress a Christian, not possess them. We will avoid this argument and declare that no matter which way you look at it, demons are not desirable. As Christians our spirits belong to the Lord, so this means that demons can inhabit our flesh but not have access to our spirit. However, demons do have access to the brain, which is part of the body, and this allows them to influence thoughts. Demons attempt to influence their host away from God so that these people would choose to eventually reject or discredit God. They torment the mind and body of believers, taking away their joy and causing confusion. Some even try to get their host to destroy themselves.

We have observed through experience that demons are singular in their purpose, and they are identified by that purpose. A demon of hate only hates, and it has no other traits. A demon of greed is always greedy and is only greedy. A demon of jealousy is always jealous, even of the other demons. Demons are identified by the traits they exhibit in their host. Some demons can affect our bodies as well as our minds. The Bible talks about demons that cause muteness (Matthew 9:33), deafness (Mark 9:25), seizures (Matthew 17:18). We have found many other illnesses that are caused by demonic activity, as well. There are even demons that function, deceptively, as "friends." These deceiving spirits talk to their host and may lead them as "spirit guides."

Some may credit these voices heard in their mind to be the Holy Spirit and will follow their leading even if it contradicts the Word of God (1 Timothy 4:1). Some people have two-way conversations in their minds believing they are debating with their own subconscious. This is not the state of someone in peace. People normally process things through their own thoughts, coming to a solution with their own reason and logic.

What do we mean by this? Take a minute to do a little exercise. Read the following question aloud, but only think of the answer to the question in your mind.

What is your favorite color?

The answer to that question, heard as a thought, was your own thinking. It was your own voice in your mind. If you hear another voice, or even an argument going on as dialogue in your thoughts, then you may be experiencing the torment brought on by a demon. Some people have had these conversations going on in their heads for so long that they do not think it odd or unusual. They believe that everyone's mind is just as busy and cannot fathom having a mind without the noise and activity they live with daily. Others fight with voices that direct them to do or say certain things which they end up regretting after the fact. Still others believe that their mind is clear but are disturbed by unusual activity when they first try to fall asleep. And then there are those who fight a mental battle, knowing it is not from God but also not knowing how to get rid of it. If any of the above applies to you, do not panic or even worry because peace is at hand.

We are consistently asked the same question: "How did I get this thing?" The answer is simple: sin. We will explain. We have found that everyone with a spirit of bitterness has committed this same sin. They went to sleep while they were angry and then meditated on what caused that anger. The Bible tells us in Ephesians 4:26-27, *In your anger do not sin: Do not let the sun go down while you are still angry, and do not give the devil a foothold.* It also tells us in 2 Corinthians 10:5, *to take captive every thought to make it obedient to Christ.* It is not a sin to get angry, but it is a sin not to deal with it and let it grow in our hearts.

Continually entertaining thoughts in opposition to God's plan for our life produces bad fruit. These are open doors for demonic activity. People who are hooked on pornography did not get that way without first opening the doors to it by viewing pornography. It does not mean that everyone who went to sleep on his or her anger or who ever saw pornography has a demon. They are, however, setting the stage for one to enter their heart if they continue doing the same things. An open door (opportunity) is what a demon is looking for. This access is opened and closed amid the condition of our heart. It is more than just a matter of the legal rights to which demons claim to operate. When we depend on legalism for our judgment of what can and cannot happen, we discount God's grace upon us. However, there are laws of the Kingdom that demons must obey, as we will soon see.

A common doorway that demons use to enter someone is through intercourse outside the marriage covenant. As noted previously, when we have intercourse, we become one flesh with the other person (Mark 10:8). We also know demons inhabit flesh. They do not enter because sex is in any way bad. As we established, sex is a part of God's plan for a healthy marriage. However, sex outside of marriage is forbidden in the Word of God (1 Corinthians 6:18-20). Not because He is trying to deny us of something good, but because He is protecting us from something harmful. When we participate, we open the door to demons through disobedience. Not only do we open our bodies to whatever sexually transmitted diseases the other person has, we also open our bodies to whatever demonic activity the other has. We have met people whose thinking became busy and whose ongoing physical, emotional, and mental problems started right after they had intercourse outside of the marriage relationship.

Another way to open the door to demonic activity is by operating in disobedience to God's Word and His plan for your life. Some common doors open when people perpetuate the following: greed, idolatry, rebellion, sexual immorality, lying, hatred, and of course the occult and witchcraft.

Ultimately, the open door is caused by sin. However, it does not always have to be your sin. Rape victims or victims of sexual abuse have a sense of feeling unclean even after they have forgiven their abuser. The defilement to their bodies is real and can last long after the pain of the event or the pain from the memory of it is gone. This defilement can be a demon that came in through the abuser. Acts of violence like being beaten or traumatic events like car crashes can open doors for some demons as well. A spirit of fear through trauma is common from these types of events.

It is also possible to be born into an environment where the spiritual doors are open to everyone in the household because of the sin of the leader or leaders of that household. In addition, the world's media such as television, movies, and online content, may open doors to spirits. These influences can seduce us from the truth of God and open doors to the demonic. The Bible cautions us in James 1:27, *...to keep oneself from being polluted by the world.*

**The open door is caused by sin.
However, it does not have to be your sin.**

There is not a demon sitting on your TV screen waiting to pounce on your children. However, children who live in front of the television set are seeing things that are meant to entice them into accepting certain situations as normal or acceptable when they are not. They become desensitized to the truth and are more likely to end up following the doctrine of demons later in life. *Now the Spirit expressly says that in latter times some will depart from the faith, giving heed to deceiving spirits and doctrines of demons,* (1 Timothy 4:1 NKJV).

Desensitization is more common than you may realize. We attended a service recently where a concerned doctor was describing the horror of partial birth abortions. We saw the shock of it on the listening faces. We saw that same shock on the faces of people some twenty years before when a doctor was first describing abortion to the same congregation. Many of us have become desensitized to everyday "regular" abortion and are now only shocked when we hear something more terrifying. It is easy when talking about this subject to become overwhelmed with the endless possibilities for defilement. If we pick up a demon consciousness, then we have fallen into their trap. They do exist and we need to be aware of them, but we are not to live in any fear because of them.

Remember: demons are subject to the laws of the Kingdom. One of the most important laws of the Kingdom concerning demons is that Christians have full authority over them without exception. *I have given you authority to trample on snakes and scorpions and to overcome all the power of the enemy; nothing will harm you. However, do not rejoice that the spirits submit to you, but rejoice that your names are written in heaven,* (Luke 10:19-20). *And these signs will accompany those who believe: In my name they will drive out demons,* (Mark 16:17). In addition the Bible tells us, *Submit yourselves, then, to God. Resist the devil, and he will flee from you.* (James 4:7) It is in submitting to God that you are empowered over the devil. You may want to read that again. Therefore, you do not have to worry about demons unless you are opening the doors for the demons to come in because of sin. If you have opened these doors, it is easily remedied, as you will soon see.

We are a spirit who has a soul and lives in a body. A demon is a being that wants to share our body. It will try and negatively interact with our soul. They try to deceive us into believing they are a natural part of us. Some will try to convince us we do not deserve to be free of their presence because of our unworthiness or because of something that we did. They may try to convince us that there is something inherently wrong with us, and that is why we have their affliction. Some demons also function as if they are helping us in hopes that we will accept them and allow them to stay. These are all lies. We have all authority over them, and they do not have to stay if we are willing to get free.

There are many good people teaching deliverance and most of them are successful. However, it is necessary to point out that deliverance, in certain circumstances, can do more damage than good. The demon came in because of an open door caused by our own actions or because of someone else's. If we are delivered (set free from the demon) and do nothing about how it entered, we will be clean and in order, for a time, but the demon can return and bring seven other demons with it more powerful than itself.

When an evil spirit comes out of a man, it goes through arid places seeking rest and does not find it. Then it says, "I will return to the house I left." When it arrives, it finds the house swept clean and put in order. Then it goes and takes seven other spirits more wicked than itself, and they go in and live there. And the final condition of that man is worse than the first, (Luke 11:24-26).

LIVING FULLY FREE

Unfortunately, we have met people in this condition because a well-meaning Christian ministered deliverance to them with the God-given authority to cast out the demon. However, they did not have the knowledge to expose how, when and where the demon entered. This lack of knowledge does cause people to suffer. To keep this from happening, we should practice identifying how the demon entered before we attempt deliverance. The answer will always be through sin (John 5:14).

God looks at the heart, and so should we, when dealing with deliverance. We have found that deliverance often happens naturally by leading someone into repentance with the associated change of heart. John the Baptist had already led the people in repentance for their sins and set the foundation for Jesus to minister to their hearts. Demons simply left (Luke 4:41). By exposing the door (the sin in their lives) and repenting for the actions that allowed the demon to enter in the first place, the demonic influences are forced to leave with a word (Matthew 8:16).

This is quite simple when you ask the right questions.

"When did you start suffering from this problem?"

"What happened at that time in your life right before the demonic influence appeared?"

In examining what happened, look for any action or reaction from the person involved that is contrary to the Word of God. That is generally the doorway. Listen for words that reflect an angry, hurt, wounded or rebellious heart. They will point to the doorway.

Also look for any of the following: greed, idolatry, rebellion, sexual immorality, lying, hatred, the occult and witchcraft. Lead these people into renouncing the words that they spoke that were contrary to God's purposes. Then lead them in repentance for the ungodly action or reaction. We have seen people healed and set free by this simple but effective method.

You must renounce any ungodly spoken words. These words came from a heart set against God's purposes even if it was just for the moment. Jesus rebuked Peter for speaking words from Peter's heart that were contrary to the purposes of God (Matthew 16:23).

If you have any of the symptoms listed above and believe that there is a good possibility that you are dealing with a demonic influence, we offer the prayer below and believe that it will help. However, we strongly encourage you to meet with an elder in the church that you can trust to discuss any ongoing concerns you may have. Deliverance does come when people repent and take charge of their lives, but it is also always helpful to have someone with experience in this area walk you through ways to overcome other potential roadblocks. If this applies to you, then repeat this prayer aloud from your heart:

Father, I renounce my dealings with any ungodly things, and I set my heart on you alone. I repent of (name the sin) that I have committed that opened the door to demonic activity. Forgive me for this sin. I refuse to share my body with any ungodly thing in Jesus' Name. Father, I thank You for your freedom. Amen.

It is now necessary to exercise your authority over the demons and repeat aloud, "I command any unclean thing to leave me right now in Jesus' Name."

It may be necessary to repeat this prayer more than once and be specific if you know what its name is (pornography, addiction, anger, bitterness, etc.). If you know you are dealing with a particular spirit, like a spirit of anger, then name that spirit when you command the unclean thing to leave. Do not whisper or politely ask it to leave. Treat it as if it were an intruder entering your house to do you harm. How should you address them? With the authority given to you by the Lord (Mark 16:17), not timid or shy but commanding and forceful to evict them from your home. In addition, do not give up. Wait on the Lord and follow His direction. If you have any doubt at all, we encourage you to go to the elders of a good, Bible-believing church.

STRONGHOLDS

Not every ongoing negative attribute or ungodly belief system is demonic in nature. Some people may have a stronghold instead of a demon. These strongholds can resemble demonic activity. Strongholds are birthed when people believe things that are contrary to the Truth of God, believing them to be the Truth. This happens when we are taught lies from people we trust or when we use our own faulty reasoning and logic to explain our life experiences. We then build ungodly belief systems around them that contradict the Truth.

An example would be this. I (Michael) attended a church that believed that praying for people for healing was an outdated and unbiblical practice. The church leaders told me that people who participated in this type of healing prayer were not doing God's work. Instead, they believed the actions of these ministers were self-serving at best, and devil-serving at worst. I believed them because I trusted them, and this created a stronghold of unbelief in my heart regarding the fact that the Lord still moves today through healing physical bodies.

I would not even entertain the idea that God physically healed people today by the laying on of hands and doubted the testimony of those who said it happened to them. I had written off the Scriptures that stated otherwise, which began a time of decreased effectiveness of God's Word in my life. When I read about where Jesus or the disciples healed people, I believed it was only history. I believed that Jesus (even though he was alive in my heart) had changed His methods and only used medical professionals and modern medicine to heal people today. It was some years later that I learned the truth. I was at a meeting where Jesus was glorified, and people I knew were healed by receiving healing prayer.

It took many good friends to get me to that meeting. I must admit that I was the biggest skeptic in the room. That is until I saw people healed in the name of Jesus and giving their lives to the Lord because of it. These people are healed to this day. My belief system changed, and the whole Word of God came alive to me. I am now one of those believers who lay hands on the sick and see them recover. When we tell people about the ministry we do, we see that same look of unbelief on their faces that I used to have on mine when people talked about laying hands on and praying for the sick.

Strongholds are also erected when people allow their current circumstances to create untrue core belief systems. April had been struggling in her relationship with God ever since her mom had died. The grieving process had been hard for her, and she was still dealing with it years after her mom's death. After a few basic questions, we found out that April had fervently prayed for God to heal her mom and not allow her to die. After her mom's death, April came to believe that God did not love her as He loved others whose prayers He had answered. She had a stronghold.

This stronghold began with her natural father who left little room for doubt that he favored his other children over April. It was for this reason she believed that God did not answer her prayers and so her mom died. She allowed life's circumstances to build a stronghold in her heart that was contrary to the truth. After instructing her on the truth and leading April through some simple prayers, her heart lit up, and the glow of it shined on her face. She is free and knows the Truth in a way that cannot be taken from her.

Words spoken as declarations or statements of intent can also set the foundation for strongholds. They usually come right after a life-altering event. Words like "I will never love anyone like that again," or "I will never trust another person on this earth again," or "I will never_____ (fill in the blank)." They might also be words spoken in rebellion like, "I don't care what my parents say, I am going to do it my way," or "I don't care if it is wrong, I deserve it," or "I don't care about how my spouse feels about it, I am going to do it." You get the picture. These words are normally said out of hurt or anger, but still, they are immensely powerful and often have a lasting effect. The words are a declaration of intent that is contrary to the purposes of God and will always be damaging. These strongholds are easily broken, though, when we repent and renounce the words that were spoken.

The Bible tells us how to destroy these strongholds and how to prevent them in the future.

For though we live in the world, we do not wage war as the

world does. *The weapons we fight with are not the weapons of the world. On the contrary, they have divine power to demolish strongholds. We demolish arguments and every pretension that sets itself up against the knowledge of God, and we take captive every thought to make it obedient to Christ,* (2 Corinthians 10:3-5).

If this applies to you then repeat this prayer aloud from your heart:

Father, I repent for (name the belief) that contradicts Your Word. Confirm in me the truth of Your Word on this subject. I repent of the beliefs that are contrary to Your nature I have gained through my life experiences that are not accurate. I repent for any words I spoke from my heart that were declarations against Your purposes. Forgive me for these sins. I declare that I will follow You in everything without exception in Jesus' name. Father, I thank You for Your healing mercy and grace. Amen.

If you said this prayer from your heart, God is already moving on your behalf. Look for Him in everything. You will see Him at work in your life, showing you revelation about Himself and, ultimately, who you are in Him.

People who were once involved in the occult may have offered their souls to the gods they served. They will have to renounce the occult from their heart before they can continue in the Lord. Those who have surrendered their will to these gods or made a blood covenant with them will have to renounce these acts and take steps we did not cover in this book. We strongly encourage you to see the elders in a Bible-believing Church for help with these strongholds. You will find freedom there. Remember that even with things like the occult, the damage done is a matter of the heart and not just a legal battle for dominion in the believer's life. Do not discount God's Grace. Rest assured, if your heart is surrendered to Jesus, then your soul is His.

We recommend that you do not take this fight on alone but encourage you to go to the elders of a Bible-believing Church and share your story. These elders have overcome many issues through the blood of Christ, and they will help you do the same.

We could author several books about this subject to do it justice, but we have covered the basics to help those dealing with these issues have a better understanding of the cause and effect of demonic forces.

Scripture References:

In order that Satan might not outwit us. For we are not unaware of his schemes.

(2 Corinthians 2:11)

The Lord directs the steps of the godly, He delights in every detail of their lives. Though they stumble, they will never fall, for the Lord holds them in His hand.

(Psalms 37:23)

Set your minds on the things above, not on earthly things.

(Colossians 3:2)

Truth About Deliverance and Strongholds

How you have fallen from heaven, O morning star, son of dawn! You have been cast down to the earth, you who once laid low the nations!

(Isaiah 14:12)

With whom will you compare me or count me equal?

(Isaiah 46:5)

Therefore, holy brother and sisters who share in the heavenly calling, fix your thoughts on Jesus.

(Hebrews 3:1)

And the devil, who deceived them, was thrown into the lake of burning sulfur, where the beast and the false prophet had been thrown. They will be tormented day and night for ever and ever.

(Revelation 20:10)

Then Jesus was led by the Spirit into the wilderness to be tempted by the devil.

(Matthew 4:1)

The evening meal was in progress, and the devil had already prompted Judas, the son of Simon Iscariot, to betray Jesus.

(John 13:2)

For we wanted to come to you certainly, I, Paul, did, again and again but Satan blocked our way.

(1 Thessalonians 2:18)

LIVING FULLY FREE

Keep your lives free from the love of money!
and be content with what you have, because God has said,
"Never will I leave you; never will I forsake you."
(Hebrews 13:5)

For my yoke is easy and my burden is light.
(Matthew 11:30)

And do not lead us into temptation but deliver us from the evil one.
(Matthew 6:13 NKJV)

The demons begged Jesus, "Send us among the pigs; allow us to go into them."
(Mark 5:12)

When Jesus rose early on the first day of the week, He appeared first to Mary Magdalene,
out of whom He had driven seven demons.
(Mark 16:9)

He called his twelve disciples to Him.
and gave them authority to drive out evil spirits and to heal every disease and sickness.
(Matthew 10:1)

Calling the Twelve to Him, he sent them out two by two and gave them authority over evil spirits.
(Mark 6:7)

Truth About Deliverance and Strongholds

At that very time Jesus cured many who had diseases, sicknesses, and evil spirits, and gave sight to many who were blind.

(Luke 7:21)

The Spirit clearly says that in latter times some will abandon faith and follow deceiving spirits and things taught by demons.

(1 Timothy 4:1)

But when the Pharisees heard this, they said, "It is only by Beelzebub, the prince of demons, this fellow drives out demons."

(Matthew 12:24)

I have given you authority to trample on snakes and scorpions and to overcome all the power of the enemy; nothing will harm you.

(Luke 10:19)

Like a fluttering sparrow or a darting swallow, an undeserved curse does not come to rest.

(Proverbs 26:2)

And when the demon was driven out, the man who had been mute spoke. The crowd was amazed and said, "Nothing like this has ever been seen in Israel."

(Matthew 9:33)

When Jesus saw that a crowd was running to the scene, he rebuked the evil spirit.

LIVING FULLY FREE

"You deaf and mute spirit," he said, "I command you, come out of him and never enter him again."

(Mark 9:25)

Jesus rebuked the demon, and it came out of the boy, and he was healed from that moment.

(Matthew 17:18)

The Spirit clearly says that in later times some will abandon faith and follow deceiving spirits and things taught by demons.

(1 Timothy 4:1)

And the two will become one flesh: So, they are no longer two, but one.

(Mark 10:8)

Flee from sexual immorality. All other sins a person commits are outside the body, but whoever sins sexually, sins against their own body. Do you not know that your bodies are temples of the Holy Spirit, who is in you, whom you have received from God? You are not our own; you were bought at a price. Therefore, honor God with your bodies.

(I Corinthians 6:18-20)

Later Jesus found him at the temple and said to him, "See, you are well again. Stop sinning or something worse may happen to you."

(John 5:14)

Moreover, demons came out of many people, shouting, "You are the Son of God!" But he rebuked them and would not allow them to speak, because they knew he was the Christ.

(Luke 4:41)

When evening came, many who were demon-possessed were brought to him, and he drove out the spirits with a word and healed all the sick.

(Matthew 8:16)

Jesus turned and said to Peter, "Get behind me, Satan! You are a stumbling block to me. you do not have in mind the things of God, but the things of men."

(Matthew 16:23)

And these signs will accompany those who believe: In My Name they will drive out demons; they will speak in new tongues.

(Mark 16:17)

CHAPTER 13

SINS OF THE FATHER

John was standing at the front of the church for prayer. He found himself reflecting on the events from earlier that week. He could not stop thinking about the words he had belted out to his eldest child. What he said was condemning and mean spirited, and the conversation was still echoing in John's head. He had come to realize that he had heard those words before. They had been spoken to John with the same intensity that he had repeated them, and the memory of that event still terrified him. He was able to remember almost every detail of the day, twenty-five years before, when he had first been on the receiving end of his father's harsh actions. He could even visualize right where he was standing when it happened.

John specifically remembered promising himself that day that if he ever had children, he would never speak to them the way his father had just spoken to him. He recalled saying aloud that, whatever happened, "he would never be like his father." However, while he was standing at the altar that day, John realized that not only was he like his father, but in some situations, he had acted even worse than his father had.

LIVING FULLY FREE

Through the years of their marriage, John and his wife had talked about certain ungodly traits or actions that John was dealing with. What his wife did not know was that almost all of these actions resembled how John's dad had acted when he was growing up. John knew the Word of God and he loved his wife and children very much, so these actions seemed to conflict with everything he knew was right. He had been trying for years to repent and change how he reacted to things, but he never seemed to gain victory. As John began to grow in the knowledge of the Lord and "police" his actions, there had been changes in his life. However, because the underlying root was not identified and removed, John was still struggling with his anger and was not sure why.

We prayed with John at the church that day and were able to share some truths of the Word with him. Then we led him through some simple prayers that brought an incredible change. Everyone in John's life noticed an immediate difference in him for the good. It has now been over three years since that time and John is still free. Now he is teaching others what he learned that day and how to apply it.

To get the understanding that brings healing, we need to start with the culprit, or the root, of John's condition: sin. It is no more complicated than that. The consequences of John's father's unrepentant sins are at work in John's life. This may be a strange concept to many Christians, but it is clearly stated in the Word. To understand what we are talking about, we need to look at a principle found in the Old Testament. The Bible tells us in Numbers 14:18, *The LORD is longsuffering and abundant in mercy, forgiving (people their) iniquity and transgression; but He by no means clears the guilty, visiting the iniquity of the fathers on the children to the third and fourth generation.* This same concept is found in Exodus 20:5, *...you shall not bow down to them nor serve them (idols). For I, the LORD your God, am a jealous God, visiting the iniquity of the fathers on the children to the third and fourth generations of those who hate Me.*

This is a hard concept for many of us to understand because most people have the thought that what we do only affects us. We tend to believe that how we act and what we do will only hurt or help *us*. This thinking gives us the false security or "license" to do what we want. But, in actuality, these beliefs are evidence of someone focused on self and attempting to justify their own selfish actions. Again, what we must begin to do is change/renew our thinking to what God says it should be. On this subject, we can see in the Word that God sees the end from the beginning, meaning that He can look over the totality of time and see the fruit of our decisions. Most of us have little or no consciousness of the lasting effect every one of our actions has on others.

Even fewer understand how these actions affect our children, even those who are yet to be born. This is especially true for those who are not God-conscious. If we could see the lasting "ripple" effect our choices have on others, most of us would immediately change our ungodly actions. Many of us did not have the benefit of instruction about these types of things during childhood, but this idea of our decisions making an impact on future generations can be found throughout scripture. If we are conscious of this, it greatly impacts how we relate to the people and world around us. We have the capacity to establish great blessings for future generations in our family, but unfortunately, we also have the capacity to establish a pattern of harm if we do not diligently care for the state of our hearts.

It is important to point out that God is not referring to judgment in either of the scriptures referenced above. What He is clearly stating is that the sins of the fathers can be carried down through the generations. This is not about judgment or punishment, but simply a principle we need to understand. He confirms that He does not bring judgment on the children for the sins of the fathers in Deuteronomy 24:16, *Fathers shall not be put to death for their children, nor children put to death for their fathers; each is to die for his own sin.*

This does not release us from our own individual accountability, so when our children walk outside the purposes of God, they will stand in judgment for their own actions. Thank God that even this situation has a solution. There is one certainty that is a never-changing fact found in 1 John 1:9, *If we confess our sins, he is faithful and just and will forgive us our sins and purify us from all unrighteousness.* It is not Gods' plan that any should perish, and He desires that we repent as confirmed in 2 Peter 3:9, *He is patient with you, not wanting anyone to perish, but everyone to come to repentance.*

God does not need to change His thinking to line up with ours; we need to change our thinking to understand His principles. The consequences of the sins of John's father were still active in John for two reasons. The first is that some of John's ungodly character came from the actions of his father and were the learned responses that John had acquired growing up. These ungodly characteristics were most likely learned by John's father from his dad, who probably learned them from his father and

Sins of the Father

so on. This is the sowing and reaping principle at work. John's father sowed ungodly things into John's life and John's son reaped the fruit of that seed. John was aware of the principles of sowing and reaping. He was changing as he grew in the knowledge of the Word of God, but he did not know how or where this process had started.

Some of this ungodly action was in John from the sins of his ancestors and he was simply unaware of it. It turns out that John's grandfather, whom he had never met, was very anti-Semitic. John's father was offended by his own father's actions towards the Jews and vowed not to follow in his footsteps, which he did not. Because Johns' father was ashamed of his fathers' actions, and because he did not share in his father's beliefs, John was never told about his grandfathers' ungodly trait. Ironically, John had adopted the same beliefs as his grandfather, even though he had not been taught these by his father.

Only now, years later as an adult, did John understand why he had been so easily drawn into this world of bitterness and anger. There were other areas of ungodly characteristics in which John was struggling. He did not understand why they were also issues in his own life. For example: Before John became a Christian he would go with his friend for a few beers. John was unable to stop drinking when his friends did and never understood why he had such a tough time with it. John later found out that both his grandfather and great-grandfather were alcoholics.

Now, although we have been using the illustration of John and his father, the consequences of the "sins of the fathers" are not just limited to the father's side of the family. John's Aunt had contracted AIDS from drug use, and as a result of her decisions,

John's cousin was born with AIDS and later died from it. The term "sins of the fathers" can easily be translated to "the sins of our parents," for as the scripture states: when we are married, "the two shall become one flesh." The husband and wife are then seen as "one." This text refers to heritage and family lines, or genealogy, not gender.

The answers to John's problems were quite simple when John grasped the principle of repenting not only for his actions, but for the sins of his fathers as well. The Bible tells of this path in Leviticus 26:40-42 NKJV, *But if they confess <u>their iniquity and the iniquity of their fathers, with their unfaithfulness</u> in which they were unfaithful to Me, and that they also have walked contrary to Me, and that I also have walked contrary to them and have brought them into the land of their enemies, if their uncircumcised hearts are humbled, and they accept their guilt- then I will remember My covenant with Jacob, and My covenant with Isaac and My covenant with Abraham I will remember; I will remember the land.*

This is not a matter of repenting for our forefathers' sins alone but is an issue of covenant faithfulness. Thankfully we do not have to repent for each and every sin they committed. How could we possibly know what they were anyway? Instead, we should repent on behalf of our forefather's unfaithfulness to God, which is the root of the iniquity. We can then make a declaration of renewed faith/faithfulness to the Lord, as well as a declaration of repentance. As evidenced in scripture, this declaration is not necessary if our fathers or mothers have honored their covenant with the Lord (1 Corinthians 7:14) and remained faithful to Him.

As we have already discussed, this was not the case with

John's father, mother, or his forefathers. They had been unfaithful towards God, and John needed to repent for his forefathers' unfaithfulness. It is important to point out that this is not an issue of sin or sins. Sin is just the symptom of that unfaithfulness. It is the consequences of that sin (symptom) that transverse the generations until someone repents for unfaithfulness. This also has nothing to do with the judgment your father, mother or forefathers will face on behalf of their own sins. As stated before, we are all accountable for our own decisions and actions before God.

The Bible tells us in 2 Corinthians 5:10, *For we must all appear before the judgment seat of Christ, that each one may receive what is due him for the things done while in the body, whether good or bad.* You cannot repent on anyone's behalf or ask Jesus to enter their hearts and then claim salvation for them. What you are doing is simply declaring a covenant with the Lord over your family line from this day forth for both you and your descendants. *But if serving the LORD seems undesirable to you, then choose for yourselves this day whom you will serve, whether the gods your ancestors served beyond the Euphrates, or the gods of the Amorites, in whose land you are living. But as for me and my household, we will serve the LORD.* (Joshua 24:15) Whatever might have existed in your family before now has been forever changed because of your covenant with Jesus Christ! *Therefore, if anyone is in Christ, he is a new creation, old things have passed away; behold, all things have become new,* (2 Cor. 5:17-18, NKJV).

Let us stop here and discuss a common point of misconception. Some of us have been taught that when we ask Jesus to be our Lord, it is personal (for us alone). What you are declaring to the Lord is that not only will *you* serve the Lord, but also that you will commit to raising your family, if you have one, to do the same (Ephesians 6:4). In accordance with the scriptures, we are to pass the instructions from the Lord to each new generation without exception (Psalms 78:3-6). We are not responsible for what the next generation does with what we teach them, but we <u>are</u> responsible to God to bring this instruction.

We all need to understand this: we do not just represent ourselves before the Lord, but because of this principle of generational blessing, we are going to be followed by many more believers because of our covenant with Him. This is where we choose to be different from our forefathers, in that we now state the unfaithfulness to God is over in our household and family line from this date forward. It is much more than just a statement of our own faith. We need to expand our thinking and our vision of who "we" are. We are not just "me, myself, and I" and need to stop seeing ourselves as such. If we are believers in Christ, we are now connected to the infinite "family" of God. We must start seeing ourselves in the light of His family line and not just through the lens of our own earthly family.

It is obvious that this transference of the consequences of sin is not a blessing but a curse. Because of that, this process is often referred to as a "generational curse." It is a fact that these "curses" can range from things like abject poverty and AIDS to any of the things listed in Deuteronomy 28:15-68. We use the terminology of "blessings and curses" because the Word of God is clear: if you follow a godly path then you will be "blessed," and if you choose other options, you will be "cursed."

As you read this chapter, have identified some behavior patterns or ways of thinking that you believe have roots in your family history? There is hope for healing! We are going to show you how to break the oppression of generational issues in your life. However, we must start by explaining some foundational truths about this process. These curses will not and cannot be broken by you or anyone else by simply repeating words or claiming, "it is broken." Only someone with a repentant heart who is under the "curse" can break his or her "generational curse." It is only reversed when the one who is the subject of this generational sin truly repents on behalf of both his and his father's unfaithfulness. It is not a matter of just words or actions but <u>is a matter of the heart.</u>

Some teach that they can make declarations that break the generational curses off the lives of others. This is dangerous teaching! This is not scriptural, and it is not possible. It would be a type of witchcraft. They can no more break the curses off someone else's life than they can speak or accept salvation on someone else's behalf. In addition, some teach that we need to renounce each individual sin of our fathers. Again, they are missing the point. Sin is just the symptom of unfaithfulness. God looks at the heart (1 Samuel 16:7, Acts 1:24). We only need to repent for their unfaithfulness towards God and not go through some lengthy list of their sins.

If we attempt to make this reversal of the curse a matter of words and actions rather than an issue of the heart, then we fall back under the law. God never intended anyone to be saved by the law, and those who want to reverse curses by following the law will have to live under it. You must understand that these ungodly fathers did not belong to Christ. Many of these people believed that God existed, and they tried to live right by doing the right thing. By their actions, these ungodly fathers were living under the law whether they accepted that fact or not.

It was in this state that the subject of our story, John, was born. Though he accepted Christ and no longer lived under the law, the consequences of John's father's actions were still "alive and well" and wreaking havoc in his life. Some believe that this could not have happened once John accepted Christ. However, many believers walk around with "things" alive in them. They do not know what the Truth is or how to apply it in their lives so that it can "work" for them. These people admit that though they may not have fallen prey to the same sins as their fathers, they have had to do battle with them in a way not common to other sins outside of their heritage. In other words, they may have had to struggle with temptation towards certain things such as alcohol, anger, or lust, as did their parents.

This whole concept is foreign to those who have little or no concern for their heritage. In The United States we are especially vulnerable because we have become a melting pot of many cultures and heritages. Many of the younger generations do not know their heritage nor do they seem to understand the value of it. It could also be said that part of this topic is the rise of a largely fatherless generation in our country, which contributes to a general sense of being disconnected from your family roots. This same problem is evidenced by the fact that many young people simply do not have an older family member to teach them.

Family history and genealogy used to be something that was especially important and was talked about extensively in families. But some of that tradition has been lost due to family

Sins of the Father

unit breakdowns or other circumstances. It used to be common to pass stories down from generation to generation as a way of remembering who we are and where we came from. There are some cultures where this is still important today and the tradition of instilling this sense of belonging to a family or "people" group larger than themselves continues. We would do well to learn some lessons from them about appreciating our heritage.

For those in the Bible, this tradition of sharing oral histories was a way to preserve their stories. Many people could not read or write, so the spoken word was the only way to share them. This allowed them to pass on the faith that they had in God from one generation to the other. They told the stories of what God had done for both them and their forefathers, which in turn encouraged and strengthened their children and their children's children. Those in the New Testament church, both Jew and Gentile, understood their heritage because of this custom. They made declarations of faith on behalf of themselves and their future heritage. They repented for their father's unfaithfulness and walked in the fruit of that repentance. We need to follow their example and do the same today.

If you believe there is a generational curse in your life, then repeat this prayer from your heart:

> *"Father, I take responsibility for my sins and the sins of my fathers with their unfaithfulness to You. I ask You to forgive me of these sins and separate them from me and place them on the cross of Christ. I declare from this day forth, my family and I will serve the Lord, in Jesus' name. I thank You, Father, for Your healing and Your blessings. Amen."*

There is another issue in John's life that may be common to some of us. John decided in his heart that he would never be like his dad. John even verbalized this decision on several occasions to his friends and other members of his family. This set in motion another principle of God's kingdom that was the reason for many of John's struggles. John pronounced his judgment of his parents both in his heart and with his mouth.

The Bible tells us that we must honor our mother and father. It is not a matter of the "law" but is a principle of the Kingdom. This is stated multiple times in the Bible and found in both the Old and New Covenant. The theme of this teaching is found in Ephesians 6:2-3, *Honor your father and mother which is the first commandment with a promise…that it may go well with you and that you may enjoy long life on the earth.* This principle of the Kingdom exists whether we are in denial of it or not, and it will not be affected by our choice to acknowledge it or not.

The importance of honoring mothers and fathers has been largely lost in our culture today; however, this was not always the case. The Bible lays out the severe penalties for those who broke this commandment, as stated by Jesus when he was quoting the commands of the law in Matthew 15:4, *For God said, "Honor your father and mother" and anyone who curses his father or mother must be put to death.*

Though these same punishments are not in effect today, when we dishonor our parents, we do open the doors for calamity in our own lives. Participating in this dishonor can, at best, cause us to fall into the very judgment we pronounced on our parents. Some parents have made it hard to honor them when your judgment is based on what they do. However, as we have stated many times before: if we have committed our lives to Jesus, we have a responsibility to do what is right no matter what someone else does. It is most important that, at the very least, we do not dishonor them, striving to honor that which we can.

The attitude of our heart and the words of our mouth need to line up with the honor that is due to them simply because they are our parents. We need to purpose not to dishonor even those who are not honorable. If we set our hearts against either or both of our parents, then we have opened ourselves up to judgment. In a world where half of marriages end in divorce, honoring both parents requires our complete attention. The issue is not a matter of our ability to judge right from wrong in our parents, calling sin, sin. We are told to do that in the Word. However, judging the motives and intent of their heart is wrong.

God gave you your parents and He is aware of the conditions into which you were born. Children under the age of accountability (around ages 12-13) may dishonor their parents before they have an understanding of God's purposes. It is the parent's responsibility to teach the children to honor them. However, after the age of accountability, children are responsible to God for honoring their parents. Those who choose not to honor them have many significant issues that seem to dissipate once they repent and begin honoring their parents. This includes the grandparents and in-laws if you are married.

The Bible encourages us to judge actions according to the Word of God. However, it cautions us not to judge the hearts of those who commit these actions, or we too will fall into judgment. This is clear in Matthew 7:1-2 which says, *Do not judge, or you too will be judged. For in the same way, you judge others, you will be judged, and with the measure you use, it will be measured to you.*

The only way you can judge someone else is to set yourself up as a judge over them. Some take judgment to the next level and not only judge others but also rally other people to believe the same way they do about the people they judge. We start telling others about the fault we find in an individual or group in hopes that they will join us in our judgment. In sharing the factual reasons for our judgment with others, we establish strongholds against that person or group. A stronghold is a fortified belief system.

Some who spread judgment do not even have the facts. They are just perpetuating rumors and have become another link in an ungodly gossip chain. Whether what people are judged for is the truth or not, is not the issue. The issue is the heart from which judgment was given. If it was one of love for the people, then I need to remind you that love always protects and love keeps no records of wrongs (1 Corinthians 13:5).

Judgment is what John did when he declared in his heart he would not be like his father. Given the circumstances, this statement was understandable. However, it was the attitude of John's heart that made it an ungodly judgment. Because of his heart of dishonor and judgment, John set the stage for the negative effects of this principle to become manifest in his own life. By his own belief and subsequent actions, he set in motion a series of events that were all destined to manifest in John that which he judged in others. This would continue until John repented and allowed his heart to be changed. The Bible talks of this in Romans 2:1-2, *You, therefore, have no excuse, you who pass judgment on someone else, for at whatever point you judge the other, you are condemning yourself, because you who pass judgment do the same thing.* It is an attitude of the heart that needs to change.

This does not mean that we are not to correct a brother or sister in the Lord who is in error or sin. The Bible encourages us to do this in Matthew 18:15-16, *If your brother sins against you, go and show him his fault, just between the two of you. if he listens to you, you have won your brother over. But if he will not listen, take one or two others along, so that 'every matter may be established by the testimony of two or three witnesses.* Before you go, ensure that your motive is for their well-being and not for your own justice. Do everything in love (1 Corinthians 16:14).

The Bible tells us in 1 Corinthians 4:5, *Therefore judge nothing before the appointed time, wait till the Lord comes. He will bring to light what is hidden in darkness and will expose the motives of men's hearts.* At that time, each will receive his praise from God. If we have judgment in our heart, it will be exposed. It is not that Jesus will condemn us, but our own hearts will reflect the darkness of our judgment when in His presence. If this applies to you then repeat this prayer from your heart.

> *Father, I repent for dishonoring my parents. I repent for every word spoken against them in disrespect. I also repent for the judgement and negative attitudes of the heart toward my parents. I ask You to forgive me for these sins and declare that I will honor them from this day forth in Jesus' Name. Father, I thank you for my parents and ask You to bless them, in the name of Jesus. Amen.*

LIVING FULLY FREE

Scripture References:

For the unbelieving husband has been sanctified through his wife, and the unbelieving wife has been sanctified through her believing husband. Otherwise, your children would be unclean, but as it is, they are holy.

(1 Corinthians 7:14)

Fathers do not exasperate your children; instead, bring them up in the training and instruction of the Lord.

(Ephesians 6:4)

What we have heard and known, what our fathers have told us. We will not hide them from their children; we will tell the next generation the praiseworthy deeds of the LORD, his power, and the wonders he has done. He decreed statutes for Jacob and established the law in Israel, which he commanded our forefathers to teach their children.

(Psalms 78:3-6)

But the LORD said to Samuel, "Do not consider his appearance or his height, for I have rejected him. The LORD does not look at the things man looks at. Man looks at the outward appearance, but the LORD looks at the heart."

(1 Samuel 16:7)

Then they prayed, "Lord, you know everyone's heart. Show us which of these two you have chosen."

(Acts 1:24)

It is not rude, it is not self-seeking, it is not easily angered; it keeps no record of wrongs.

(1 Corinthians 13:5)

Do everything in love.

(1 Corinthians 16:14)

And now these three remain: faith, hope, and love. But the greatest of these is love.

(1 Corinthians 13:13)

CHAPTER 14

TRUTH ABOUT SALVATION

A common theme that Christian churches can agree on is that everyone should accept salvation and make Jesus their Lord. However, it is amazing what some people believe and teach about how to receive the precious gift of salvation. This misunderstanding is why some people are confused about it or may declare they do not need it.

There are a thousand reasons you could come up with to not pursue salvation. Every one of them is from your mind's reasoning and many are for purely selfish reasons. A lot of people look at those that proclaim to be a Christian and because they see ungodly behavior, they have the same attitude that Gandhi had when he stated, "I would become a Christian, if it were not for the Christians." What a sad statement. It is not our intention to contradict any reasoning you have about why you would not want to receive salvation. If we did, another idea could just as easily take its place. We could present more Scriptures that would paint a picture of Jesus, what He did for you, why He did it, and what your life would be without it. But we believe, since you're reading this book, you already know enough to pursue salvation.

But let's just clarify something: Salvation is not from our own reasoning, but is born in the heart, our own soul.

I could tell you many stories from my years as a pastor when I was at the bedside of people that were passing from this life. It was evident which ones had a relationship with Jesus and which ones did not. Lets just say that those who had rejected the gift of salvation so graciously offered to all of us, chose to live their life as a slave to the kingdom of this world, only to die with nothing. We could paint a picture of Hell, and that would most likely elicit a response on your part, but then your motivation would be out of fear. Fear can motivate you not to do something wrong, but it is seldom a motivator to do what is right. This is <u>not</u> how Jesus wants you to begin your relationship with Him. Instead, we want to tell you the truth about salvation.

Salvation is not a prayer, it is a relationship journey with Jesus Christ into eternity

Salvation is not a prayer, a commitment to a church or denomination, or even agreement with a belief system, no matter how noble. It is a journey with Jesus Christ into eternity. It is initiated from the heart of God to your heart to be in a relationship with Him and that is where it will remain: in your heart. It requires a decision of your will to surrender both who you currently have become and who you planned to become in exchange for the original blueprint of God for your life. God's Spirit then inhabits your very being and becomes the mentor of your yielded heart (2 Corinthians 1:22, Roman 8:14). It is not bondage to a new belief system, but freedom itself.

Your surrender and His presence are confirmed in a covenant between you and God, a New Covenant. Everything about your being and your purpose is reborn, and because of that, it is sometimes referred to as being born-again (John 3:3). Salvation is a lifestyle that starts the day you surrender your heart to Jesus and continues daily as your soul matures. It is complete with the redemption of your spirit and soul into eternity with Jesus.

The freedom to ask God into your heart, was purchased for you by the blood of Jesus over two thousand years ago. The son of God chose to die on a cross, agreeing to take the punishment for the ungodly things that are in our hearts (sin) that is not compatible with the presence of God (Hebrews 10:19). If it were not for His sacrifice and without these ungodly things removed, (washed away) if God were to come into our hearts, His very presence would be more than our souls could bear, and we would die.

Jesus laid down His life to redeem us from sin and to reconcile us, once again, to the Father. Salvation not only restores us into the right relationship with Him, but it puts us back on the path that we were designed and created for. It brings *new life*. Without God in our hearts, we would not be able to complete our original purpose, and we would quickly resort to following Him another way. Our flesh would prefer a clear set of rules. Such as a specific list of written dos and don'ts like the Israelites had in the Old Testament (the written law) (Acts 13:38,39). But what a laborious chore. When we accept Jesus' salvation, we also benefit from the fact that His death and resurrection set us free from the curse of being subject to those Old Testament laws.

LIVING FULLY FREE

Salvation, which is an exchange between us and our Savior (our old life for His new life), brings a New Covenant of freedom. Jesus paid the price and fulfilled the requirements of the law as an atonement for our sins. This is both a mystery and a miracle.

Since Jesus took the ungodly things from your heart, He is the mediator of this New Covenant (Hebrews 9:15) and He is the one we call on for salvation (Romans 10:13). Salvation is an eternal experience with treasures beyond our understanding. We highly recommend it. The Bible speaks of this in 1 Corinthians 2:9, *But as it is written, "Eye has not seen, nor ear heard, nor have entered into the heart of man the things which God has prepared for those who love Him"* (NKJV).

How do we receive salvation? We simply call upon Jesus, surrender ourselves and hearts totally to God, ask for forgiveness of our sins, and then receive the new life that He promised us. Your old life will be over, and a new life will begin. When we come to Him with a repentant heart, He said He would take out our old hardened heart of stone and replace it with a new heart of flesh! (Ezek 36:26) At that point we have become a new creation in Christ and a part of the Kingdom of Heaven.

If you have decided to give your life to the Lord, then repeat this prayer from your heart:

> *"Father, I (state your full Christian name) surrender 100% of my heart to You from this day forth. I believe Jesus is Lord. Jesus, I choose to walk away from my old life, and I offer to You those things (sins) that would keep my heart from being fully occupied by your Spirit. I ask You to forgive me for living contrary to Your purposes and forgive me for the sins I*

have committed. I will live for You from this day forth. Jesus, You will be Lord of my Life. As my first act of surrender, I choose to forgive anyone who has sinned against me while I was living contrary to You and I ask You to bless them, in Jesus' name. Father, I thank You for Your salvation. Amen."

If you said this prayer from your heart, you have just entered into a Covenant with God and you are now responsible to Him as He directs you. He did not take control of your heart; you still have control of that. He will lead you from your heart when you yield to His Spirit. So, start following the promptings from your heart and not your head. Do not confuse your heart with your feelings; we are not to be led by our emotions either. God's Spirit will guide you as you walk with Him, and you are in for the adventure of a lifetime.

There are things we suggest you do to maintain your relationship with Him. For two people to understand each other, they must communicate. Talk with God. Take the time to talk with Him on a regular basis and be willing to listen to His reply in your heart. It is called prayer, and you should do it all the time.

Secondly, get to know Him. One of the best ways to do this is to read the Bible, or at least listen to it on a streaming device. Everything about His character and nature is in there. You will find Him much easier to understand the more you know about His characteristics. He is quite amazing, and His wonders never cease. If you have never read it before, may we suggest that you start with the book of John in the New Testament. And even if you have read it before, start again! Now that He is in your heart, the Bible comes alive in ways unimaginable, as you are now seeing things through different eyes.

LIVING FULLY FREE

You are now part of a new family: the family of God. Take the time to find a good church or home group that teaches the Word of God and attend as often as possible. Connect and fellowship with other believers so that you can encourage and strengthen one another. He is now in your heart and will lead you to a church that feels like home, but it may not happen if you do not look.

Finally, we encourage you to follow in Jesus footsteps by participating in a water baptism. (Acts 2:38, Rom 6:3) Baptism is a public declaration of faith that symbolizes the washing away of the old (buried with Jesus in His death) and the birth of your new life (being resurrected back to life) with Jesus. It may sound like a strange act, but those who have done it testify that it empowered their hearts, and they were stronger because of it.

Let us say personally that we know the purposes of God are great in your life. During this journey, you will enrich the lives of those you meet, and you will experience a love you have never known before. Welcome, you are family!

Scripture References:

Set his seal of ownership on us and put his Spirit in our hearts as a deposit, guaranteeing what is to come.
(2 Corinthians 1:22)

Because those who are led by the Spirit of God are sons of God.
(Romans 8:14)

Truth About Salvation

In reply Jesus declared, "I tell you the truth, no one can see the kingdom of God unless he is born again."

(John 3:3)

Therefore, brothers and sisters, since we have confidence to enter the Most Holy Place by the blood of Jesus

(Hebrews 10:19)

"Therefore, my brothers, I want you to know that through Jesus the forgiveness of sins is proclaimed to you. Through him everyone who believes is justified from everything you could not be
justified from, by the law of Moses."

(Acts 13:38-39)

For this reason, Christ is the mediator of a new covenant, that those who are called may receive the promised eternal inheritance—now that he has died as a ransom to set them free from the sins committed under the first covenant.

(Hebrews 9:15)

For, "Everyone who calls on the name of the Lord will be saved."

(Romans 10:13)

And I will give you a new heart and I will put a new spirit in you. I will take out your stony, stubborn heart and give you a tender, responsive heart.

(Ezek 36:26)

LIVING FULLY FREE

Peter replied, *"Each of you must repent of your sins and turn to God, and be baptized in the name of Jesus Christ for the forgiveness of our sins. Then you will receive the gift of the Holy Spirit."*

(Acts 2:38)

Or have you forgotten that when we were joined with Christ Jesus in baptism, we joined him in his death?

(Rom 6:3)

CHAPTER 15

ADDICTIONS & OTHER ISSUES OF THE HEART

This section is devoted to dealing with some problems that are common to our heart but have not been addressed completely in the previous chapters. They include Anorexia and Bulimia, addiction to alcohol, drugs and cigarettes, abortion, chronic anger, and sexual abuse. Healing for these things is simple when you deal with the root cause. Even if these issues do not affect you, knowing what brings healing in these areas will empower you when ministering to others. God sets patterns in His Word, and we have followed them. Do not make ministry in these or any areas a methodology or a science, but instead be led by the Holy Spirit in everything. We have seen God move supernaturally in each of these areas. Do not limit God in any way.

There are many other issues of the heart not directly addressed in detail in this book. However, the <u>outline</u> for healing for most issues of the heart that are not addressed within the preceding chapters of this book can be found in the few issues listed below. Seek God for all answers. Philippians 4:19 *But my God shall supply all your needs according to his riches in glory by Christ Jesus. In whose name you are healed.*

ANOREXIA AND BULIMIA

Sandra had been in recovery from ongoing bouts with Anorexia ever since she was sixteen. Now at 22, she was still battling with her eating disorder. Her mom, who loved her deeply, had enrolled her in many different programs but the problem always seemed to return. Sandra was quick to answer all your questions with a classic textbook response. She knew more about the illness than some professionals did. What she did not know was the root cause of her illness. After a brief time of ministry, we were able to recognize what appeared to be a harmless event that had happened in her life. However, in reality, this was very traumatic for Sandra. We presented her with the truth about the choices she had made concerning that event; she repented for them and has been free for many years now. Sandra now helps other girls with the same problem.

Anorexia and Bulimia are eating disorders that have their root in rebellion and its aftermath. The scripture says: *Some became fools through their rebellious ways and suffered affliction because of their iniquities. They loathed all food and drew near the gates of death* (Psalm 107:17-18). Others in the ministry tell us it is caused by many reasons from self-hatred to demons. These "other causes" do exist in some of these people but are just the aftermath, or symptoms of a rebellious heart.

What can be very confusing is that these people (usually young girls from the age of 12 to 18) have the same problems that plague most teenagers and young adults. It is easy to credit any one of these other problems as being the cause. However, they are not. These girls are sweet and show love to others, but their plan is often contrary to God's perfect plan for their life. A person's persona and their heart's condition can be two different things.

We have found that the symptoms of Anorexia and Bulimia start anywhere from a few months to years after these people pass the age of accountability (12-14). It is at this age they become responsible to God for their actions. They may rebel right after a dramatic event that takes place in their lives, and you can no longer live with themselves as they are. Because of this event they determine in their heart to live contrary to what they know is the truth. This event may have even happened before the age of accountability, but the manifestations of the symptoms do not show up until later.

Their decision to rebel in their heart is followed by words or declarations that are rebellious in nature, sometimes slandering one or both parents and others in authority. Healing comes when they recognize the rebellion, repent for their actions, and renounce their ungodly words. Those who will not easily admit they rebelled in their heart will often admit to being self-seeking or living for themselves. Even though they may appear concerned about others, they are rarely worried about the consequences of their actions. Once they repent for rebellion, they may have to repent for any subsequent sins that were born from the rebellious heart.

In addition, guilt and shame may be the result of these problems and will hinder the healing process as a stronghold. The way to get free of this is to take it to a third party. When we are ministering to someone like this, we ask him or her to identify with someone they loved or a good friend about their age. We then ask them if this other person went through what they have gone through and repented for it, should they feel guilty and ashamed of it? They all answer with a resounding, "No." Then we ask, if their loved one felt the shame or guilt they were feeling now after they got free, would they be believing the truth about themselves or a lie? They all respond with "a lie." We then ask, "Are you believing the truth or a lie when you carry guilt and shame after you have repented?" They see the truth and respond with, "A lie." Sometimes have them repeat aloud, "I believed a lie," or "It was a lie," many times until the truth of that statement sinks into their heart. You can see it happen before your eyes. Freedom is that easy. If this applies to you then repeat this prayer from your heart:

> *Father, I repent for the sin of rebellion. Forgive me this sin and put it on the cross of Jesus Christ. I renounce the words I said in rebellion. I repent for dishonoring my mother and father and I will honor them from this day forth. I repent for the sins I have committed because of my self-seeking heart in Jesus' name. Father, thank You for healing my heart and body. Amen.*

SEXUAL ABUSE

As head of the prayer team, Jackie had ministered to most of the women in the church at some time or another. She was well respected and dearly loved. What no one knew was that Jackie had a secret she had been carrying her whole life. Jackie was sexually abused from the time she was eleven years of age until she was sixteen. At that point, she finally found the courage to fight back and refuse the relatives who had abused her.

Because of the years of abuse, she had a tough time valuing

her own self-worth. She experienced problems in her relationships with men because of the abuse. As a Christian, she was able to forgive those who hurt her. However, she always felt that something was wrong with her, or this would not have happened. We led Jackie into prayer and showed her some Truths in the Word that broke a stronghold under which she had been living. She has been free ever since. She is now ministering to other women who have been abused.

The number of people who come for ministry because of scars from sexual abuse is overwhelming. We encounter so many people with this problem. Like Jackie, these people suffer many other complications that come from the effects of the abuse. They include little or no self-worth, fear, anger, bitterness, depression and even rage, just to name a few. Some have lost their childhood and may be emotionally stalled in childish behavior or, on the contrary, may act more mature than their years. Either way, their damaged life needs God's healing touch.

It is easy for you to receive healing. First, you need to forgive those who abused you. Chapter 5 gives an in-depth explanation on forgiveness. What they did to you was sin. You will not be forgiving what they <u>did</u> but will be forgiving <u>them</u>. They do not deserve forgiveness, but this is not about them. Forgiving them will set you free, not them. Take your time with this process and when you are ready, the prayer for forgiveness is below. Forgiveness always brings healing, however, there is more to be done.

Father, I choose to forgive (name/s of person who abused you). What they did to me was sin. Take this sin from them, put it on the cross of Jesus Christ, and separate it from them.

On the Day of Judgment, I will hold no accusation against them. Even now, they are free. Father, have mercy on them and bless them, in Jesus' Name. Thank You for Your love and Your healing, amen."

Next, we need to deal with the stronghold built in your mind. You will know it as the belief that "You were somehow responsible" for what happened to you or even that it was "Your fault." Or you may know the stronghold as the constant thought that "Something is wrong with you," or "you are somehow bad," "you must be awful, or it would not have happened to you." Jackie believed all of these. To someone who has not been abused, it is easy to understand that a child is not responsible and is not bad. However, to the abused, this way of thinking is foreign. No one going through this struggle thinks of these beliefs as strongholds, but that is exactly what they are. They strongly stand in opposition to the truth and hold you to a lie.

This lie becomes the stronghold. Even if I were standing face to face and we told you that you were not responsible or that there is nothing wrong with you, you would react the way most do, in disbelief. So how can you get free of these strongholds? It will happen naturally and effortlessly when you see the truth. It will require a technique used in the Bible. Nathan the prophet went to King David to confront him about David's adultery and conspiracy to commit murder. David was unable to see it for himself, so Nathan told David a story involving someone else, and David's eyes were open. That is what we are going to do.

Think of someone you know who is the same sex and age as you were when you were first abused. It could be a relative, neighbor or a child at church. Think of this person and answer this question:

What could this child do to deserve the same abuse that happened to you? Think about this for a moment. Just what could they do? Is there anything else? Are you sure? The answer is, of course, "nothing."

Take this a step further and say that the child you are thinking of is now your age. They, too, believe they were responsible for the abuse. They believe that something was wrong with them that somehow caused it, or it would never have happened. Would this child believe the truth, or would they be believing a lie? Are you sure they would be believing a lie?

We agree with you. They would indeed be believing a lie, and so are you. You are both in the same trap. Do not be afraid, getting free is easy. What we want you to do is repeat aloud, "It is a lie," "I am not (whatever applies) "responsible" or "bad," "'That is a lie." It is imperative that you keep repeating this over and over out loud until you realize the truth of it. One time is never enough. At first, it might seem awkward or even difficult to say and you may not feel any different. However, do not stop! Speaking the "truth" breaks strongholds.

As you continue to repeat this simple truth, it will completely displace the lies. You may physically feel lighter when you are able to see the truth of it. Some people begin to cry or laugh as they are released from the bond of deception that has held them captive for so long. They feel the sense of freedom and joy flooding their heart. Do not give up. Keep saying it aloud until it sinks in. You will know when to stop. Freedom is just on the other side of this. It really is easy.

Many other problems are born from this abuse, such as fear of the ones who hurt you, to an inability to trust and love people of the same sex that abused you. These are easily corrected after the stronghold is broken. They are all addressed in other parts of this book, and we encourage you to visit them, as necessary.

ADDICTION TO ALCOHOL AND DRUGS

Addiction to alcohol and drugs plague most of the modern world. Unfortunately, addiction to these chemicals has affected the church as well. Everyone knows at least one person or many people who are addicted to one or many of these chemicals. What we do not know is how many people in the church are secretly battling with substance abuse. They may be mastering it for a moment while fighting daily to stay on top of their addiction. There are many good programs helping people with their addictions and we are thankful for all of them. If we mention anything that contradicts them, keep in mind that we are supportive and thankful to God for the people who get free through them. Even if we have different beliefs about how to get and remain free. We agree with all of them that accountability to others is necessary when dealing with any sin. However, we do not promote programs that exchange one bondage (addiction) for a lesser one (lifetime in a program). However, if you are currently involved in a group where you are safe to express your heart and have accountability, stay until you know that you know you are free.

Most chemically dependent people did not start out with the plan of becoming addicted. Some were experimenting with something they knew had the potential to hurt them and later it did. Others were hurting inside or physically in pain and could no longer live with themselves in this condition and went the way of drugs (prescription or illegal) or alcohol to mask the pain they were feeling. At some unknown time, the addiction became as big if not bigger than the problem they started with. Eventually the addiction itself becomes the overshadowing problem. After that happens, the character of the one addicted deteriorates rapidly and greatly. The addiction becomes entangled with deceit, selfishness, and desperation to keep the addiction going while the character of the one addicted disintegrates, even if the outward appearance changes little.

The initial root cause of addiction (the inability to live with oneself) can seem insignificant compared to all the other problems that arose because of the addiction and the eventual need to support it. These other problems are woven into one web that has become a trap. By this time, the deception is complete, and everyone knows how deeply he or she is addicted except the one caught on the web. Their problem, many claim, is their own and they have no real comprehension of their effect on others. Unless God moves miraculously in their lives, and we have seen it happen often, intervention and subsequent recovery programs are the only hope for these people.

However, there are people who have not reached this point of hopelessness and are not yet looking for freedom from their battle. When they finally want to be free, it is easy when the root cause is exposed, and the people renounce the addiction. Most people who know they are addicted have taken ownership of their addiction and it is what helps keep them in this state. They have made "their addiction" part of their identity and that is a lie. Most will tell you that their addiction is different from someone else's. This belief is part of the trap. It is a stronghold.

The initial cause of addictions is rebellion. Surprisingly, most people battling addictions know this in their heart and it is not hard to bring them to this understanding. To break ownership of "my addiction" and the belief (stronghold) that their addiction is somehow different, we have them replace the word "addiction" with "rebellion" and then call it what it truly is, "my rebellion." We ask them to tell us how their rebellion is different from others. They cannot. They then understand their addiction is not different from others and that they have been taking ownership of a lie. It takes the power away from the stronghold.

Once they have understanding they need to repent for their rebellion. They may then have to repent for the sins they have committed while under the influence or while driven to support the addiction. Most people have already said they are sorry for these subsequent sins, and some have even repented, but it is necessary to repeat this repentance from the heart. In addition, guilt and shame may have become a result of these problems as well and can hinder healing from taking place. The way to get free of this is to take it to a third party. We ask, "If someone you love or a good friend repented for a particular situation, should they feel guilty and ashamed of it every time they see you?"

They all said, "No."

We ask, "If they felt shameful and guilty after they were forgiven, would they believe the truth about themselves or a lie?"

They all respond, "A lie."

We then ask, "Then are you believing the truth or a lie when you carry guilt and shame after you have repented?" They then understand and respond, "It was a lie." I have them repeat "I believed a lie" several times until the truth of it sinks in.

Finally, there is a spirit, or spirits associated with addiction, and every spirit must leave. The door in which it entered (rebellion) has been dealt with and the spirit must be commanded to go. There may be a spirit for each substance to which they were addicted. In addition, other spirits may have entered because of the ungodly activities during the addiction. I strongly encourage anyone with these problems to share their heart with the elders of a Bible believing church. They will help you through this process.

If this applies to you then repeat this prayer aloud from your heart:

Father, I repent for my rebellion against You and all authority. It was a sin. Forgive me this sin, put it on the cross of Jesus Christ and separate it from me. I also repent for the other sins I committed because of this rebellion. Forgive me these sins and place them on the cross in Jesus' name. Father, I thank you for Your freedom. Amen.

It is then necessary to exercise your authority over the demons and repeat aloud, "I command (name of spirit) to leave me right now in Jesus' Name."

ADDICTION TO CIGARETTES

Elaine had been battling with cigarettes for over twenty years. She had been through many programs and had success for short periods of time. She was wearing a nicotine patch and chewing gum when we met her, and she proudly declared she had been free two whole months. She then described this freedom with its agony, cravings, and her nerves always on edge.

We shattered her delusion and let her know that under no circumstance did the experience she described resemble freedom in any way. Professionals in the medical field have said that getting free from cigarettes can be harder than any drug. This is surprising because we have seen so many people get free with such ease. We led Elaine through repentance and then she repeated a simple prayer. We saw her six months later and she said she had not even thought of a cigarette in months, much less had one. Instead of being drawn to others while they smoked, she was disgusted with the habit. She is now helping others get free.

No one started smoking believing it was the right thing to do. Everyone knows it is bad for your health and for those around you. Smoking is unique because most people who are addicted started smoking when they were young. Most people who started smoking did it out of rebellion and then confirmed it with a declaration of their anger or disgust with their family members or someone they loved.

Surprisingly, many of these people can remember the words they said the day they started smoking. "I do not care what my mother or father thinks. I am going to (fill in the blank) anyway. It is my life!" Or something like that. This addiction is not about cigarettes; it is about a heart that is in opposition to the truth of God. Those who made this declaration and decided to smoke have given over to their own desires and are now addicted. Some of these people have also had to overcome alcohol or drugs at some time in their life.

Getting free of this addiction is easy. It requires that the person struggling understand they rebelled and repent for it. They then must renounce the words they said in rebellion or in dishonor to their parents or both. This takes care of the door at which this spirit of rebellion entered and getting free is easy once the person then chooses to give up smoking. You then must command the spirit to leave.

Most people are surprised when they hear us say, "You can continue to smoke if you want to." You should see their faces in reaction to our comment! The people are usually confused and stand there with this look of total bewilderment on their face with their jaw dropped to the floor. The first time we did this, we were at the front of a church teaching healing, and you could feel the very air being sucked out of the room by the large gasp of everyone in the congregation.

Understand that once the person is free, the drive is gone and then they must choose not to smoke again. The chemical of nicotine is not the issue. The root issue is rebellion. Once you have dealt with the rebellion, God removes the dependence on the chemical and you are set free. If we told you not to pick up a cigarette again, you would be set up to fail as some have. You know you should not smoke; you must be willing to quit by your own free will, not commanded to do so.

After the addiction is broken, we still get back reports of some people who, by habit, still reach for a cigarette at the times they would normally have one, after eating, etc. They no longer have the desire to smoke but they do have the habit of reaching for one. With the addiction gone, this habit is easily overcome.

We have found that with some people, guilt and shame may have played a part as a stronghold in the addiction and that can hinder healing from taking place. The way to get free and break the stronghold, is to take it to a third party so that they can have perspective.

When people come to us, we ask them if someone they loved went through what they went through and repented for it, should they feel guilty and ashamed of it? They all respond with, "No." Then we ask if their loved one felt shameful and guilty after they got free, would they be believing the truth about themselves or a lie? They all respond with, "A lie." Then, we ask, "Then are you believing the truth or a lie when you carry guilt and shame after you have repented?" They finally understand and respond, "A lie." We have them repeat, "I believed a lie" several times until the truth of it sinks in. It really is this easy when people repent from their heart. If this applies to you then repeat this prayer aloud from your heart:

Father, I repent for my rebellious heart. I yield to Your will from this day forth. I repent for the words I spoke that were contrary to Your truth and I renounce them. I repent for any dishonor towards my mother or father. Forgive me these sins and put them on the cross in Jesus' Name. Father, I thank You for Your healing. Amen."

ABORTION

Beth was telling us about the many things that God had set her free from after she came to Christ. She suddenly lowered her voice and whispered that she once had an abortion. This caused us to whisper back, "Have you received ministry for this?" "Oh yes," she replied with her voice at a normal level again. "I am forgiven, and it is over." However, it was clear to us that it was not over as her whisper declared. Guilt and shame were all over her face and had kept her bound ever since it had happened. She had a stronghold that was robbing her of life.

People had told her not to feel guilty about it anymore, but their words were empty to her. Though she did not want to feel guilty, she did not know how to get free of the overwhelming feeling of guilt that covered her like a dirty wet blanket. We gave Beth some instruction and led her in a simple prayer and you could see the weight of it leave her shoulders. We have seen Beth since that time and she is dedicated to helping other women become free, just as she is.

Abortion not only destroys the baby's life, but it can wreak havoc on the mother's life as well. To have an abortion most women must distance themselves from the idea that they would be taking the life of their baby, or many could not live with themselves. They accomplish this by shutting down part of their heart.

Afterwards, they live in fear that the part of their heart they shut down will be too painful to ever deal with. Others do not feel like they deserve to be healed of such a crime. Some feel that they need to suffer a little longer before they should be free. Still others have a fear of ever having children again or believe that they do not deserve them. The women who do get pregnant again may live in fear wondering if something bad is going to happen to this baby because of their previous abortion. Of course, all these fears are lies. They rob the believer of life.

Healing is easy when you deal with the heart. Abortion is a sin. However, there can be many other factors involved, such

LIVING FULLY FREE

as unforgiveness towards those who pressured them to have an abortion, a spouse, boyfriend, or parents. They could have ungodly feelings towards the doctors or nurses who told them everything was going to be alright, but it was not. In addition, they may have to deal with lies that were told to keep it a secret. All the above will be complicated by guilt and shame.

Getting free from this sin is easy when you follow God's truths. First, repent for taking your baby's life. Secondly, forgive all of those who you feel pressured you or were the reason for you to get this abortion. You do not need to forgive yourself. You might need to read that sentence again. Accepting God's forgiveness will accomplish everything that you need for yourself. Now, repent for any lies that you told to keep it a secret. Finally, you will need to deal with the guilt and shame (stronghold) as described in the next paragraph.

We have found that guilt and shame are common side effects of abortion. The way to get free of this is to take it to a third party. We ask these women, "If someone you love went through an abortion and repented for it, should they feel guilty and ashamed of it every time they see you?" They all reply, "No."

We then ask, "If their loved one felt shame and guilt after they were forgiven, would that mean they were believing the truth about themselves or a lie?" They all respond with "A lie." We ask them, "Then are *you* believing the truth or a lie when you carry guilt and shame after you have repented?" They finally understand and respond with "A lie." We have them repeat "I believed a lie." several times until the truth of it sinks in. It really is this easy when people repent from their heart. If this applies to you then repeat this prayer aloud from your heart:

Father, I repent. Forgive me for the sin of abortion. Take this sin from me, put it on the cross of Jesus Christ, and separate it from me. I choose to forgive (name of those you hold accountable) for what they did. Place this sin on the cross. I will hold no accusation against them. Father, bless them. In addition, I repent for any lies or deceit to hide this sin from others. Forgive me for these sins in Jesus' name. Father, I thank You for Your healing and for setting me free. Amen.

CHRONIC ANGER

We have all gotten angry at one time or another. It is not about if we get angry, but why, and how we react when it happens. Anger, in and of itself, is not evil or wrong. The Bible includes scriptures where God gets angry. 1 Kings 11:9-10 says, *And the LORD was angry with Solomon, because his heart had turned away from the LORD."* However, when we get angry, we are cautioned to resolve it quickly. Ephesians 4:26-27 reminds us, *In your anger do not sin. Do not let the sun go down while you are still angry, and do not give the devil a foothold.*

Repeated anger, being angry all the time, or anger as a common response is a sign of a much bigger problem. James 1:19-20 says, *My dear brothers and sisters, take note of this: Everyone should be quick to listen, slow to speak and slow to become angry, because human anger does not produce the righteousness that God desires.*

People who are easily angered know that it is wrong. However, they may be unaware of the damage their recurring anger does to the relationships of people who receive their wrath. Those who receive ministry for their anger admit they do not like how they react, and they all say they want it to change. Almost as much as the ones to whom their anger is addressed.

Intimacy is often lacking in those who live in fear while walking on eggshells around the individuals who are easily angered. The one easily angered is also lacking intimacy in their own lives, whether they are aware of it or not. Those who are always easily angered may have never understood real intimacy to start with, so they feel little or no loss. In addition, we have met people who use anger as a shield against the vulnerability of intimacy.

Anger comes from expectations that do not get met.

Why do people get angry? Anger comes from expectations that do not get met. It is that simple.

People who are easily angered or are angry all the time will continue "reacting" until they are willing to change their thinking when stirred. How does one do that? To change their reaction, their thinking must change accordingly. When the urge to become angry hits, immediately change your thinking by asking yourself, "Is the expectation (not met) realistic for the circumstances?" If you are not fully aware of the circumstances (most of us are not) you will need to gain understanding by asking questions and obtaining knowledge instead of reacting. You can then honestly evaluate your reaction.

For some, anger can be repressed until it explodes unexpectedly. People who get upset/angry about issues and suppress their feelings for days, weeks, or even months can react in anger with an outcome unmerited to the event causing it. It may even be for reasons not related to the current circumstances. Some compromise themselves (for the sake of peace) for so long until they cannot live with themselves and react in anger. The freedom from anger for these people is the same. However, for each individual ongoing event that causes a reaction over time, understanding is needed. The same question needs to be answered throughout the days, weeks, or months. Are the expectations reasonable based on the circumstances? In these situations, questions about the circumstance should proceed any reaction to it. Questions start a conversation, assertions end them.

In another scenario, it is not uncommon for people to react in anger to circumstances based on how they believed the correct response should have been from the other(s) involved. We have all said it at one time or another. "I would never do that, or say that, or act in that manner." We expected them to respond as we would have based on our judgement. But these people are not us and certainly may not think like you at that moment. If you have been married for a while, most spouses have experienced this at one time or another. So, is your reaction realistic when you expect them to think and react like you? We use phrases like, "Any good or decent person would not have acted or reacted like you did," so we became angry. We used "our belief" of what would have been the right reaction as a basis for our anger towards others. They never stood a chance against your anger.

The feeling of anger can sometimes be confused with hurt. Hurt comes from loss and is associated with pain. Someone's action, or lack of it, angered you and you identified it as hurt.

Why is this important to resolve? Because the Bible tells us not to let the sun go down on our anger (deal with it quickly) and give the devil a foothold (Ephesians 4:26-27). If our "hurt" is really anger turned inward, should we not deal with it quickly? In addition, it is possible to become angry from hurt by thinking about what hurt you and replaying the experience over (and over) again in your head adding things you should have said or done at the time. Re-living the event in your thoughts can produce anger. Hurt often makes you feel vulnerable, while anger provides a sense of power and control. Neither one is healthy.

If someone throws a bucket of icy water on you and you become angry, you can accuse them of making you angry. However, the only thing the other person did was make you wet. You chose to get angry all by yourself. This may be a radical example, but you get the point. You are in control of your anger, no one else!

Is it right to expect an eight-year-old or twelve-year-old to act the same as an adult, and then become angry when they do not? As parents of four girls, we had to ask ourselves similar questions to this more often than we wish to admit. When we ask questions, the relationship with our children grows closer because of it. My girls can still recall the times in their young lives when their dad reacted in anger instead of inquiry.

Again, we all get angry at one time or another and sometimes for good reason (injustice). Anger and disappointment are not bad in themselves if the reaction is reasonable to the circumstances and dealt with accordingly. However, during those times, how we react and the words that we say display to others, if not ourselves, the condition of our heart. The truth as directed by the Word is to be slow to anger, manage your words, and forgive all.

If you have failed at any of these, freedom is available through this prayer.

Father, I have allowed anger to rule my judgement, and I have also gone to sleep on my anger. In addition, I have said words in my anger that should not have been said. I repent and will seek understanding before I react. In addition, I have judged others who were angry with me without cause. I choose to forgive them for this sin and the words that they said to me in anger. Father, in turn, I ask You to forgive me for my words and my actions committed in anger that did harm. Thank you, Father, for my forgiveness and freedom.

APPENDIX
List of Healing Prayers

Chapter 1
The Truth

Father, if there is anything in this book that You want me to have, then I ask You to open my eyes, ears and heart to hear and receive what You are saying to me. Give me the ability to look at my life honestly and the strength to make the changes that are needed so that I become who You created me to be and reflect who You are to others. Father, I thank you for the healing that is coming to my heart and for fulfillment in my own life. Amen.

Chapter 2
A New Beginning

Father, I am afraid the things in my heart will not change and the conditions in my life will continue as they are or even get worse. I have tried everything I know to do and have not found lasting answers. I am willing to give You all my fears and concerns and I lay them down at Your Altar.

Father, I ask You to help open my heart to hear any truths You have for me or to correct any false beliefs. I am willing to change my direction where You show me a truer path from Your Word.

I ask You to give me Your peace and show me Your love. Father, I thank You for what You are going to do in me and in others through me, in Jesus' name. Amen.

Chapter 3
Preparing the Heart

Father, I confess the fruit of my life is not what it could be and that my thinking needs to change. I also recognize by the words of my mouth that my heart needs to change. I do not have consistent peace and that needs to change. Jesus, I am willing to open my heart to You and trust You to make the necessary changes within my heart. In Jesus' name, I pray. Father, I thank You, for the change that is coming to my life. Amen.

Chapter 4
Truth About Repentance

Father, I confess that I have hidden sin in my heart. You said in Your Word that You would forgive me if I confessed my sin and that You will cleanse me from all unrighteousness. Father, I take responsibility for this sin (name of the sin or sins), I repent and will not repeat these sins again. Father, I ask You to forgive me. and to place these sins on the cross of Jesus. I thank you for washing me clean and making me whole, in Jesus' name. Father, I thank You for Your forgiveness and Your love. Amen.

List of Healing Prayers

Chapter 5
Truth About Forgiveness

Father, what my ex-husband (his name) did to me was sin. Take this sin from him, put it on the cross of Jesus Christ, and separate it from him. I forgive my ex-husband and on the Day of Judgment when I am before Your throne, I will hold no accusation against him. Father, forgive my ex-husband (his name) and have mercy on him. Even now I release him of this sin. Father, bless him in Jesus' name, Amen.

Father, I choose to forgive (name of the person) for what they did. What they did to me is sin. Father, take this sin from them and put it on the cross of Jesus Christ and separate it from (name of the person) and on the Day of Judgment when I stand before Your throne, I will hold no accusation against them. Even now, they are free, in Jesus' Name. Father, I ask you to bless them. Amen.

Father, I repent for (name of the sin). Father, forgive me this sin, separate it from me and put it on the cross of Jesus Christ. Father, You said you would forgive me just as I forgave (name of the person you just forgave). Father, I thank You for forgiving me of this sin, in the name of Jesus. Amen.

Father, I have spoken many words against (name of person or persons) that should not have been said no matter how accurate they were. This is sin. I renounce the words I spoke against them and will not repeat them in the future. Father, forgive me for this sin.

Chapter 6
Who Has Your Heart?

Father, I confess that I have taken back part of my heart from my spouse. It is contrary to Your nature, and I ask You to forgive me for hardening my heart. I am willing to lay down my list of expectations at your altar. I will not make them requirements to meet before I give them my love and my heart. I (your full Christian name) choose to give (full Christian name of your spouse) 100% of my heart from this day forth, in Jesus' name. Father, I thank you for restoring my marriage and the intimacy in my relationship with my spouse. Amen.

Father, I confess that there is a lack of intimacy in our relationship, and I want that close intimacy with You again. I am willing to lay all the conditions that I was expecting You to meet at Your altar. I ask You to forgive me for allowing my heart to be hardened towards You. I (your full Christian name) choose to give 100% of my heart to You, Father, from this day forth, in Jesus' name. Father, I thank You for Your love that endures forever. Amen.

Father, I confess that I have not put all my trust and faith in You. I also have been (say the ones that apply) self-serving, selfish, self-centered, greedy, trusting in myself and what I can produce. I have trusted in my wealth, my income, or have been trusting in the things of this world instead of You. That is idolatry and I repent in Jesus' name. Father, forgive me for this sin. I give You all my heart and will serve You alone from this day

List of Healing Prayers

forth in Jesus' name. Father, I thank You for your forgiveness and Your love. Amen.

Father, I have been carrying the burdens of my circumstances and relationships. I ask You to forgive me for disobedience by worrying and not trusting in You. I now choose to lay those things I cannot change at Your altar. Father, I lay my spouse at Your altar. I lay my children at Your altar. I lay my job and my finances at Your altar. I lay (the circumstances you cannot change) at Your altar. You are my supply, and You alone can move in my circumstances. I give these to You and trust you with them in Jesus' name. Father, I thank You for caring for me. Amen.

Chapter 7
Truths of the Kingdom

Father, I have allowed doubt and unbelief to influence my life, and I repent for it now. Doubt and unbelief are not of You, and I refuse to follow them any longer. I will put my faith in You and Your Word, and I will follow Your instructions alone. Father, I have allowed hopelessness into my life by not using the love and faith You have given me. I repent. I will apply them in this situation and every other one from this day on. Finally, Father, I have not loved my neighbors as much as myself and I repent. I will love them as You direct me to do. Father, this is sin, and I ask you to forgive me this sin. I ask that you reveal to me Your love for them, in Jesus' name. Thank you, Father! Amen.

Chapter 8
The Trials of Life

Father, I have not considered it pure joy when I have gone through various trials and have even become angry and frustrated with You through them. I repent for any words I said such as I would never trust, never love, never give my heart again or never (fill in the blank). Father, I have made the people on the other side of this trial the enemy. This is sin. I repent and ask for Your Heart towards them.

Father, I have given the devil credit for this trial as if You were not the author and perfecter of my faith. I repent and refuse to even mention His name.

Father, I repent for these words and ask you to Forgive me for them. I will put my trust in You through this trial. I will give You thanks in everything from this day forth, in Jesus' name. Father, I thank You that You said You will never leave me or forsake me and that You will lead me to maturity in You. Amen.

Chapter 9
The Power of Words

Father, Your Word tells me to say things that edify, to build up, that correct in love, or confirm. Words of condemnation, lies, slander, and gossip or accusation are not of You. People have said words for and against me that were sin. I choose to forgive them for this sin and release them from it. Father, bless them in Jesus' Name.

I have said words about (<u>name of person you spoke badly about</u>) that did not edify, and did not correct, and did not confirm. I have allowed judgment and condemnation in my heart towards others. They are sin and I choose to repent. Forgive me for this sin. I will only say words that bless (<u>name of person you spoke badly about</u>) from this day forth. I take responsibility for those words and renounce them in the name of Jesus. Father, I thank You for your healing and forgiveness. Amen.

Chapter 10
<u>The Power of Thoughts</u>

Father, I have not taken the time to diligently seek to know who you are. Because of that, I have believed things that are not your truths. Forgive me for empowering the lies of the enemy. I ask you to expose any beliefs that are not of you. Lord, I have not taken authority over my mind and thoughts as you commanded me to. Father, I repent, and I thank you for a new beginning. Lord, I ask you to reveal yourself to me. To open my eyes to see you for who you are in Jesus' Name, Amen!

Chapter 11
<u>Truth About Covenants</u>

Father, I renounce the ungodly covenant I made when I participated in sexual intercourse with (name of the person). I repent and I will not continue in it. It was a sin. Place this sin on the cross, separate it from me, and forgive me for it, in Jesus' name. Thank you, Father, that this covenant is dissolved. Amen.

Chapter 12
Truth About Strongholds & Deliverance

Father, I repent for giving Satan glory. This is a sin, and I ask you to forgive me for it. I will no longer give him credit for anything, but will always give thanks to You, in Jesus' name. Father, I thank You for restoring me in every area of my life. Amen.

Deliverance

Father, I renounce my dealings with any ungodly things, and I set my heart on you alone. I repent of (name the sin) that I have committed that opened the door to demonic activity. Forgive me for this sin. I refuse to share my body with any ungodly thing in Jesus' name. Father, I thank You for your freedom. Amen.

Strongholds

Father, I repent for (name the belief) that contradicts what Your Word states. Confirm in me the truth of Your Word on this subject. I repent of the beliefs that are contrary to Your nature I have gained through my life experiences that are not accurate. I repent for any words I spoke from my heart that were declarations against Your purposes. Forgive me for these sins. I

List of Healing Prayers

declare that I will follow You in everything without exception in Jesus' name. Father, I thank You for Your healing mercy and grace. Amen.

Chapter 13
Sins of the Father

Father, I take responsibility for my sins and the sins of my fathers with their unfaithfulness to You. I ask You to forgive me of these sins and separate them from me and place them on the cross of Christ. I declare from this day forth, that my family and I will serve the Lord, in Jesus' name. I thank You, Father, for Your healing and Your blessings. Amen.

Father, I repent for dishonoring my parents. I repent for every word spoken against them in disrespect. I also repent for the judgement and negative attitudes of the heart toward my parents. I ask You to forgive me for these sins and declare that I will honor them from this day forth in Jesus' Name. Father, I thank you for my parents and ask You to bless them, in the name of Jesus. Amen.

Chapter 14
Truth about Salvation

Father, I (state your full Christian name) surrender 100% of my heart to You from this day forth. I believe Jesus is Lord. Jesus, I choose to walk away from my old life, and I offer to You those things (sins) that would keep my heart from being fully occupied by your Spirit. I ask You to forgive me for living contrary to Your purposes and forgive me for the sins I have committed. I will live for You from this day forth. Jesus, You will be Lord of my Life. As my first act of surrender, I choose to forgive anyone who has sinned against me while I was living contrary to You and I ask You to bless them, in Jesus' Name. Father, I thank You for Your salvation. Amen."

Chapter 15
Addictions and Other Issues of the Heart
Anorexia and Bulimia

Father, I repent for the sin of rebellion. Forgive me this sin and put it on the cross of Jesus Christ. I renounce the words I said in rebellion. I repent for dishonoring my mother and father and I will honor them from this day forth. I repent for the sins I have committed because of my self-seeking heart in Jesus' name. Father, I thank You for healing my heart and body. Amen.

Sexual Abuse

Father, I choose to forgive (name(s) of person who abused you). What they did to me was sin. Take this sin from them, put it on the cross of Jesus Christ, and separate it from them. On the Day of Judgment, I will hold no accusation against them. Even now, they are free. Father, have mercy on them and bless them, in Jesus' name. I thank You for Your love and Your healing. Amen.

List of Healing Prayers

Addiction to Alcohol and Drugs

Father, I repent for my rebellion against You and all authority. It was a sin. Forgive me this sin and put it on the cross of Jesus Christ and separate it from me. I also repent for the other sins I committed because of this rebellion. Forgive me these sins and place them on the cross in Jesus' name. Father, I thank you for Your freedom. Amen.

Addiction to Cigarettes

Father, I repent for my rebellious heart. I yield to Your will from this day forth. I repent for the words I spoke that were contrary to Your truth and I renounce them. I repent for any dishonor towards my mother or father. Forgive me these sins and put them on the cross in Jesus' name. Father, I thank You for Your healing. Amen.

Abortion

Father, I repent. Forgive me for the sin of abortion. Take this sin from me, put it on the cross of Jesus Christ, and separate it from me. I choose to forgive (name of those you hold accountable) for what they did. Place this sin on the cross. I will hold no accusation against them. Father, bless them. In addition, I repent for any lies or deceit to hide this sin from others. Forgive me for these sins in Jesus' name. Father, I thank You for Your healing and for setting me free. Amen."

Chronic Anger

Father, I have allowed anger to rule my judgement, and I have also gone to sleep on my anger. In addition, I have said words in my anger that should not have been said. I repent and will seek understanding before I react. Father, I have judged others who were angry with me without cause. I choose to forgive them for this sin and the words that they said to me in anger. Father, in turn, I ask You to forgive me for my words and my actions committed in anger that did harm. Thank you, Father, for my forgiveness and freedom. In Jesus name, Amen.

www.ingramcontent.com/pod-product-compliance
Lightning Source LLC
Chambersburg PA
CBHW070736170426
43200CB00007B/539